The Cities of the Plains

An Anthology of Iowa Artists and Poets

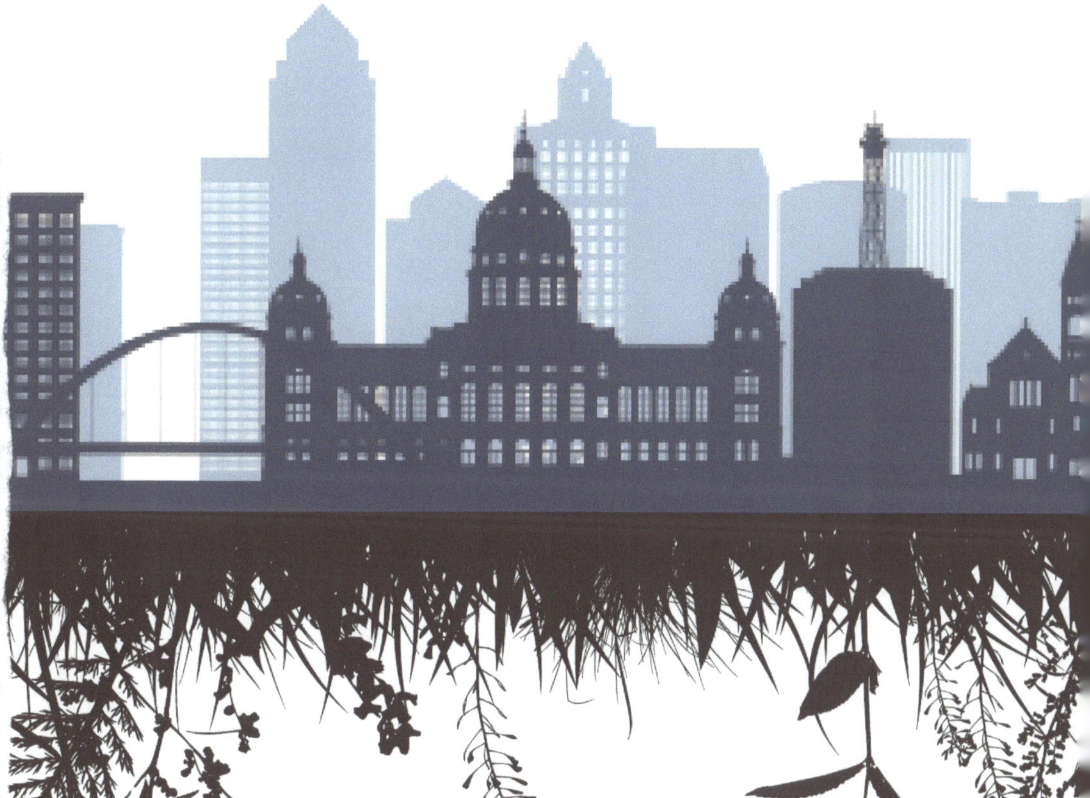

Edited by Paul Brooke

ISBN 979-8-218-38985-7
Cover Design by Paul Brooke
Interior Design by Paul Brooke
No part of this book may be reproduced
except in brief quotations and in reviews
without permission from the publisher.
First Published in 2024 by Grand View University
Printed by Ingram
Supported by a Grant from the Iowa Economic Development Authority, the
Iowa Arts Council, and the National Endowment for the Arts.

The Cities of the Plains
An Anthology of Iowa Artists and Poets

Table of Contents

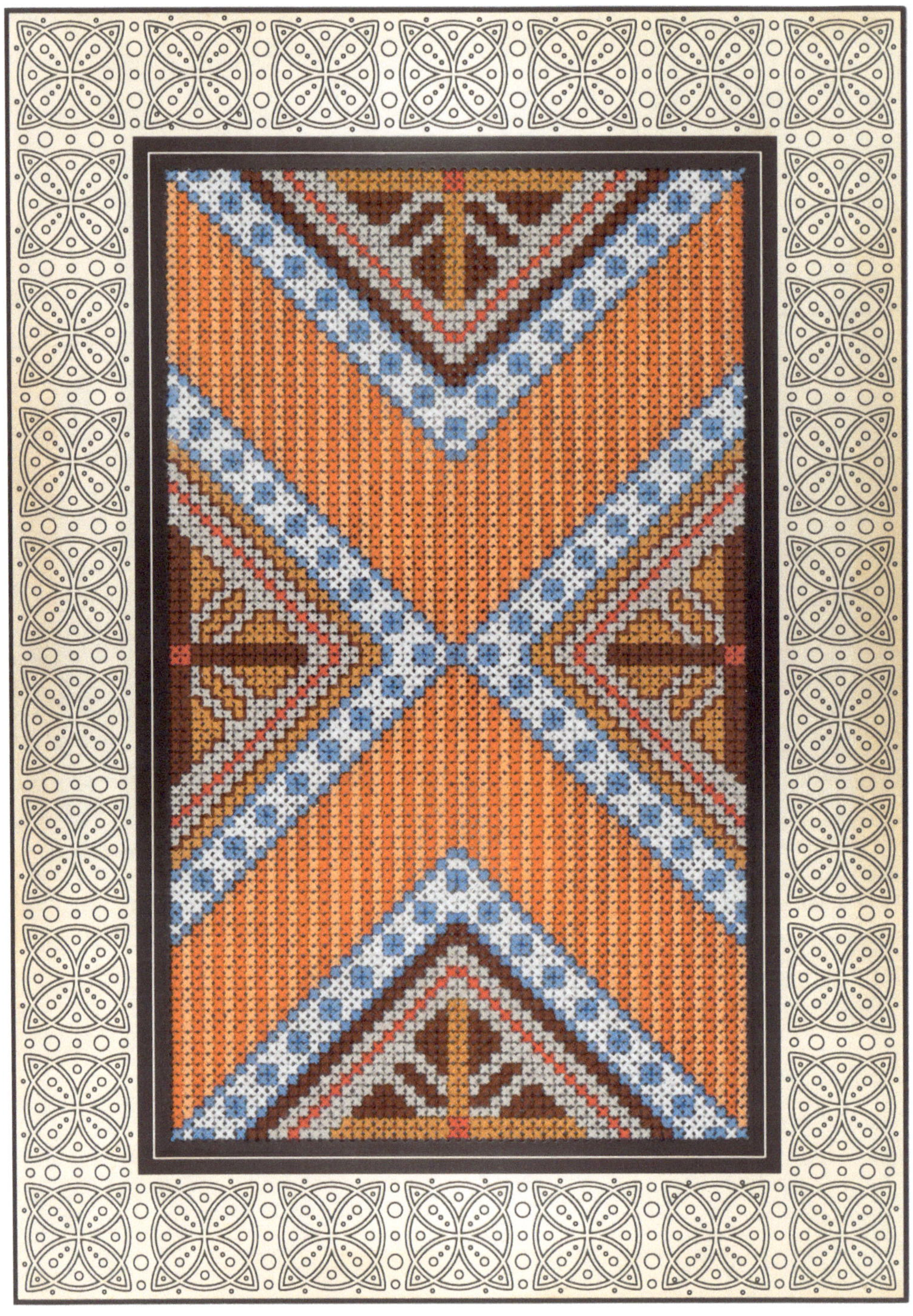

Tibi Chelcea   Randomly Accessed Memory #35, Embroidery on
Custom-Designed Circuit Board

Introduction

I first conceptualized this anthology driving past my birthplace of Eldora, Iowa. This is where Mona Van Duyn, the Pulitzer-Prize winning poet, was raised as a child (she was born in Waterloo). There was a poem that she recorded called "The Cities of the Plains," a poem strangely about Lot's wife. A line came to mind: "fabulous bouquets of persons" and I imagined—suddenly—an anthology filled not only with our state's best poets but also our best artists. I thought about elevating these talented persons, these fabulous bouquets. Thus the idea was born.

Six months later, I applied for an Iowa Arts Council grant through Iowa Economic Development Authority and was chosen to create this anthology. I set out to create the most diverse collection of artists and poets the state of Iowa has to offer. And I remembered early in my career being selected for Michael Carey's *Voices on the Landscapes* (1996) and knew it was time for a reboot. Today, this anthology offers a glimpse of the power and talent of our artists and writers. Many of the 57 artists/poets span multiple disciplines. Many have won prestigious awards. All are astonishing.

Iowa, I believe, is the right place to cultivate a prolific art and writing career. There is space in which to create work and the time in which to do the work necessary to achieving success. People outside of the state often belittle or dismiss Iowa as an artistic haven but, in fact, it is. We do the hard work and create art that matters. Van Duyn practiced that work ethic and sought to make poetry that endured. She found that in the Midwest.

Van Duyn lived in Iowa and Missouri for the bulk of her life and she had an ear for language as much of her work was grounded in place. She noted the changes she was witnessing in her own time, her own ecosystem. One poem that always spoke to me was "The Burning of Yellowstone." Here she describes how the fires in Yellowstone are affecting the sunset in the Midwest: "Fallout of deep red peony litters the treeline./We take each other's hand, eyes wet, and hear/how gently the world informs its witnesses...of its debt to the artistry of their beholding..." The poem's timeless quality and its relevance to understanding the impact of those fires weighs heavily today as we experience the same issues from the Canadian and Northwest wildfires.

Many of the poems and the art included here are grounded in place and have that same beautiful aesthetic of language as Van Duyn's: "Parked cars, like aquarium pebbles, circle the pond./A roar, a dry sprinkle, and a good machine/ goes by, cutting grass in a ten-foot strip" (*A Time of Bees* 28). Poems in this anthology also sing the earth and honor it, poems like Geneva Toland's "song for the prairie" or Shelly Reed Thieman's "The Numerology of Gardening" or Marilyn Baszczynski's "pears." Art pieces celebrating the beauty of the earth are Anna Stoysich's "Loess Hills Storm" or Patricia Tiffany Morris' "Stained Glass Landscape" or Catherine Reinhart's "Inland Surveying" or Louise Kames' "Winter Willow." Amazingly, as I designed the interior of the book for this anthology, many of the art pieces matched beautifully with the poems because of their shared aesthetics and themes.

Van Duyn once said, "I believe that good poetry can be as ornate as a cathedral or as bare as a potting shed, as long as it confronts the self with honesty and fullness." Poems that felt ornate and well crafted were Dawn Terpstra's "Sonnets for a Week Between Seasons," Tasha Jacson's "The Inferno Elegies," and Charlie R. North's "To the Bone." Many of the art pieces were incredibly complicated in terms of their design and their aestheti were Tibi Chelcea's "Randomly Accessed Memory #35," Matthew Matthew Kluber's "Friday I'm in Love," Jocelyn Chãtcauvert's "Switchgrass," and Lydia Nong's "Exodus."

Van Duyn often tackled politics and seemingly offered a new vision of our culture: "When all the white rats in the world have confirmed our flaws,/and the separateness of our wish, or its treaty with laws,/where either night causes day or there is no cause" (*A Time of Bees* 21). I think that there are poems that echo this sentiment like Caleb Rainey's "If You Give a Black Boy a Dollar" or ML Hopson's "A Black Child's Walk to See the Freedom Train." Likewise, artists give us those same insights like in Vi Khi Nao's "Boatwoman" or Joan Webster-Vore's "Fences" or Indigo Moore's "Wake Up" or Seso Marentes' "Lost Chicano Tribe of Iowa" series.

Finally, Mona Van Duyn created beautiful poems that matter today and felt timeless. That is the mark of a poet of genius. "Passing Thought" examines the past, using cooking as a metaphor:

> But when the chaos spits something up
> which goes over the side and lands on the stove—
> the spraddled fern of celery top,
> bloodclot of an over-ripe tomato,
> tough twig of splurged-on country ham slice—
> the pure accident of its splat

is wiped away quickly, guiltlessly away,
being nothing more meaningful than that.

It is often the simplest expression that recalibrates our understanding of a concept. It is often the simplest presentation of art, the stripped down essential quality that stuns us like Molly Wood's "Poppy 150" or Amenda Tates manibus series or Elizabeth Rhoad Read's "Bound Restraint" or Catherine Reinhart's "Inland Surveying" or Igor Khalandovskiy's "Snow Forest." Poetry that fulfills this practice includes Tracie Morris' "Becoming to Iowa," Ray Young Bear's song poems, Vince Gotera's "How Clara Met Santiago: A Pantoum," and Jen Rouse's "My Uterus Eats Itself Like a Ravenous Thing."

I think about Mona Van Duyn practically every day now. She gained momentum late in life, winning prizes well into her seventies, including the Pultizer and Poet Laureate of the United States. "I bless all knowledge of love, all ways of publishing it." This anthology embraces all knowledge of love and it embodies the creative soul of the state. There is so much to celebrate in this collection and by pairing art and poetry it heightens the experience for the reader/viewer. I cannot express the joy I received working with such talented authors and artists. It shot me full of excitement and pride to witness—firsthand—the abundance of genius in Iowa. We are incubating talented artists and poets!

Paul Brooke, Spring 2024

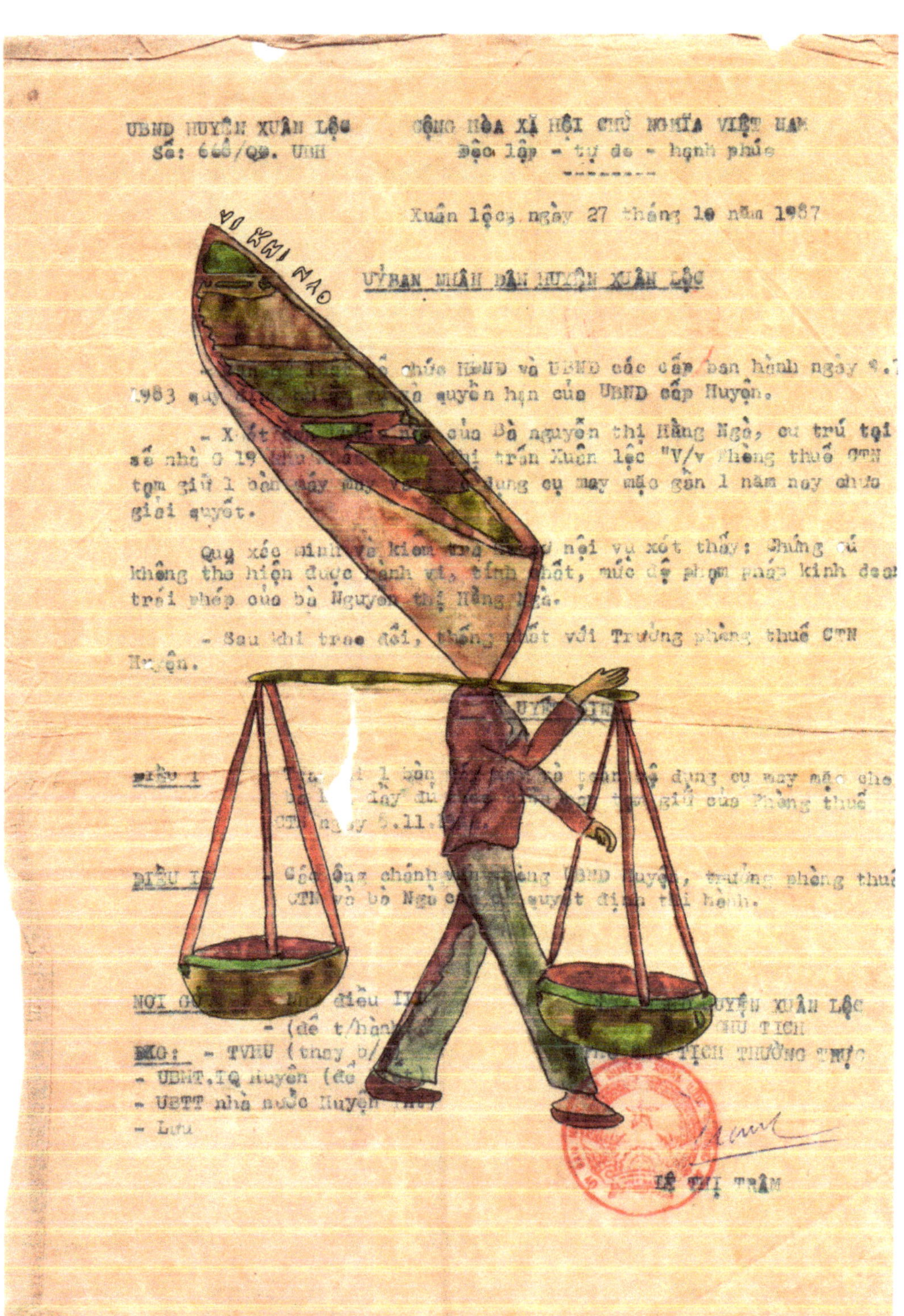

Vi Khi Nao   Boatwoman

from *Radiant Paralysis*

In your dew-bathed
smile, youth unfolds
Fragments of myself,
a story yet untold
Hồ Chí Minh's art
from war did arise
And I,
from my father's lecture,
found art in disguise

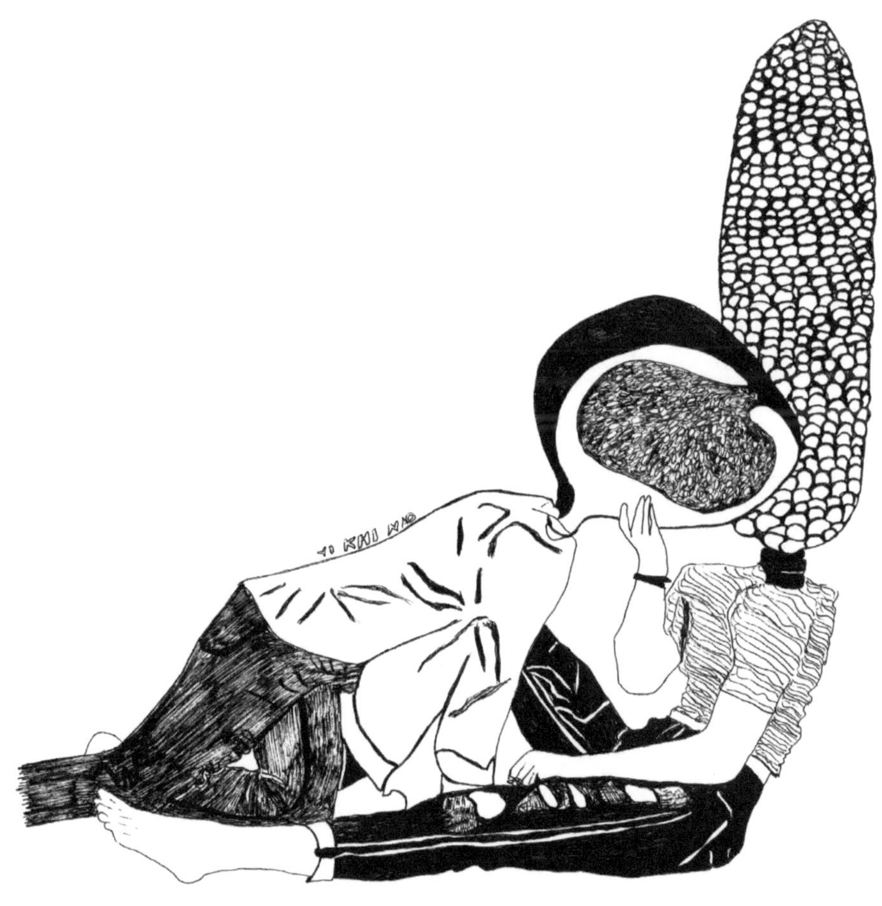

Vi Khi Nao   Miss Fig and Miss Corn

from *Radiant Paralysis*

Peasants toil, straw hats
shading their heads
Archival release of fire,
history spreads Lethal,
I've become, a city
elevated high
Fueled by a song,
my country's spirit won't deny

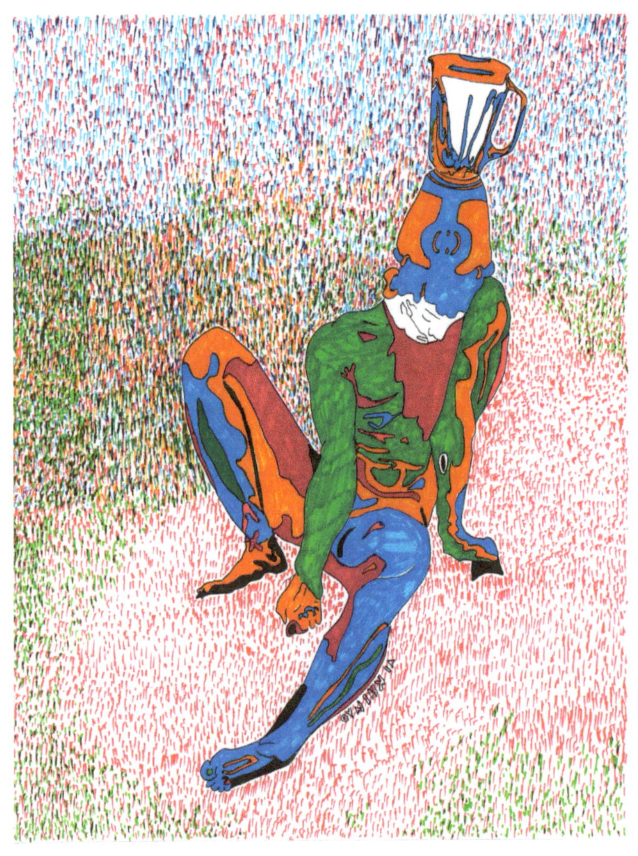

Vi Khi Nao   Blender Dude

from *Radiant Paralysis*

From the wide basin,
Điện Biên Phủ's embrace
Tết offensive's echoes
in my creative space
Aged rice fields, cost less,
yet they thrive
A lacquered bowl of rice,
a domino theory alive

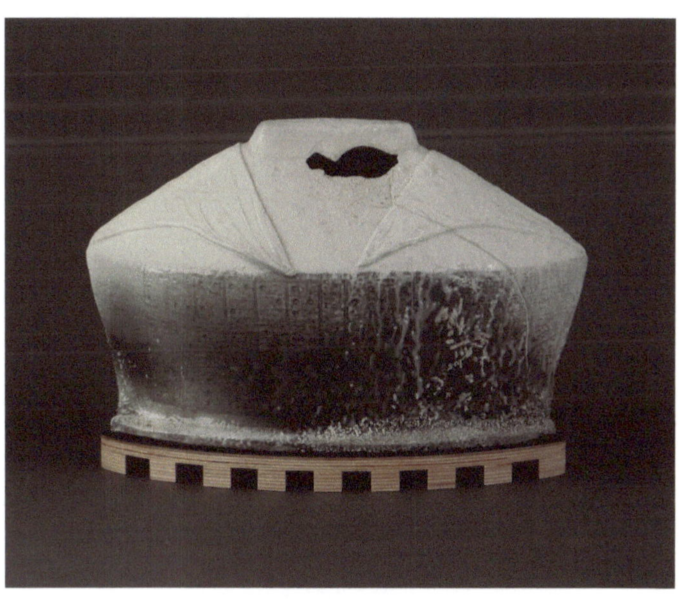

Ingrid Lilligren   Summer Return

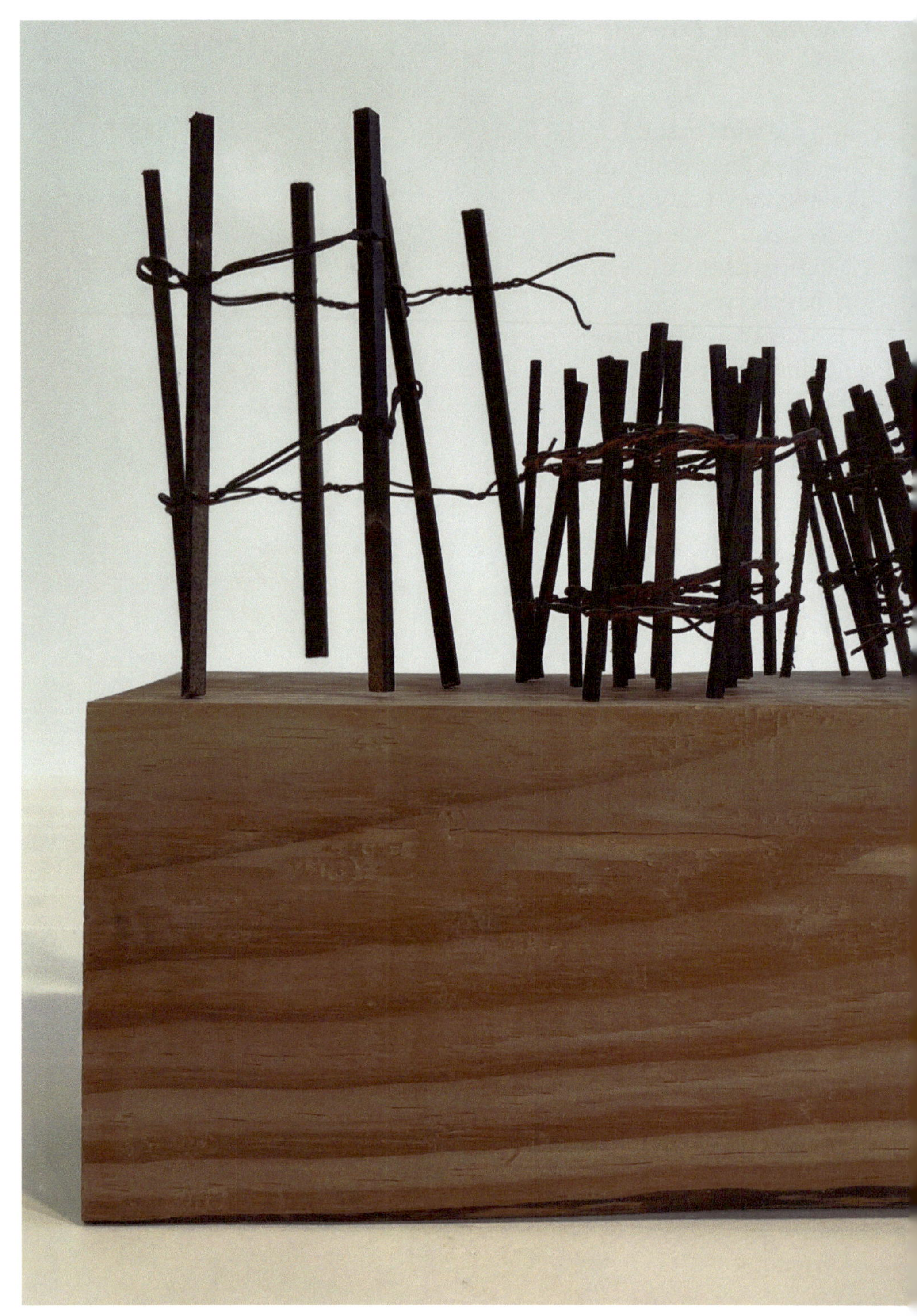

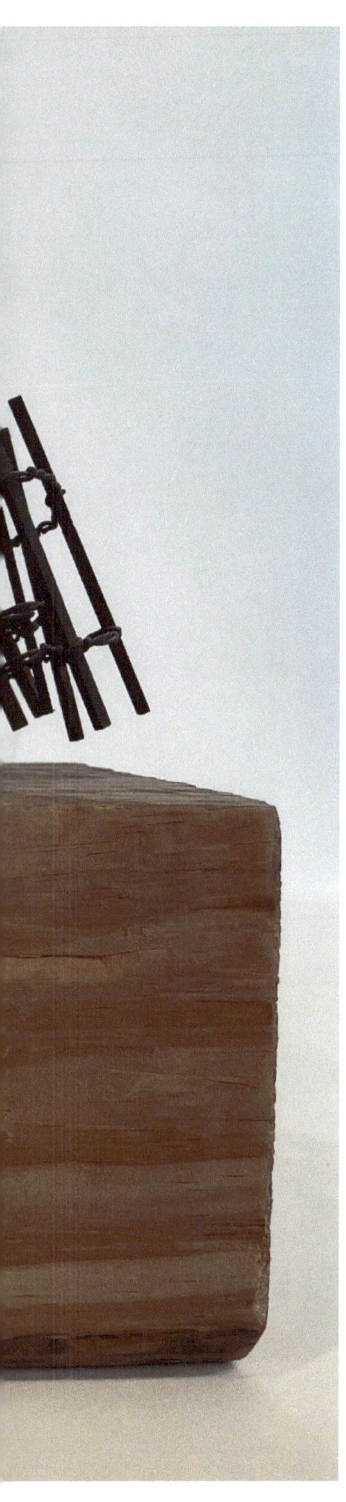

Caleb Rainey

Obsidian Skin

A rock formed
from the flames
of a burning cross.
Generational heat
hardened and passed

down. George Floyd
must have mistaken
himself diamond,
not knowing his Black
        made him look
too tough, too dirty, too guilty. I

found myself on the ground.
Black and translucent
next to him as they hoped
to make us hollow.

If You Give A Black Boy a Dollar

Caleb Rainey

If you give a Black boy a dollar / he's gonna wanna shop.
He'll think of hot wheels / and video games,
new kicks / and a bike to do tricks with.
His wish list is limitless, / but he'll settle for food.

If you let a Black boy shop for food / he's gonna wanna eat.
He'll think of fried chicken, collard greens, / Mama's mac and cheese,
Grandad's black eyed peas, / Granny's banana pudding.
The hunger inside / him gowing
soul food dream, / but he'll settle for McDonald's.

If you let a Black boy eat / he's gonna wanna a drink.
He'll imagine Kool-Aid / and lemonade.
On a special day / grape soda.
The thirst will make his mouth dry,
tongue twisting itself, / desperate / rain dance waiting for a drop.
But he'll settle for water, / pray its clean this time.

If you let a Black boy drink / he's gonna wanna live.
He'll see himself / playing ball, winning rings and trophies,
          leaving a legacy.
He'll see himself / designing skyscrapers, creating a clouds rival,
          reaching for the sun.
He'll see himself / in space, stepping on planets,
          discovering the beyond.
He'll see himself / paint a galaxy, constellations on a cotton canvas
          capturing magnificence.
He'll see / his future.
He's gonna wanna live.

But Black boy will settle for a dollar, / all that you're willing to give.

Blk Boi Joy

Caleb Rainey

this that Black Boi Joy, that running
wild with a free smile, that playing
the dozens with my cousin's, that top

five debate–where the culture's
at stake–that watching
Dragon Ball Z, knowing each line
in the scene, that dreaming of better
like Wakanda forever, that whatchu mean?
          i'm doing me, that laugh too loud

even in a crowd, that giving
dap with a pat on the back, that currency
everyone wants from me, say it don't

belong to me. the world wants to swallow
me, but they choke
on my royalty. this is my inheritance
can't nothing stand against
this Black Boi Joy.

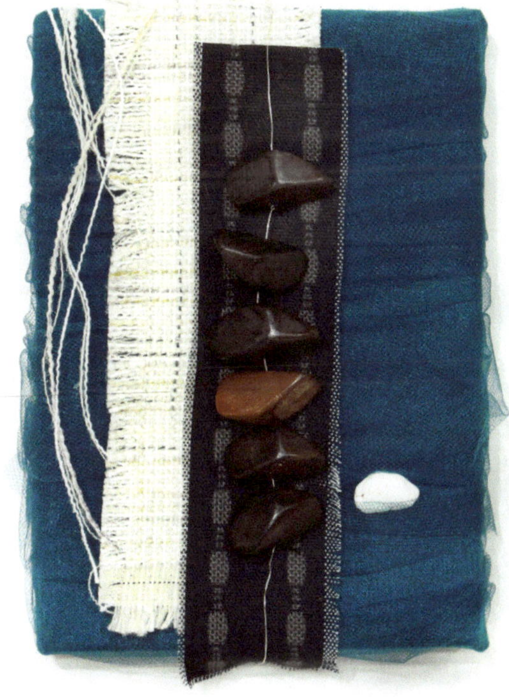

Akwi Nji   Uprising Does Not Always Roar Like a Fire

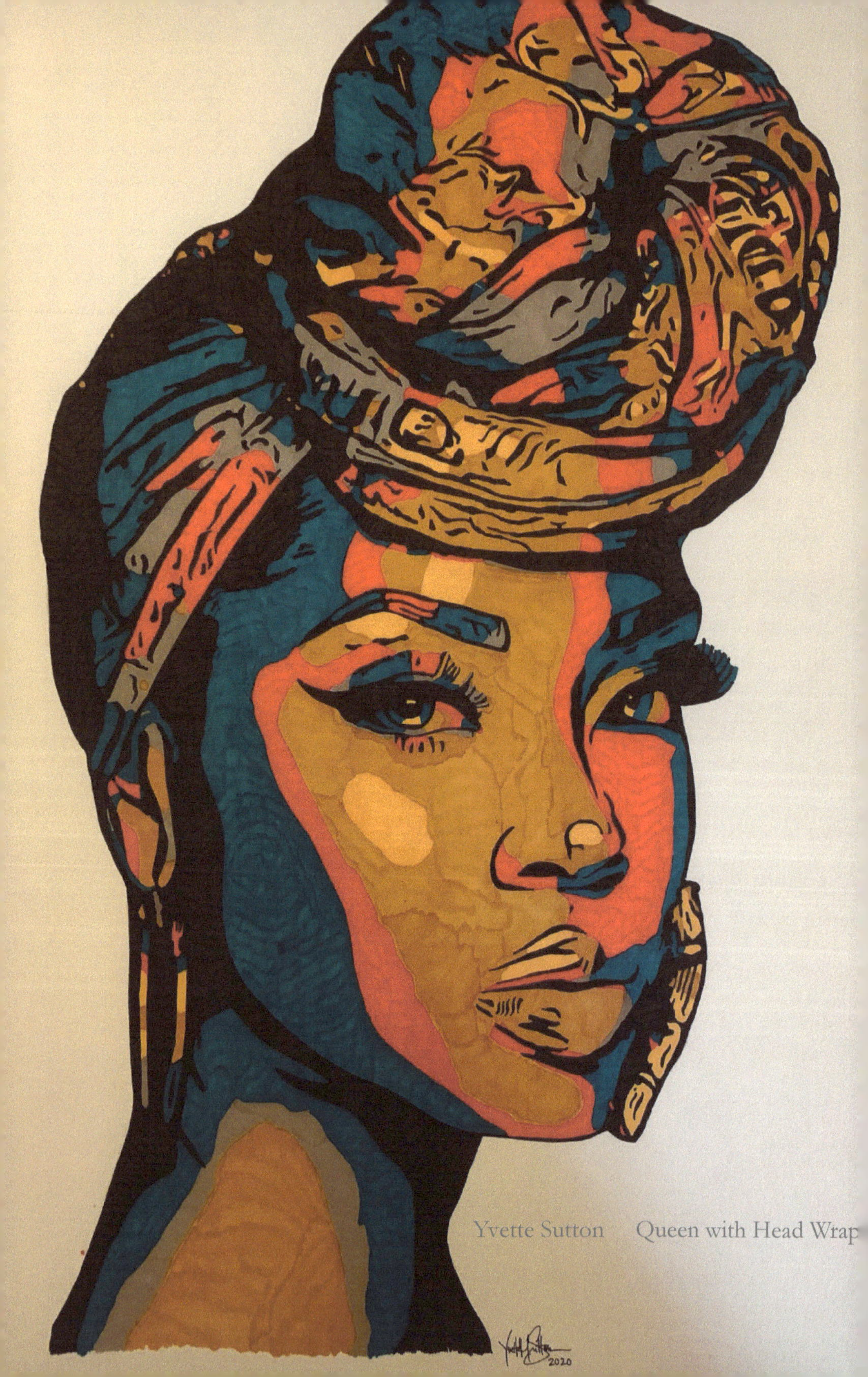

Yvette Sutton   Queen with Head Wrap

Vibe with Me

Akwi Nji

Live. Live in earth's exhale,
fall in love with earth-mother,
the sigh beneath bare feet.

Discover oceans spring from seeds,
our palms, our psalms of freedom.
Our ancestors, our ancestors are callin.

I am alive in every way.
I am alive in every way.

Shake off the chains n write, craft,
architect empires,
new ways of being, writing, playing.

Play.

Currency-synergy. Free-flow, vibe-glow.

Demo old structures,
deconstruct the constructs.

Fresh start, let's go.

Build foundation,
with growth-potential activated,
authenticated.

Captivated, this vibe.
Expansion of intuition, divine energy,
infrastructure. For us. By us.

A new revolution.

Live. Live in earth's exhale,
fall in love with earth-mother,
the sigh beneath bare feet.

Discover oceans spring from seeds,
our palms, our psalms of freedom.
Our ancestors, our ancestors are callin.

I am alive in everyway.
I am alive in every way.

Vibe with me.

A revolution. A revolution is comin.

You feel me?
What are we here for?

Vibe with me.

You feel it? You feel this energy?
What are we here for?
Vibe with me.

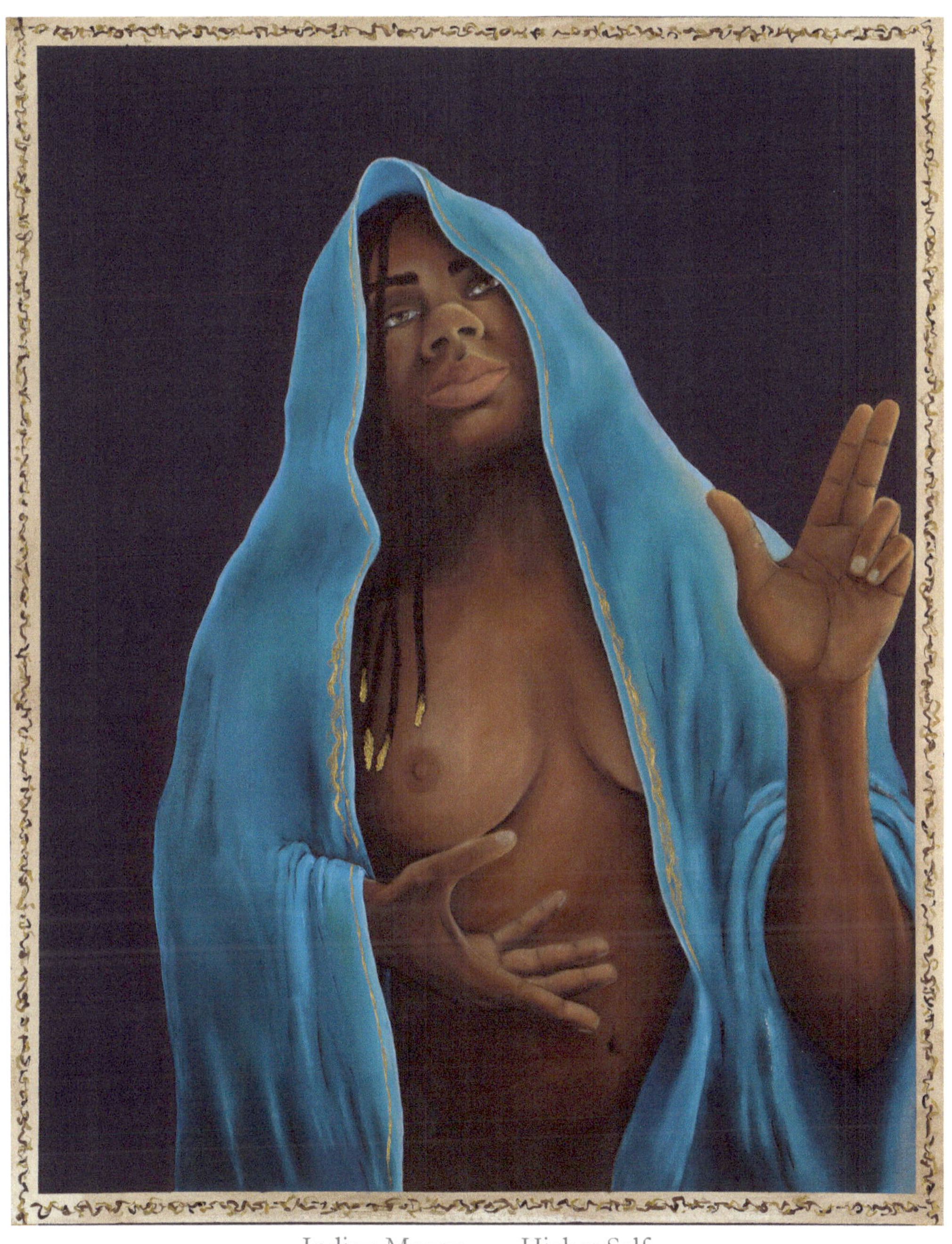

Indigo Moore   Higher Self

Black n Blaze

There are many angles
from which we can examine
Blackness, the word black.

Black.

Absolutely dark,
absorbing all light,
the color of soot or coal, ink.

Dark.

Burned. To scorch, which is to blaze,
glow, shine, gleam.

The same root produced the word
Pale... as in light.

Do you hear?

The same root that produced absolute darkness
produced light.

Bright, shining, glittering light.

The connecting notion being, perhaps,
they say

Fire.

So let us be born from fire. Blazing and beautiful,
moving in harmony, mesmerizing,
captivating.

Born from light and birthed into blackness, into purity and joy.

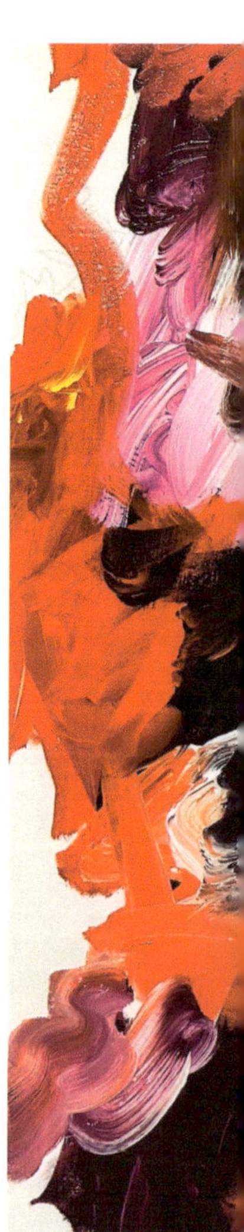

Daughters of Ra,
we love and self-love, with urgency and intimacy.
Comets sprout from footprints
blazing paths, illuminated.

We who are born from fire,
we blaze.

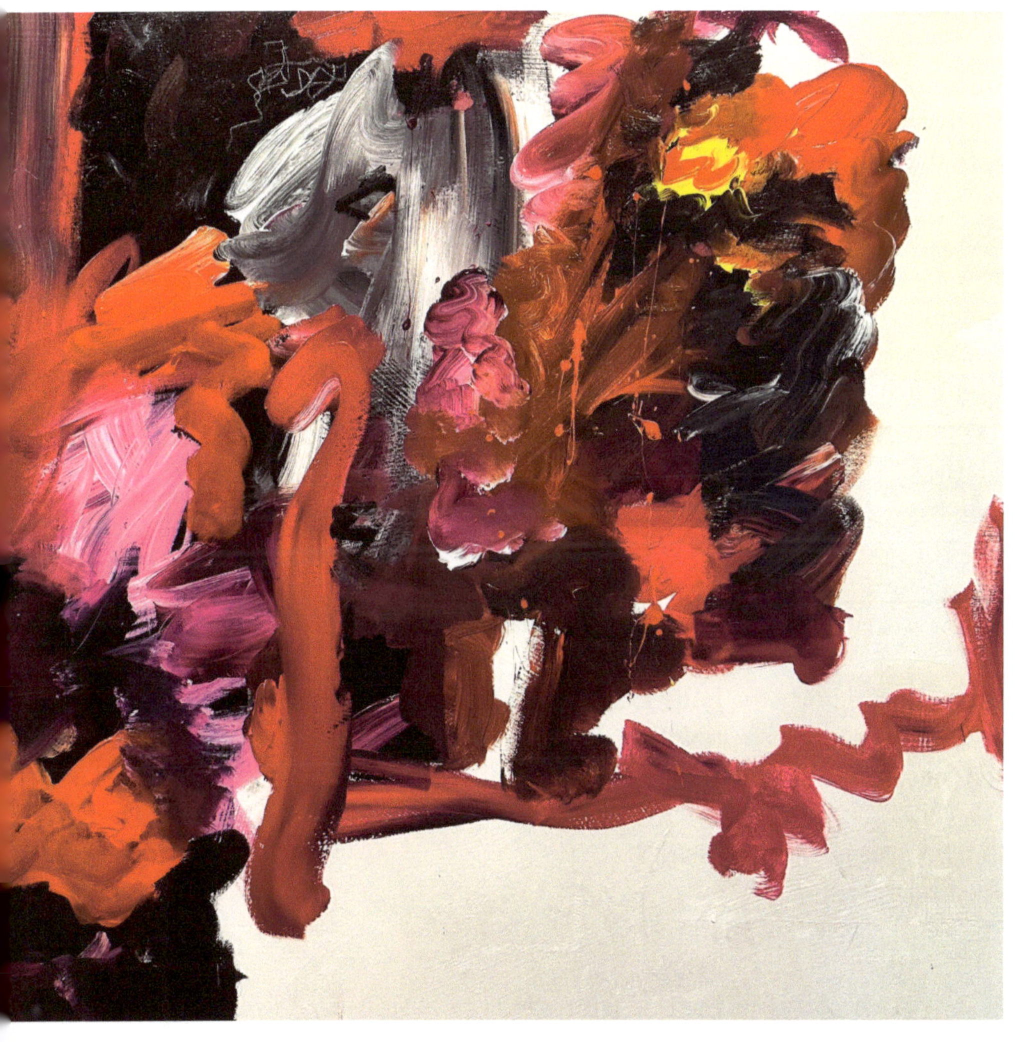

Akwi Nji   Vibe with Me

Birth of a Nation

There was first a nation birthed,
and then the nation birthed a word,
and another
and another

until each word strung loosely together
delivered a sentence,
became a lash dancing ancient choreography
became a moment of silence
became a hymn.

Do you hear?
The words turned into lashes
with the power to take breath from the body.

Can you see
how a word becomes a death sentence
dancing ancient choreography?

a sentence
a sentence
a lash
a silence
a hymn

Can you see the breath, the body, the breath, the body?

The body the body the body that was his body until it was made,
suddenly, a ravaged field with
soft bleeding sunset of skin.

Can you see the smoke rising?
The breath rising.
The word rising into hymn.

Here is the bounty, the bruised fruit,
the body the body his body rising.

The nation rising into uprising into uprising into uprising

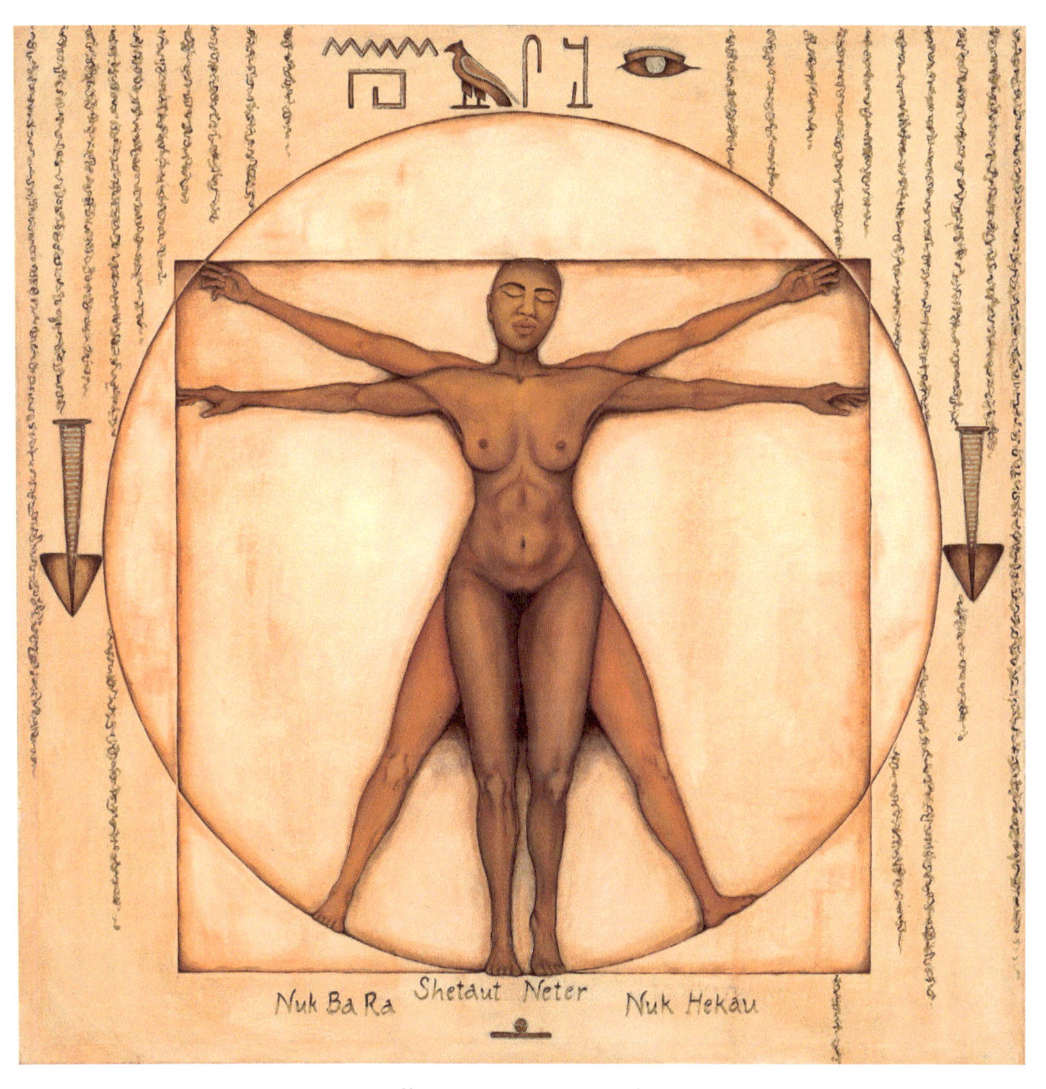

Indigo Moore   Wake Up

Ritual Fires

Insects spark skyward from late summer soil,
heavy fog lays across tassels—swallows
weave a blanket of feasting through droplets
spun into a hot-sided morning. I
am somehow dry tinder, combustible,
framed against August's wall of water.

I am night's ember
                    carried on clay,
desire kindled for earth to lay upon,
to quench my burning tongue between dawns.

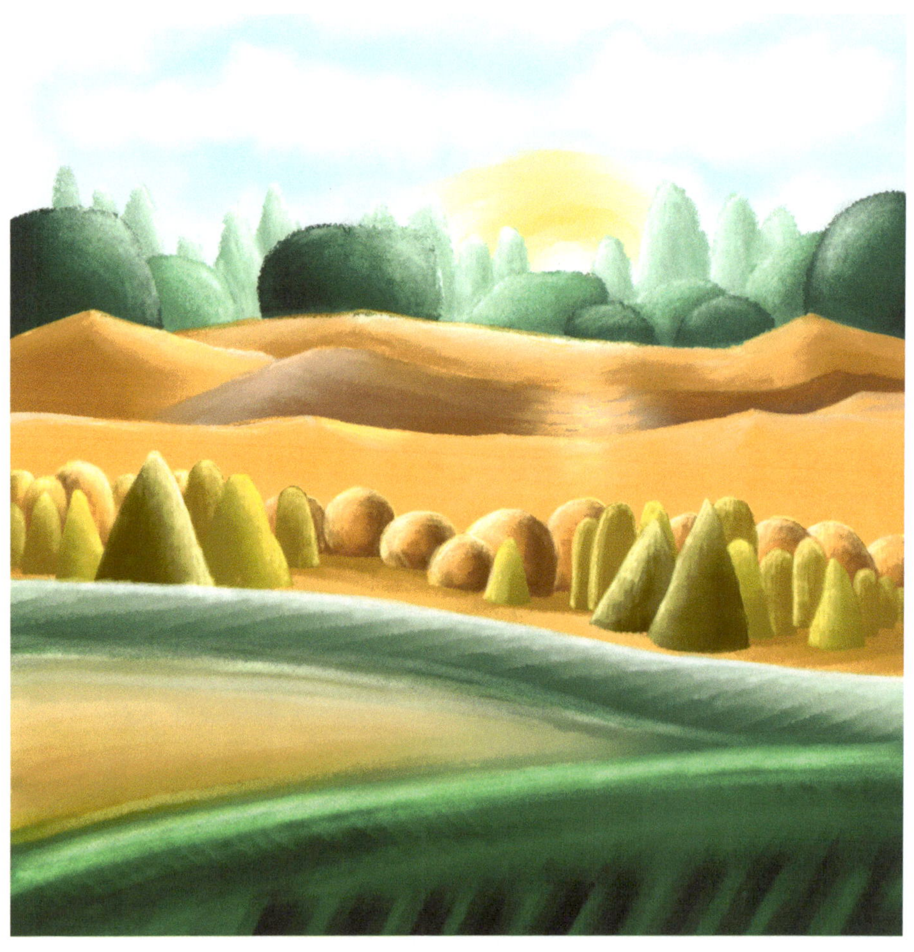

Patricia Tiffany Morris   Grant Wood Landscape

I seek the grace of morning mist, hovering
at new salvia like a hummingbird:
yet I linger, warm beneath covers, light

my signal fire for the horizon,
cluster of stars to navigate the dark.

*

Past the blazing stars, I navigate dark
forest paths, stepping into sun, valley
of ash, now damp across a rolling hill.

Blackened char threshold, I cross to breathe
the burn of a prairie, this ruin,
prescribed, restorative blaze extinguished

before autumn winds wander, its presence
pushing and stirring this apocalypse.
In the spring I will caress familiar

tender shoots among cinders, soothing
grief gentled with emerging hope, like
a mother praying over her garden.

Antler to stir the soil, a song for rain,
I keep prairie fire, my better lover.

*

I keep prairie fire, my better lover,
in a dress of crinoline and gossamer:

my ashy tongue coated and heavy
with birdsong, a distant thunder. Watch

wind-swept oaks bow and sway, an orchestra
whipping dirges with debris, homelessness

skitters the cinders, a field mouse
and her pups won't wait for miracles—

scrap of hollow log lays near the hollies.
Red-feathered Phoenix, sing your cardinal song

this evening, rejoice in smokeless horizons,
twilight of sinking orange embers,

praise blackened soil's stubborn fertility,
praise rainfall, rising currents of honeybees.

*

Praise rising currents of honeybees, rainfall
after the ditches are burned, April ritual
to clear rose hips clinging to last season,
lantern flowers from beneath another sky.

Nothing ever happens on the edges,

small town fades slowly into copse and sedge:
where tamarack and cattails mark the slough,
where chiseled stones and ancient yews stand
sentry to eternity, resurrection

into glory possessed of more grace

than found upon this earth, in this town.
I know lives stolen too soon and too young:
kin-bond through blood's distant river, we wore
red ribbons through eyelets—I remember her.

*

Red ribbon through eyelets, I remember her
on the 4th of July, blonde ponytail,

blue-starred scrunchy, white denim shorts, t-shirt
declared Made in America. She played

flute in the parade, ran the 5K,
took a shift at the snow cone booth, staining

her shorts like a purpled bruise. She would be
Miss America someday. She would be

a Med Tech someday, saving accident
victims, the wounded and sick. She could have

been her own hero. Midnight on a blacktop,
deer leaping from a ditch, distant fireworks

cascading red, white and blue. She loved
how they bled together at the end. New light.

*

How they bled together at the end, new light
hues of orange, magentas, purples
burn with night's coming grief. I clasp this dark robe

void of warmth, comfort, voices whispering
close from those beloved.
                              Weren't they blazing stars
here for short, fragrant seasons? Their blossoms
known best by God's smallest-winged creatures?

I walk the night seeking constellations,
listen as greater white-fronted geese call
their star routes
                    to the south. I believe

in cartographies of those lost, the paths
they must fly, the distance between grieving
and the mysteries. How my simple lines
trace the air like wings ignorant of flight.

*

My wings trace the air ignorant of flight,
how they blend together at the end: random
ribbon through my eyes. I love: remember
rituals after spring ditch fires burn,
my ashy tongue coated and heavy.
Old cinders, like dreams, lantern the skies
I seek. I sing cloud songs for rain, stir
my blessings with rich soil, with bones and seed:
my mother-heart prays over graves and gardens.

I am
night's ember carried on clay,
a signal fire kept for new horizons:
warm beneath covers, I linger, touch
a cluster of stars to navigate the dark,
to spark morning soil with flying wings.

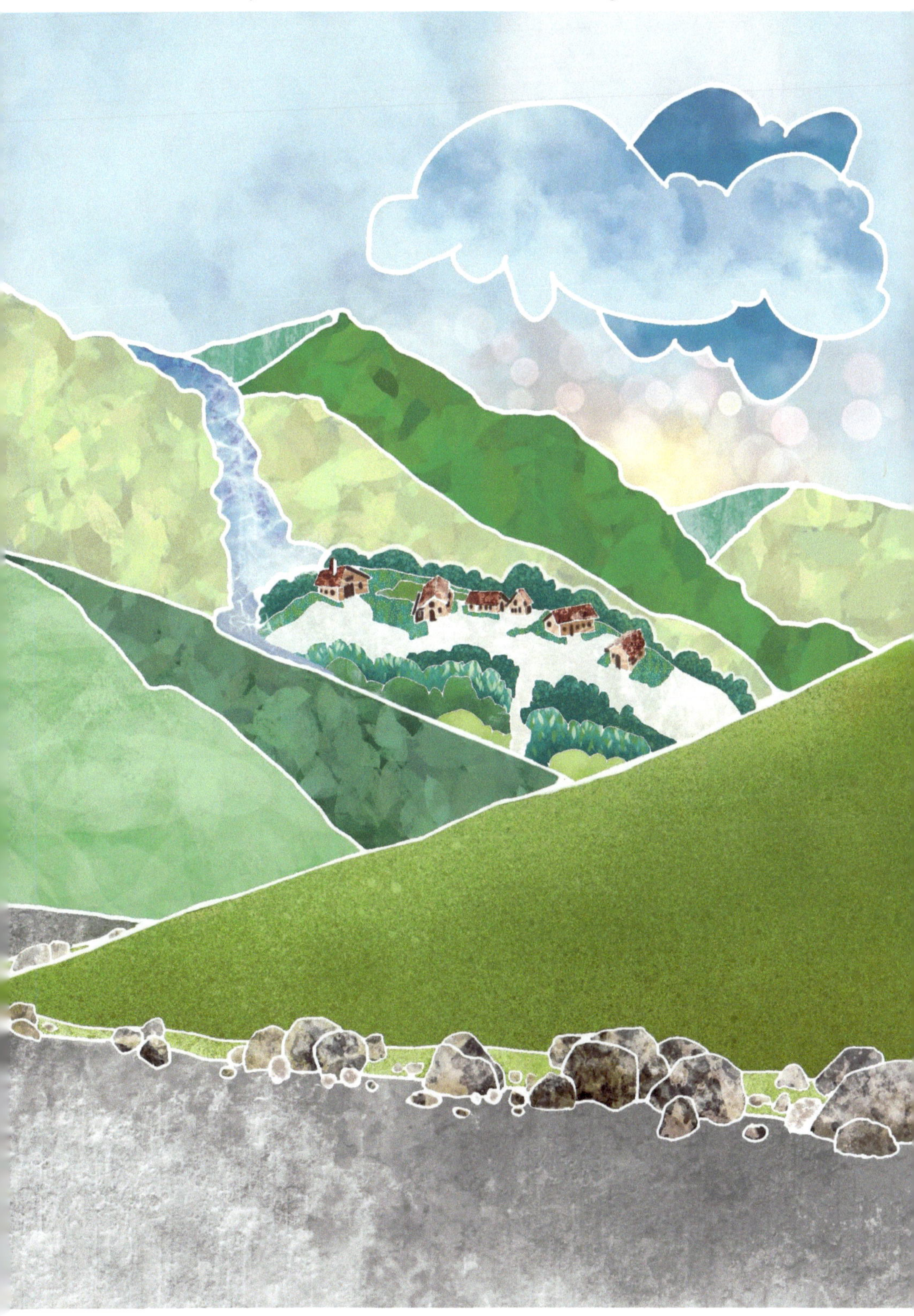

Sonnets for a Week Between Seasons

10,000 fly beneath the stone gray floor of sky,
white-winged cacophony swirls toward open water
stretched as an ocean inlet between landlocked cliffs.
Urgent, furious squall, they scatter as they land,
drift across the surface like a season's final snow.
Flocked music rises as I watch from a high bank,
a cemetery nearby, grave markers inscribed
with scripture, stones shimmer this Sunday like haloes
these souls may have earned in life. Bald eagles perch
in waterside pines to scan ice for dark pockets
opening to depths encased by winter. They chatter,
swooping with their acrobatics, predatory
and beautiful. I wonder what language eagles
speak, the snow geese and angels? My voice, unworthy.

———

Snow geese and angels, my unworthy voice stills, a
vagrant foreign to these shores. Have I visited
in memory with ancestral migrations—stars

guiding me to nesting grounds near a river bank?
I have spent years with this lover winged next to me
searching for signs—iris spikes pushing garden loam,

mockingbird calling from a bare-branched maple tree.
For a final day eagles crowd thick ice, scattered
like mounds near water pockets. They stare past winter

to the bottom of a sprawling lake set to turn:
in the shallows, small-eyed creatures will soon look back,
tree pollen will bring honeybees, wild and hungry.

But for today, paired wigeons and gadwalls dabble
shallows, trumpeter swans push past thin-crusted ice.

———

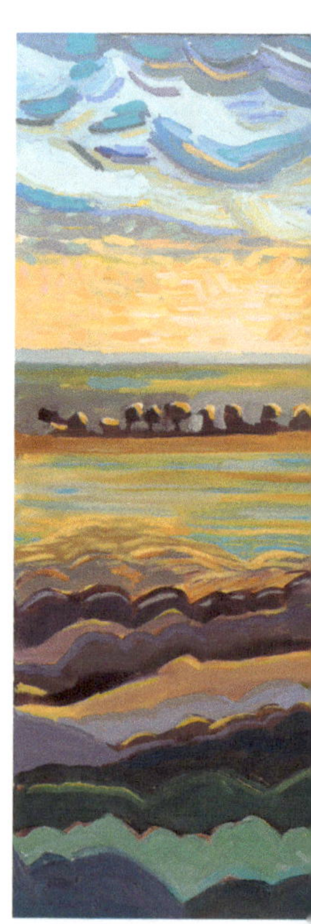

In the shallows, trumpeter swans push past thin ice,
white-lush bodies float as feathered clouds against sky.
We share binoculars and scope. A water bottle.
We don't remember last year's melt but conjure
a date before catbird and blackbird migration.
The cap you wear has hung in our house 30 years—
how tufts of hair stuck out then, your eyes, cobalt blue:

I believed our words, then and now, written across
daybreaks, trees we planted, their taste in spring water,
their smoke in poems
                          returned to earth and burned for sky.
When I lean on you, walking up hills, through marshes,
when I hear birds you can't or remind you of names,
words you don't recall, I feel love's seasons inside
my bones, the weight of age upon my tongue. You, here.

———

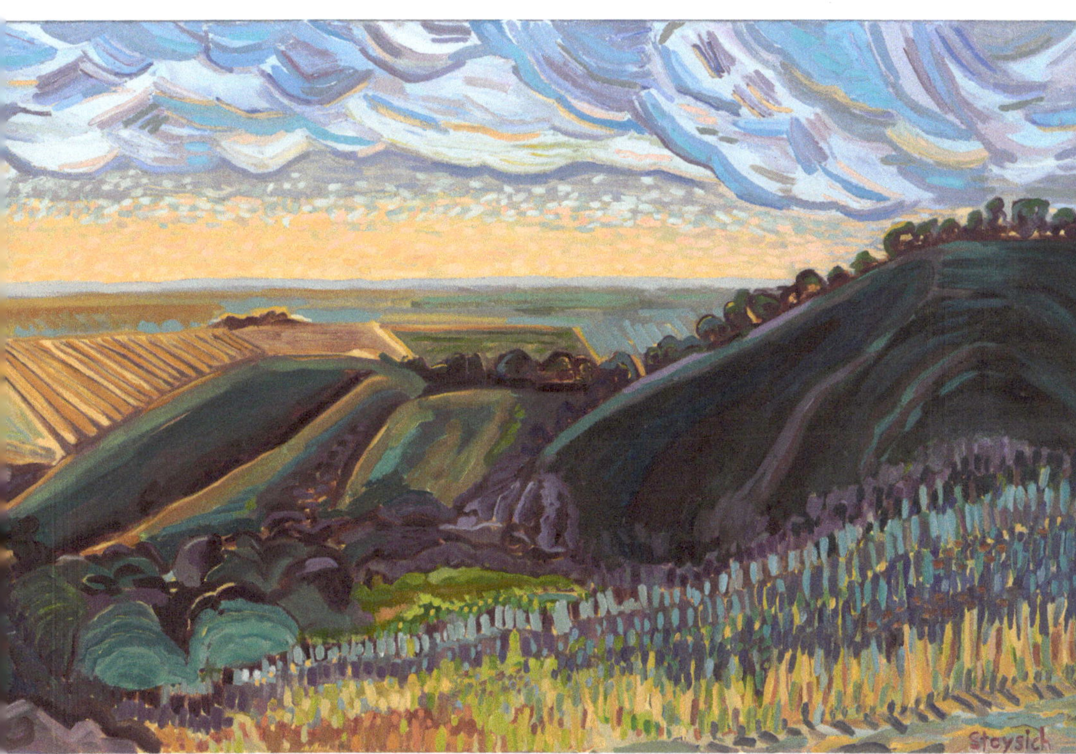

Anna Stoysich   Loess Hills Storm

My bones, the weight of age upon my tongue—here you
guide me to the book of our days, found pages—sun
and sacred hum of darkness. We acted parts: lines

memorized in former lives, dreamed Venus led us
to a forest cradling the children who made us
better—forgetting the pain of new birth and breath,

demons drowning in a river.
                              Dark shadows fill
my sleep. I move next to you this night, my blood warm
with decades of desire. It's nesting season.

Old oak hides great horned owl eggs while time incubates
our small hopes—that aging is like moonlight upon
a tread-worn porch, where lovers are always lovers
beyond wisteria vines and bleeding hearts. When
we hear peepers singing, the world begins again.

———

We hear peepers singing: the world, begins again.
I clean the closet of old jackets, dirty boots,
a long tasseled cap, a little girl's cowboy hat.
A sun dog in the west, a ring around the moon,
a long time comin', but I know change goin' a come.
I wear sunglasses and embrace a new brightness,
bending, fertile as a tree awaiting equinox.
I linger, scent of your wet hair on my pillow.
I line up sandals, paint my toenails Morning Glow,
long for Luna moths to crawl summer window screens.
I borrow the language of blossoms from bloodroot,
spring anemones, my tongue coated in pollen.
Tonight, 5,000 birds will fly beneath the Pink moon—
migratory lines coalesce, then break away.

———

Migratory lines coalesce, then break. Away
on a Friday, new language takes wing, rises from

musty silence. I drive to the abandoned farm

where my blood calls like a mother. I ride currents

of a younger self, galloping, whooping between
hay bales. I race grandfather along the river—

his palomino flying, white tail streaming

like a banner until the crossing. My old mare,
lathered, her ribs heaving between my legs, slows

to follow grandpa's horse into muddy water:
horses and riders become one in rushing current.

My legs lift with water's pull—grandfather lunges
as my horse goes under, her cargo releases—

floats delicate as feather grass, a heron's neck.

———

Delicate as floating feather grass, a heron's neck
tenses then strikes a silver flash in the shadows.
You and I still navigate our fields and forests,
love and loss—fleeing muffled voices, breath choking
in a throat, hostage to water. I will wonder—
always wonder, about spinning toward the delta,
what mysteries or benevolent dreams wait near
the end. I ask on the holiest days. God's ears
open to echoes from floating girls, from eagles,
angels on horseback along a river.

We push
together through ice, through years with wind against us.
Our bodies tire. We're content to land as snow
geese drift beyond. Listen! Furious squall above—
10,000 fly beneath the stone gray floor of sky.

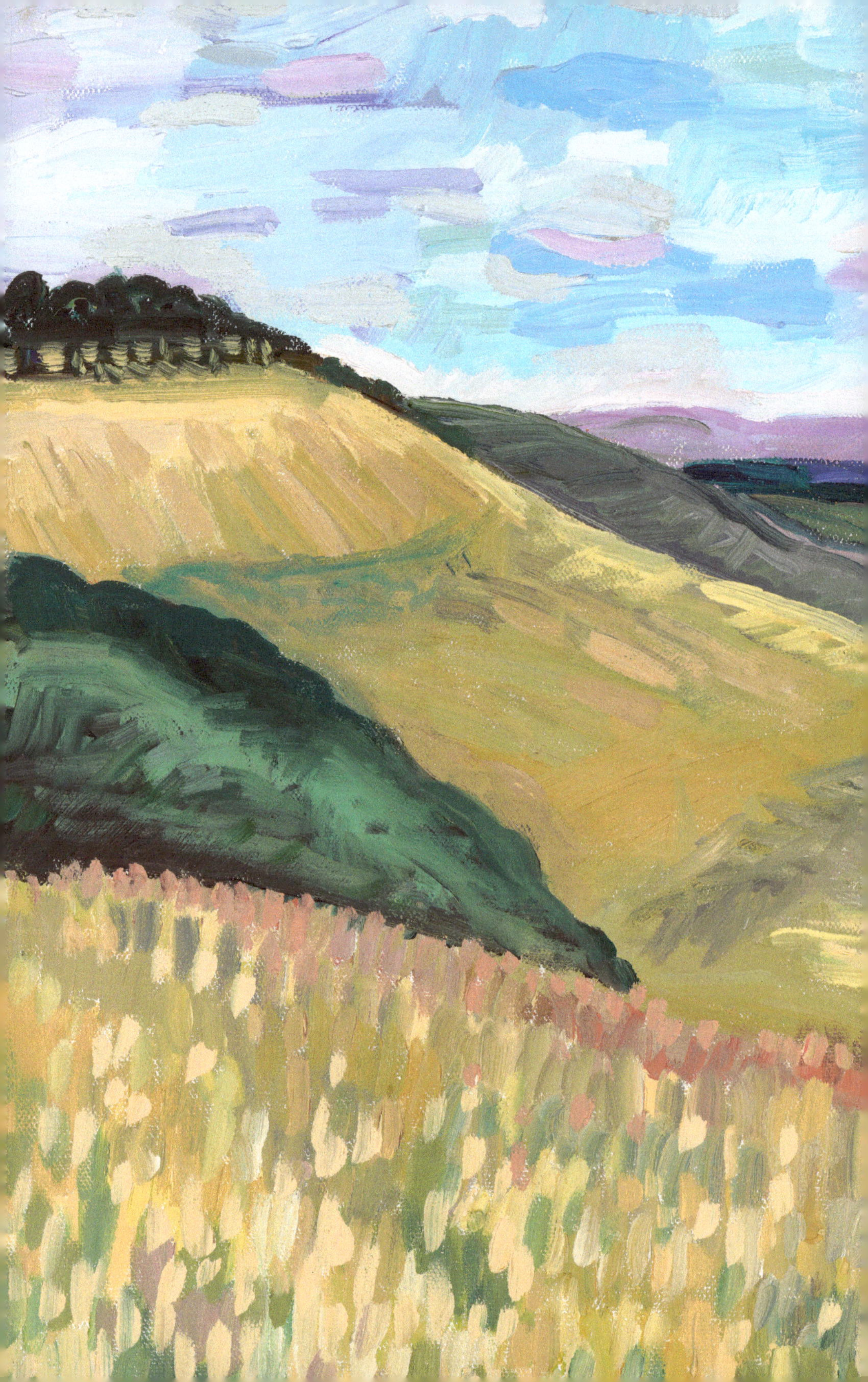

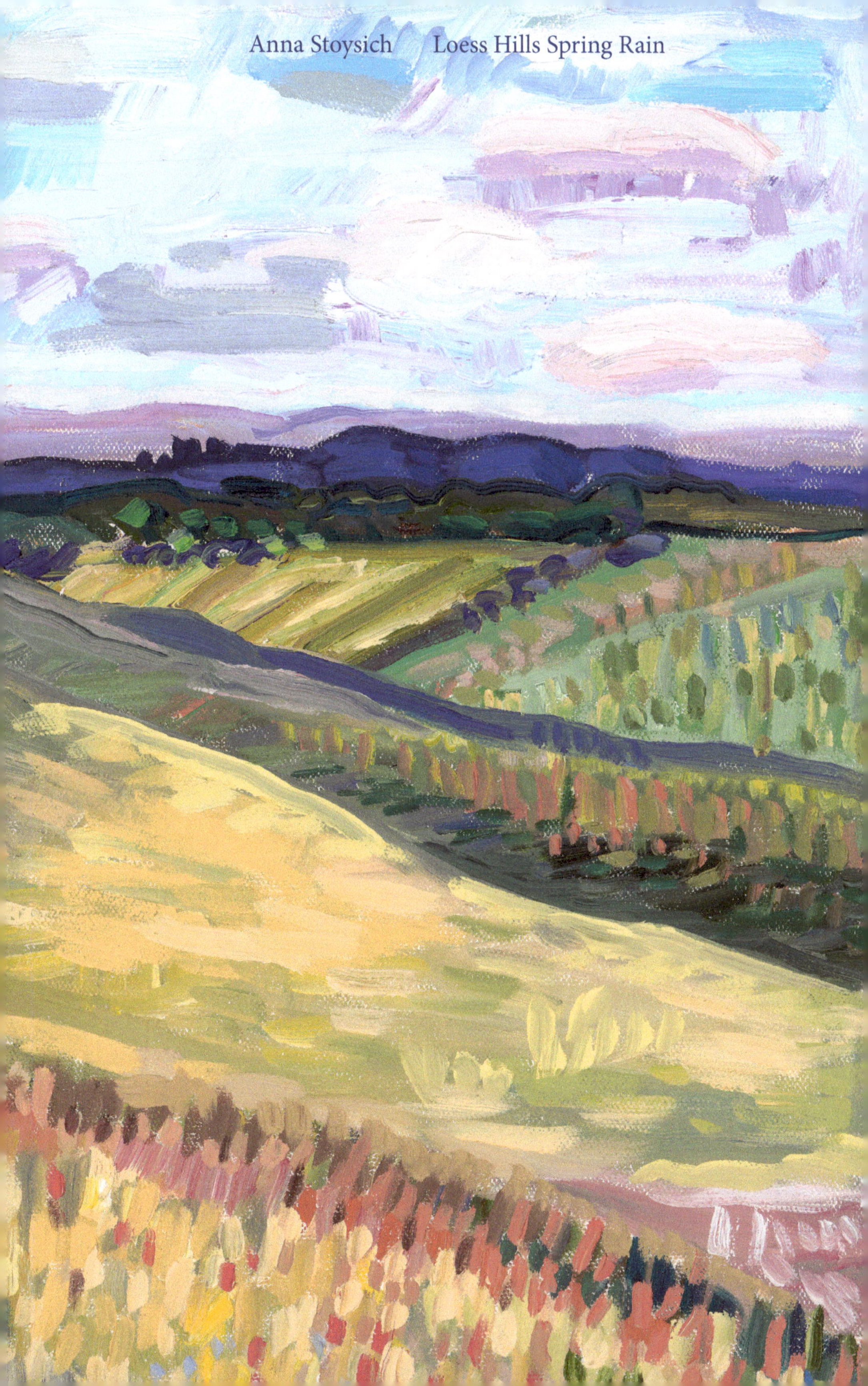
Anna Stoysich   Loess Hills Spring Rain

song for the prairie

i.

i wish i could have seen you in all your glory
when you were more sea than stem, ten feet tall and a hundred feet deeper,
i hear you kept wind beholden, or were you beholden to the wind?
i have nothing to give but this voice, this song i give the few cornflowers
still in bloom along the highway the lines breaking
your sea into clumps, i am so thirsty,
you are so thirsty,
the riverbeds crack in the heat, chapped lips
split tongue, i wish i knew
how to love you,
though what right do i have to wish that
to claim that, but i do wish i do wish
to be here where you are, pushing my toes
into your tendrils, trying to grow back
everything lost, everything toxic now,
i only have this song
i give to the hawk
hunting along the highway
their tail a bright flame
a sky a sunrise
a blooming golden-
rod glory
this love
i give it all

ii.

we went searching for a song
to sing the seeds fresh planted
this marriage we keep
to grow life
to feed ourselves
and if done right
everything else
how do we say
thank you
you asked and i said

we sing what we have
sing what we know
we make it up
so we sang and hoped
it was enough
to bond one heart to another
what is the heart of the seed
you asked and i said
light
the snow geese rebuked
their small sounds falling
like rain
they brought from south
to north
a chorus
of everything turning
towards the great
unfolding
the hawk swirling
the summer breeze
the snow melting
the dripping
spring singing
everything singing
the peepers singing
the snow geese singing
the light singing and us
the seeds
singing
small songs of praise
small tendrils
of prayer
reaching
the light

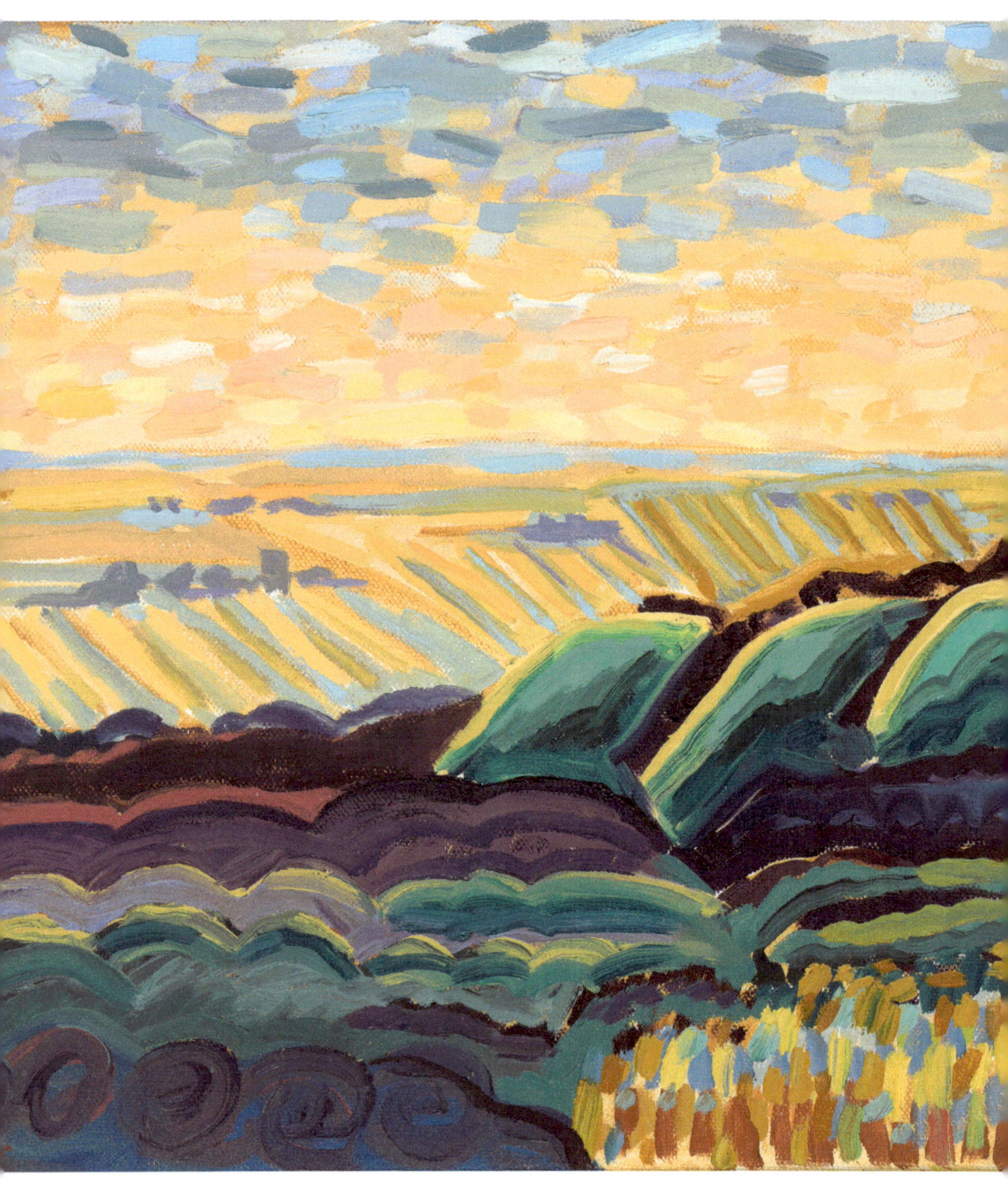

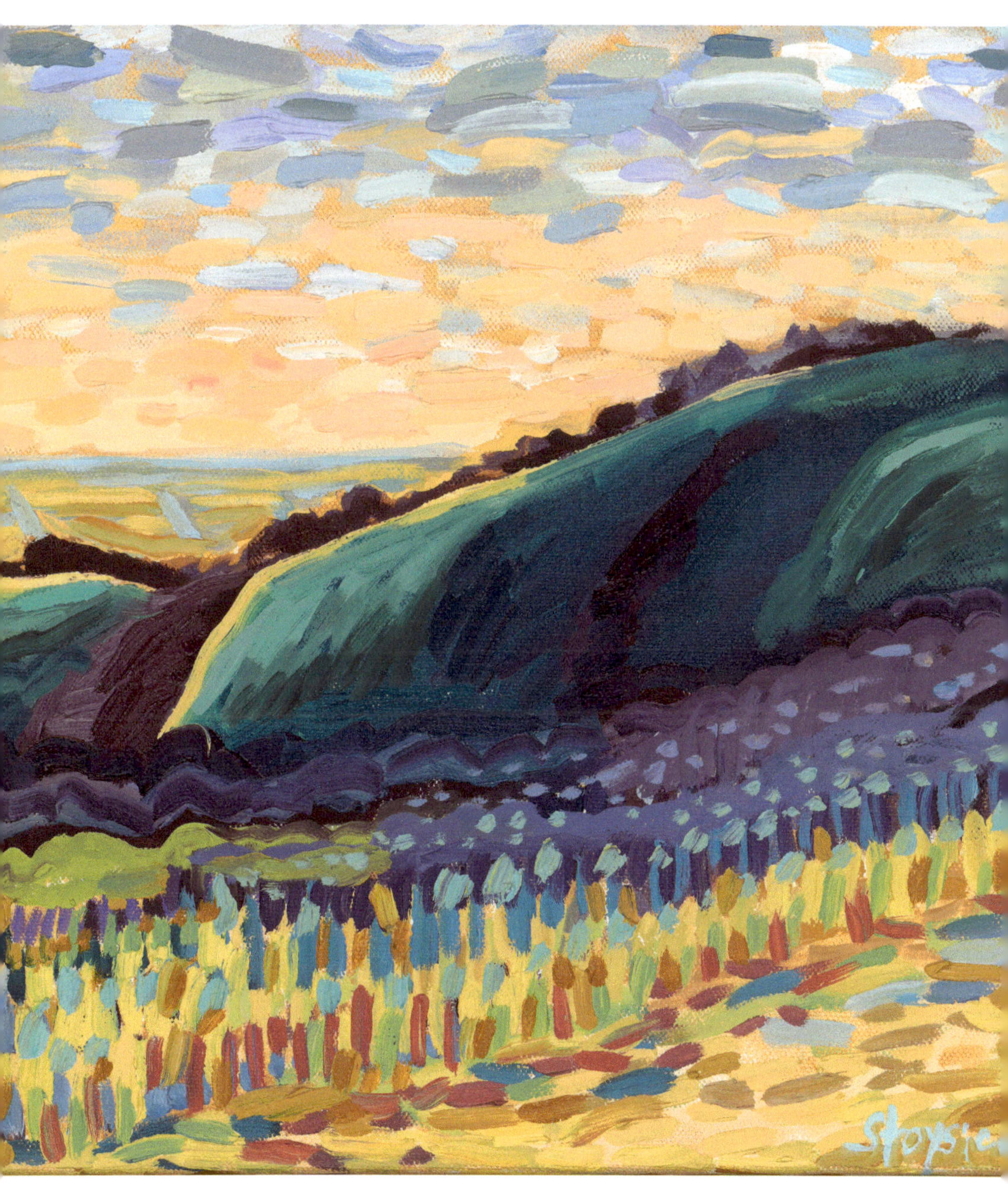

Anna Stoysich   Bright Loess Hills

Spring Congregation

I pause to ask the man with binoculars
if the bird on the lake is in fact a loon
and he says *Yes!* so we talk about migration,
about *how special* that they stop *right here,*
just for a moment, just to rest,
say their song reminds us
of northern lands, of other
times, of other homes
we *oooh* and *aah* over their ladderback
stripes, their white neck rings, time them
as they dive down for *so long!*
and never re-emerge where we expect—
the women walking by stop
and ask, *are you looking at the loons?*
We say *Yes!*
the man with binoculars and I
a team now we say *so special*
we say *right here!*
I tell them *I am from New York*
say *I didn't know* about loons in Iowa
and the women say *oh my*
say *that's quite a ways from home*
and one of the women looks at me
with such tenderness that, for once,
I am understood
the other woman ripples the stillness
asks *why'd you move?*
I say *I came here to write* and she ruffles
her hair and says *Good!,* says *We need more joy!*
and behind us the frogs start singing
in the small wetlands
someone saved just to save something
and in front of us the loon surfaces
their black back slicking the white
and water split into all directions
and the man with binoculars points
says *look*
and we all look

Early May, Iowa

Rachel Morgan

This morning I bought batteries
at the chain drug store on First Street.
The predicted rain was recalcitrant,
like a proud relative announcing
a secret everyone already knew.
On its breath, the anticipation of crops
and ornamental trees, the world petal-luscious.
In the parking lot, a young Amish woman
set out seedlings for sale, probably
planted indoors as the last snow fell.
Most everyone has started their day,
recently called from sleep, where again,
we learn to speak, remembering
what we want to say. I drove to work.
It's the last time I'll see this semester's students.
I want them to be happy, and tell them so.
I ignore the rain. Next the day of meetings,
grading, writing. Leaving work, I held the door
for someone I thought I knew, but did not.
A friend ate dinner with us. My son asked me
to sit with him. I said no, thought better of it,
and said yes. We are curled like ribbons when
he shows me a game on his screen. I don't need
to understand it, just see it. Today rests
like a stranger's head who's fallen asleep
on my shoulder. The bus ride is long,
winding into the mountains in a country
I've only seen on postcards, snowy alpine peaks,
blue-eyed sky, red flowers. Everything is beautiful
and every turn threatens to wake us both.

A Weed So Gorgeous It's Kept

Rachel Morgan

Before this, I was born in coal country
where stars and satellites fell from the night
sky and no one could tell the difference.
I was related to everyone on the coiling road
of trailers, the snake swallowing its tail.
Gravity pulls us to earth, and families net us
by birth. The tales warn of danger—
dark forests, evil spells, parentless children
wolves as wolves, and wolves in disguise.

When I moved to the prairie's patches
of corn and soy, I noticed a spidery weed
that grows best next to no other species
blooming in my garden. I pulled them.
Now, dozens of Red Columbine hang
their lacey bell-heads earthward.
We built boats, never stayed in one place,
crossed ice, sent gold records of surf, wind,
thunder, and whale song into outer space.

What will set the needle on the record's golden
groove hearing the human boy say, hello
from the children of planet earth?

I Could Lose All Father Now

Rachel Morgan

Winter dead ahead and I am walking
my father's land. Some of the leaves
are shaped like a child's mittened hand,
most are ragged like lace-space.
Between the rains' and birds' songs,
I think of him after years of not
thinking of him. We believe
different things. In a few weeks, he'll be
seventy-one and wants to still groom
the earth with his metastatic bones.

I return home, five states away and tend
my corner lot, divorced at the middle of life—
I sow grass seed when rain is forecasted,
the same time to pile up tangled brush,
messy oak leaves, and burn anything
that's just a little dead or rotting.

We are best alone. I start the brush fire
with one match, just like he taught me,
bank my bills, and continue to think
it's not how much is earned, but saved.
Ash, still glowing red rises in the heat
over the oak's living branches, past
the steep roofs in my neighborhood.
It's a letter I've written him. I'm less certain
of what fathers are for, but I thank him.
I have so much to thank him for.

# of weapons and water

Seth Thill

we skim the river for bullet shells
and the algae finds the holes in itself
stone shore, oil barrel fire pit,
heron feathers burn. mississippi, what do you
long for? whisper it into these severed ears

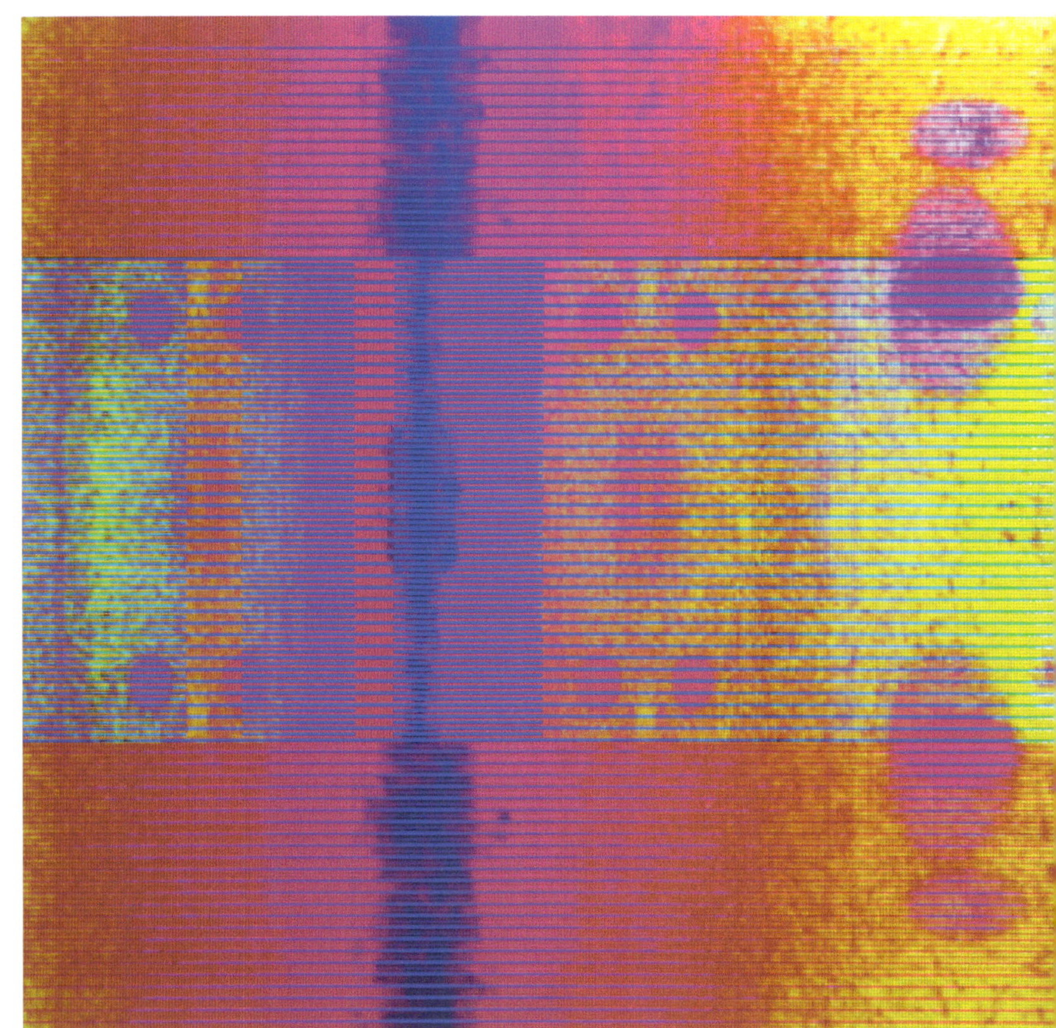

Matthew Kluber   Friday I'm in Love, Alkyd on Aluminum,

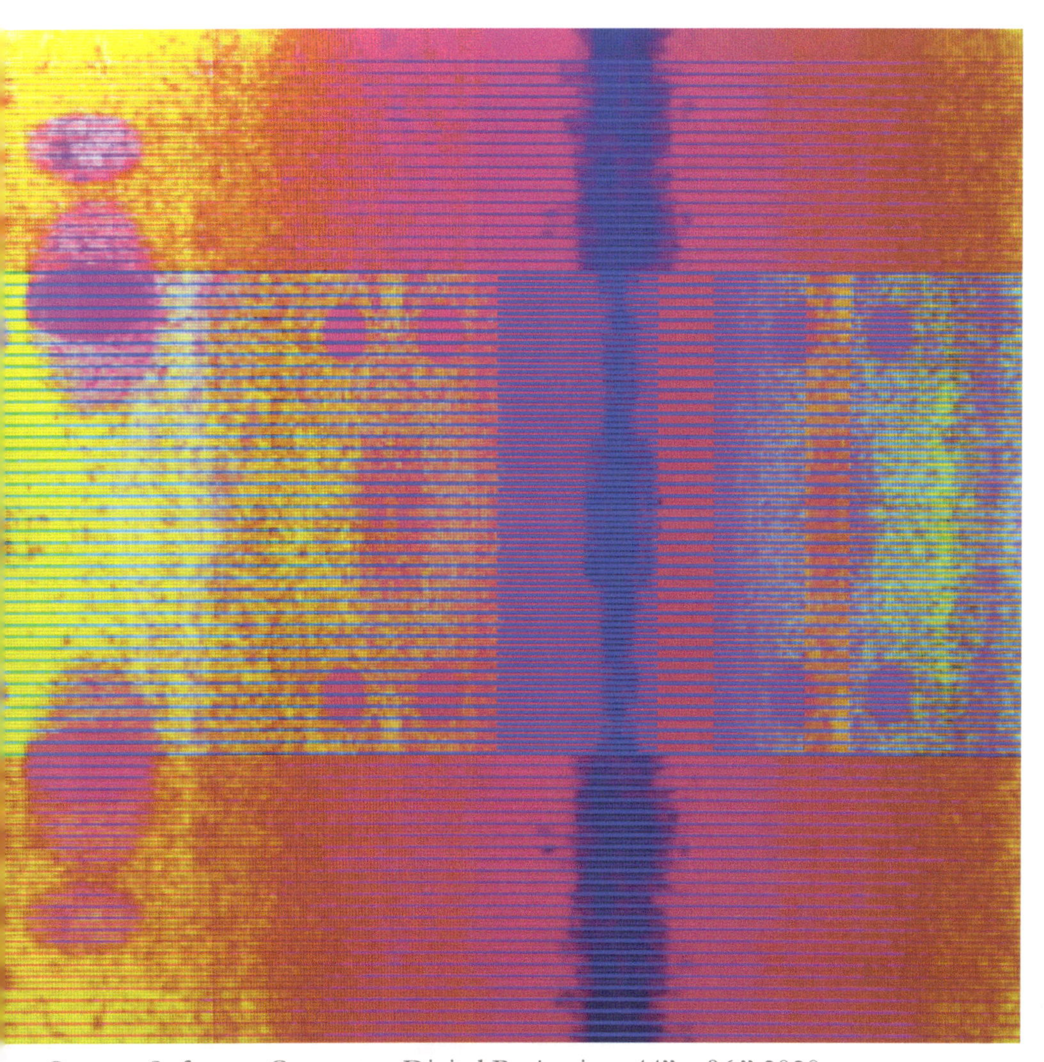

Custom Software, Computer, Digital Projection, 44" x 96," 2020

Walmart Claw Machine: 1 AM

Cheap plush, neon faces impaled
with misplaced, chasmic plastic eyes,
line my dash. I drive slow, park in faded yellow.
Aaron's half-asleep beside me, the moon
roof stretches empty miles that end

once summer air's snared moisture evaporates
in industrial cooling, industrial light.
Quarters from the cupholder awaken
the claw, shiny glass nostalgia awakens
endorphins, nothing quite awakens Aaron.

The metal drops against fabric, rigid
control vs. wildly fluid variables. Claw scrapes
a bear's white belly, but lets
go, stretches back out, rises, dangling in
rigor mortus. More quarters in and

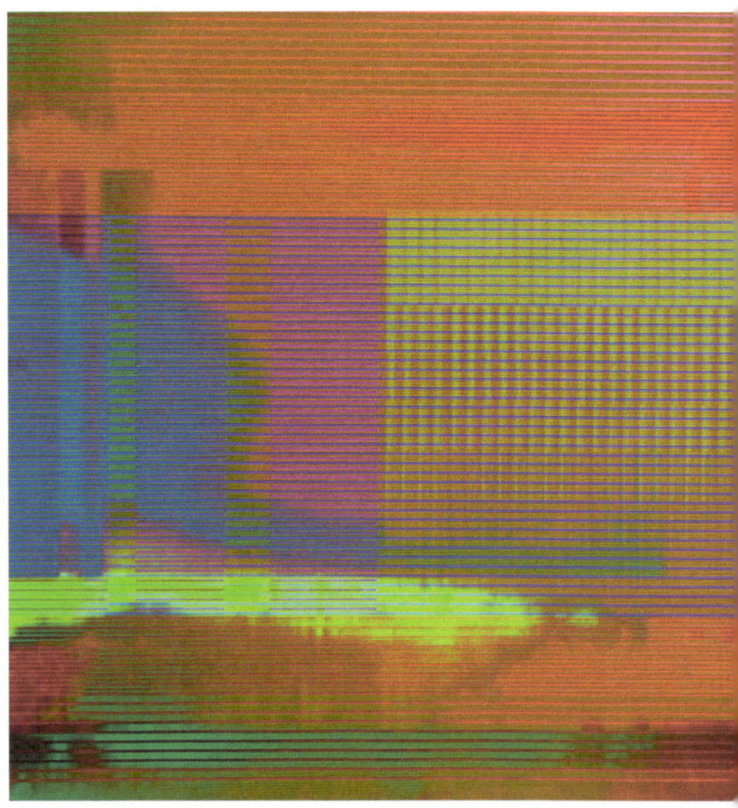

Matthew Kluber   Radio Free Sante Fe, Alkyd on

Nothing after nothing fills
the space between the prongs, between
the glass walls, the borders holding
the only victories I can imagine besides

The Doritos I buy as a consolation prize.
Bag rests on my lap as Aaron and I pass
out in the car. On the dash,
the prizes of past nights breathe sweet

nothings, and bodies wait,
with our windows open,
for plastic eyes to tell us we are enough,
for awakenings met with plush skies.

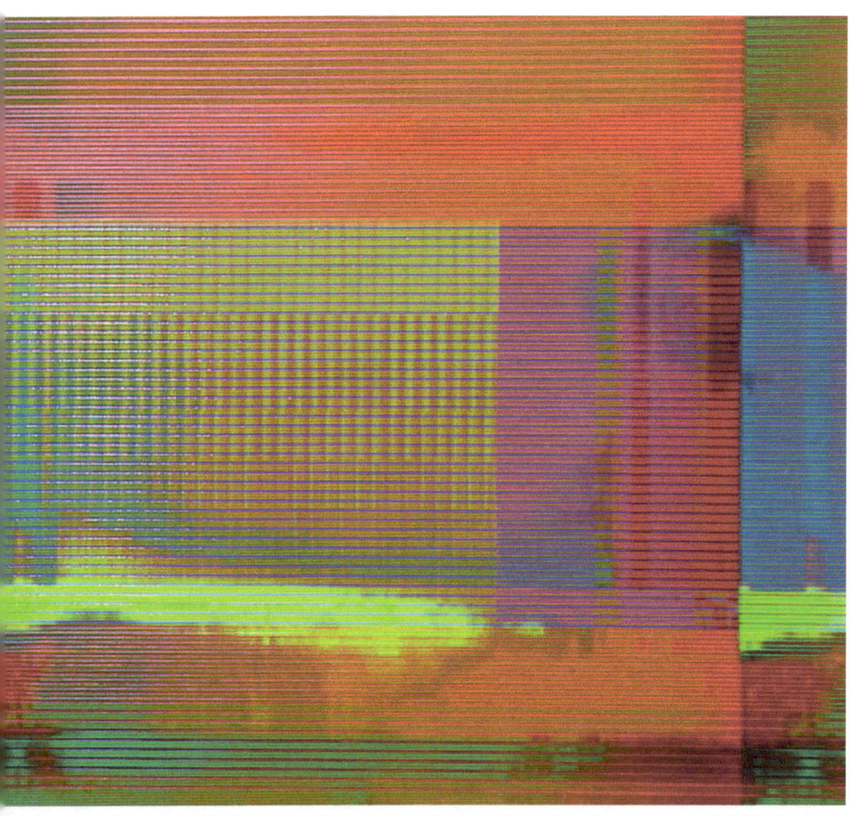

uminum, Custom Software, Computer, Digital Projection, 44" x 96," 2018

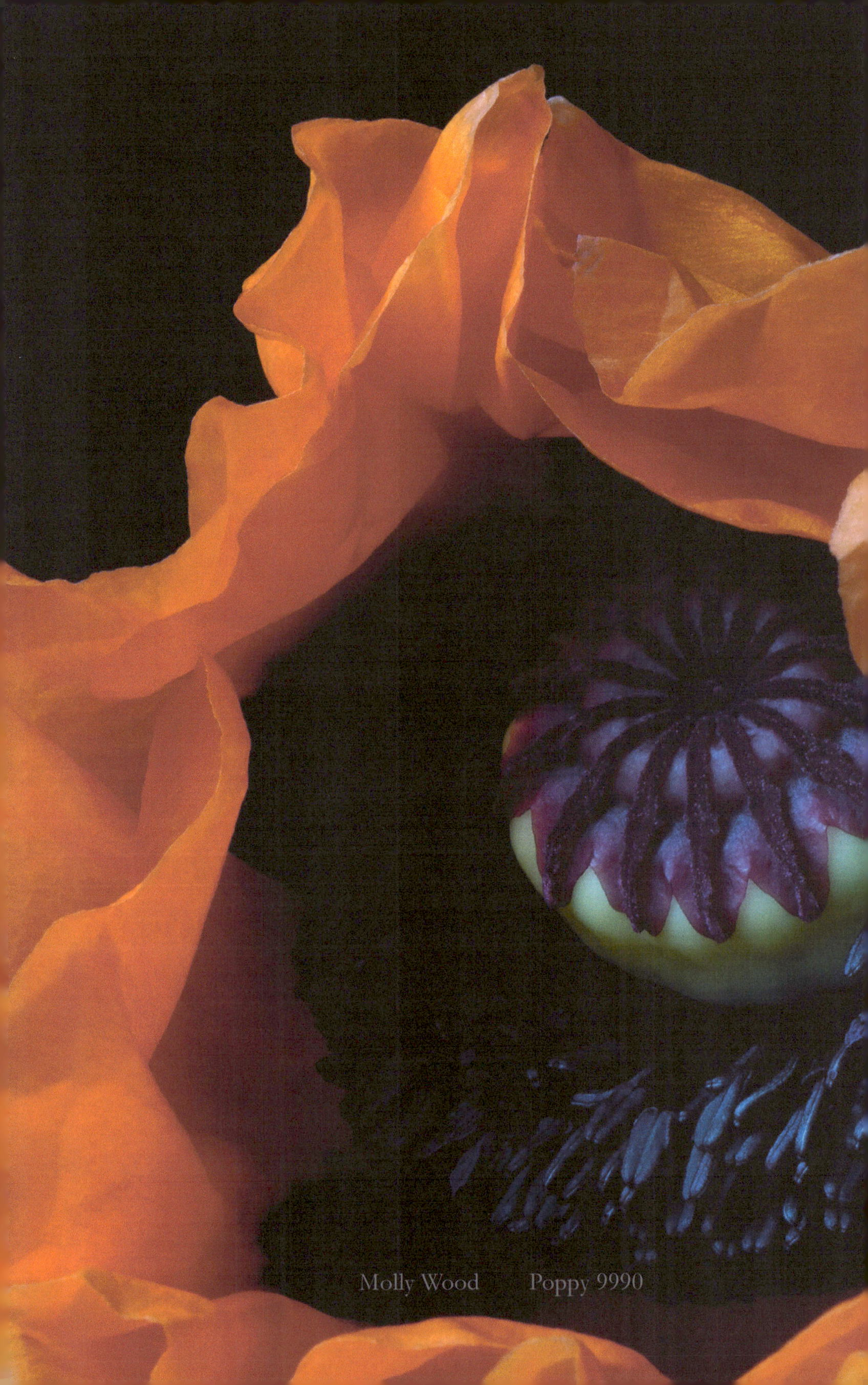

Molly Wood   Poppy 9990

The Numerology of Gardening
in homage to Teijo Nakamura

Shelly Reed Thieman

Today, even the lake I fish is manmade. Animus clouds hover like ravenous gulls. Shin deep in cool water, I hold two lines from Nakamura—*Remember, today's flower is today's flower, today's wind is today's wind*—and think of you—Today's husband is today's husband. You are three-season husband to golf.

look not
for dust in the corner
but at the wilting orchid

The kitchen floor takes on the shape of my feet after so many foretold meals. You're reading Salzi's *Old Man War* in the oatmeal leather chair with your feet propped like a czar on the ottoman. If I croaked at the stove, you would not know until your six o'clock belly rumbled like a garbage disposal.

tonight, stay indoors
this spring moon
no longer palpable

Monday stumbles from bed. You polish your shoes and clubs, cram balls in pockets of the monogrammed bag, drive away. I listen to Donovan's *A Gift from a Flower to a Garden,* polish my nails *Take a Bow Blue.* Through afternoon I plant nineteen black dahlias along the fence. You don't come home for dinner.

so familiar
the moment dusk slips
its arm around me

Jen Rouse

My Uterus Eats Itself Like a Ravenous Thing

I thought I loved bubble
gum ice cream, its perfect sunset

pink and pops of blue moon
Chiclets orbiting. I don't really know

now why I make my father
threatening in every memory.

Or why a child dropping her favorite
flavor brings me to my knees. My uterus

eats itself like a ravenous thing
with Chiclet teeth—orange and green

mirror squares—and, there, in the sheen,
the day I tripped once and could not

mourn the ice cream for fear
of that anger. A great white

shark has two uteri. Embryos
jockey for best position, cannibalize

their siblings. It is so hard to want
more. I attempted to keep two tiny

creatures alive. One who chose to stay,
firmly cemented in her idea of self.

The other like an ice cream midfall,
and I'm reaching out to catch the soft

pink eternal goo of them as they
slide through fingers. Cone to stardust.

The lining of a shark uterus flutters,
layered lamellae, soft soft. Ever before

we knew such intense hunger.

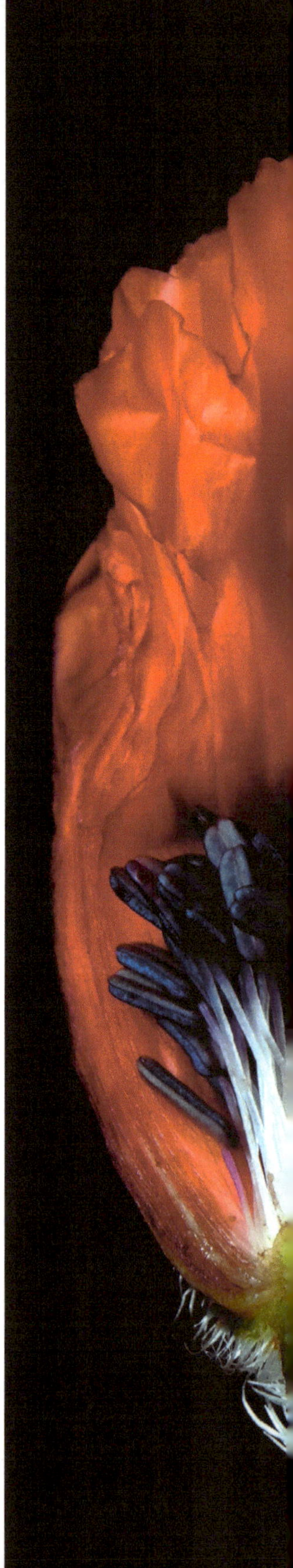

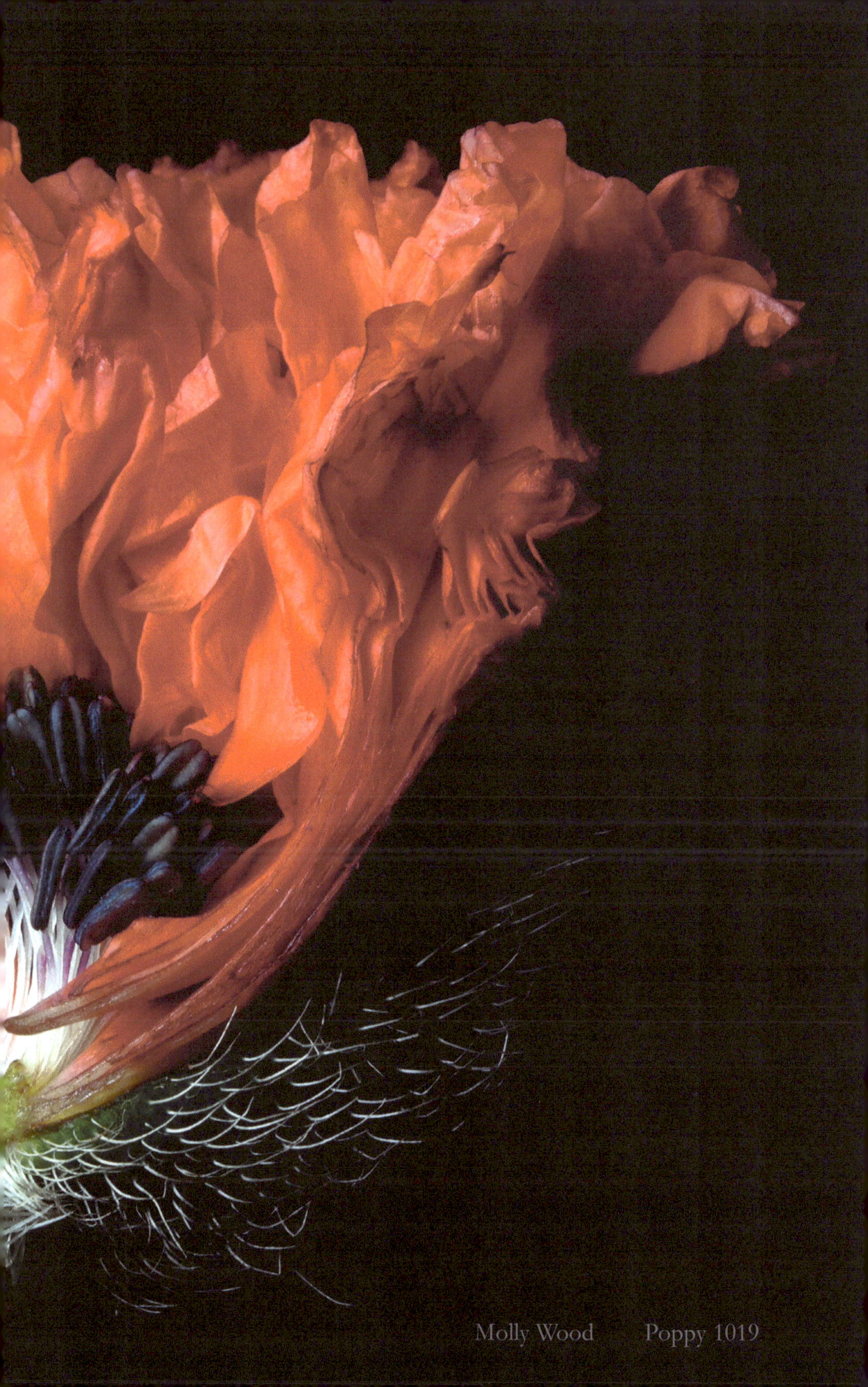
Molly Wood   Poppy 1019

Somewhere in that Process Lies the Evolution of the Mind

But wait, you are mostly still morons—shouting into the void
like jellyfish first firing their flickering orbs, developing
a sincere and combative sting, those
500 million years ago.

Let me give you the reason for build
For nervous system   For brain

= something mattered/matters/will matter

Some of you live in the murky depths of receptive
and others in the aquatic chemistry of action.

Between think and do, this arc,
this in between. Call it a maze,
call it a network of currents running hell bent,
call it the slow sardonic wit
you wait for when you've gotten
lost in your own ways of forgetting
I exist. You only hear the words when
they collect themselves in brilliant displays,
drawn to the desire to show themselves
to like selves, determined. Yes, you become
determined. You are certain you are
vibrant and worthy. You begin to
learn the language of react.

I am the constant reminder
that something has to matter,
that you will never quite walk
on water. Without me.

Pharmakon de Medici

237 cabinets. You are a woman. You are poison. Thorned in this palm, a peony unfurling. When there is a massacre, when the people split and the heavens hide their gods, you refuse to leave the throne. At tea, the devil's trumpet. And all of the ladies unlace. Just a little. There hasn't been a moment for breath. And if they would call you a great king, cunt and all, would you accept the compliment? But they will never. Behind the first door is a pair of perfumed gloves. A fork behind the second. Some science that sounds like sorcery, third. How dare you be Italian. You are a curiosity in your own cupboard. Bad mother. And you are. And you are not. Belladonna. Black widow. When you prick your own finger, what do you taste on your tongue?

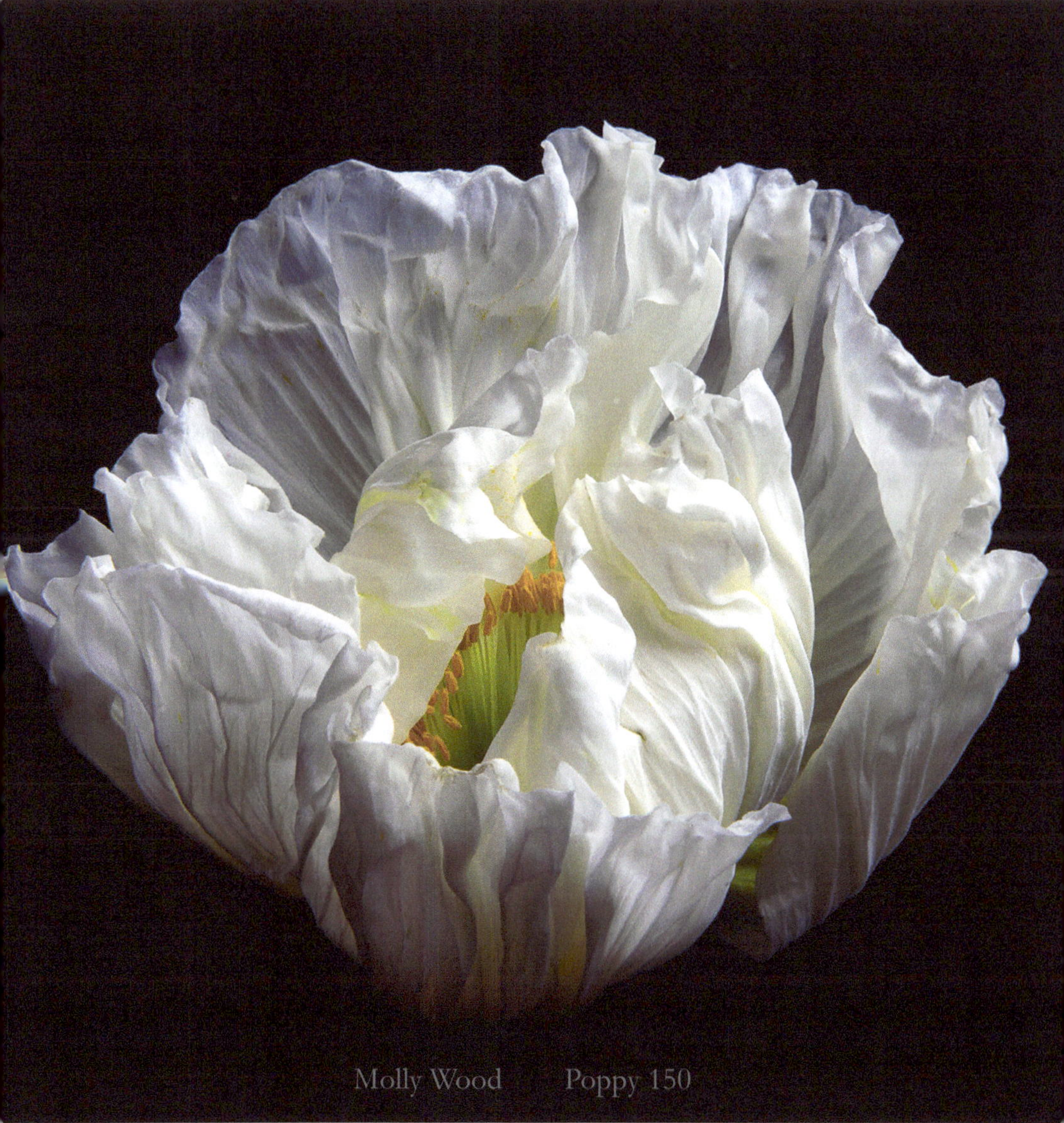

Molly Wood   Poppy 150

The Inferno Elegies

Tasha Jackson

The set of six interconnected poems represent a physical journey through the rivers of hell, which was first discussed in Dante Alighieri's epic poem known as Inferno, the first part of his The Divine Comedy (La Commedia in his native Italian). La Commedia is considered by many to be the greatest literary work in Italian history, and consists of three distinct parts: Inferno, Purgatorio, and Paradiso (Hell, Purgatory, and Heaven in English, respectively). Inferno was his story about traveling through the nine different levels (circles) of Hell, with the famous poet Virgil as his makeshift tour guide, and drew from Dante's knowledge of Greek mythology.

The Greeks imagined Hell as a physical place, rather than a metaphorical one – a hidden dimension, or a parallel universe, accessed only via specific conditions and timing. The rivers crisscrossed and flowed, both around, and through, the Underworld itself. Scholarly accounts differ widely on the order they were thought to follow within the plane of Hell, but a rough consensus puts them in this order: Acheron, Styx, Phlegethon, Cocytus, Lethe – this is the order Dante himself used in his work, so I will use it as well.

I. AcheRoN

you were only legendary
for spreading your own rumors
you thought it'd lead to Fame
but that road only curved toward Ruin
how could it not—
you looked like summer in a human form
and you watched them feed on me—
wolves tearing away at the thin flesh of
my exposed neck—
a part I'd made vulnerable, only for you—
gloating like the Cheshire cat
as you reveled in my suffering
carved relief—my ashen face

and you became someone else then—
an empty, soulless **Thing** inside
a void with arms & legs
predator coiled around its prey
that sullen shadow I would come to know
so well, that I'm beginning to forget

your sandpaper thumb
brushing my cheek
the promise
that you wouldn't let anyone hurt me
anymore
(my rescue boat against the crushing swells)
before an enemy took root
and spread its venom in your brain
just because you severed the leaden cable
that connects us, with a sword
didn't mean the nerves
hanging ragged from my chest
no longer felt your absence

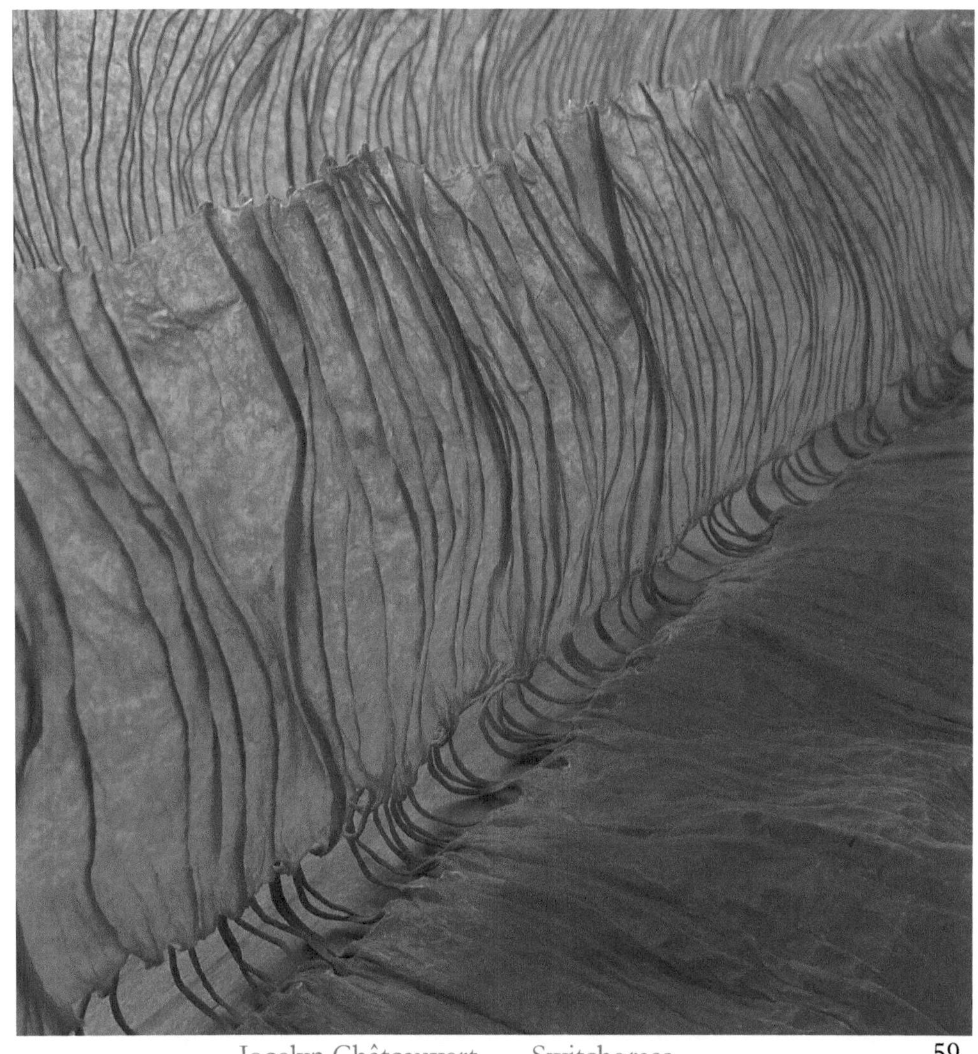

Jocelyn Châtcauvert   Switchgrass

I'm not sorry
for loving you
with everything I had
I'm not sorry
for trying everything I could
to save you—
from yourself
I always wanted it more
than I wanted to save Me

so I gladly pay the fee
with this coin beneath my tongue
to the ferryman
with eyes aflame
whose thoughts broadcast
directly through my veins
shockwaves through my limbs
each time he deigns to speak

and I begin my journey
down this dark river
it's not a journey it's a sentence
away from the shores of mad
screaming corpses
begging for mercy as they claw
at each other, blood blanketing the dirt
to a place where I can leave
my memories of you behind
good luck with that
the somber sky an iron mask
where the air is always Night
where I can imagine
in these dreams
that you never mattered to me
*you **do** know why you're here, don't you?*

so I can pretend that it was true
when you whispered—
lips grazing at my ear—

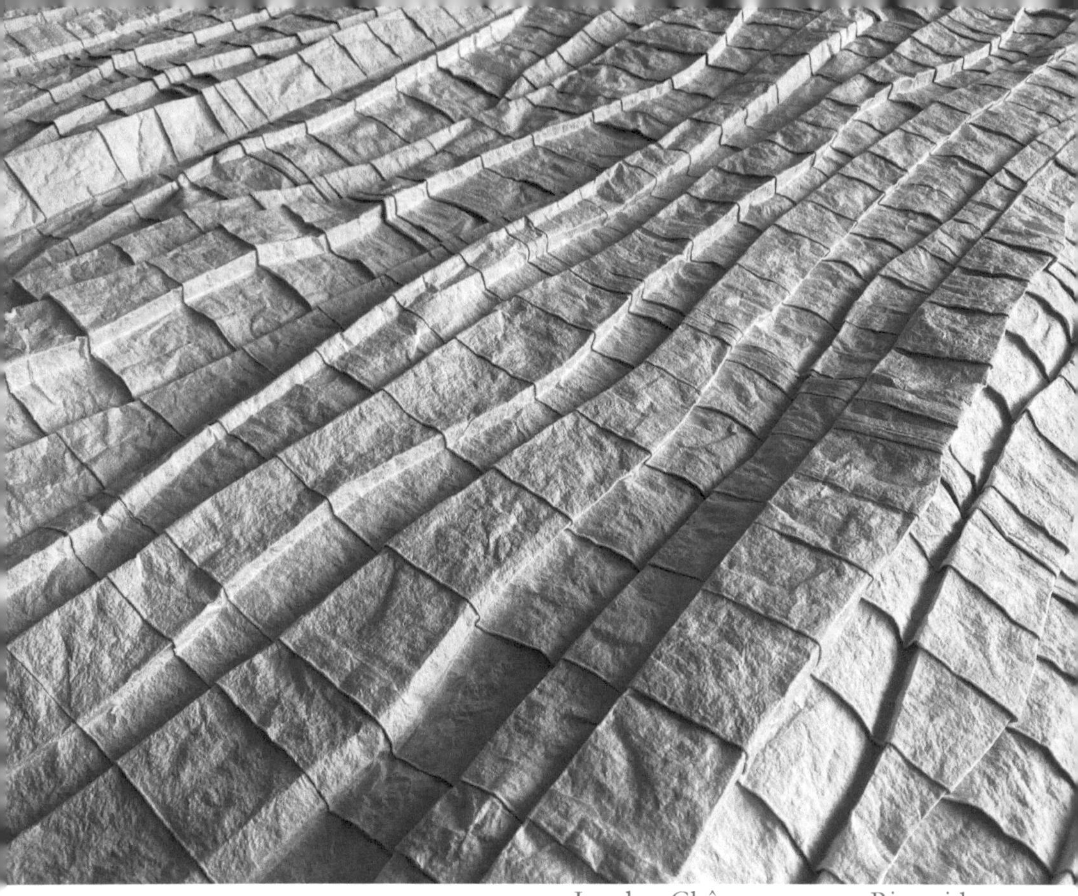

Jocelyn Châtcauvert   Riverside

that I'd be safe with you

II. StyX

disgust and hatred unfurl inside my heart
rampant symbiotes of darkness
until there's nothing left to taste
gaping wound festering in an empty chest
a vicious contagion
revenge consumes my waking thoughts
now that I'm alone
in a storm-battered grimy
ancient rowboat of my own
to carry me through churning, brackish waves
with hurricane curtains
obscuring every view
to finish what we started
before you destroyed it all

Charon paused as though awaiting
a thank-you for the ride
so I maimed him with his steerage pole
to buy myself some time
he blinked at me, a bit confused
I'm Heracles—a clever ruse

and the nightmares continue—
the two of us
expired shells in all of them
but it doesn't feel wrong
only—almost—
s a t i s f y i n g ...

the electric power of knowing your demise
was written by my hand—
fingers dripping malice—
spraying red
that I'm the one who gets to end your story
just like you ended mine—

crushing my ribs beneath
your heavy boots,
gaining leverage to rip your arrow
from my neck—
its cracking deafened me
split me to the core
now I no longer hear the screaming
coming through the floor

and this surge of revulsion
will take me right where I belong—
because I'll never forgive you
and I'll never let go
you thought you could escape me
but you don't get to choose the ending!

'cause even though I wake up
from these twisted dreams

occasionally
it doesn't mean it wasn't ever real—
for me

it doesn't mean I didn't feel anything

III. The Black Gate

the fog creeps in
a snake winding through dark sand
waves of billowing gray smoke
water slowing to a rolling boil
as I enter the canal
this worthless dinghy finally approaching
the eternal city known as Dis
has it been days, or weeks?
my plan was to escape unscathed

barnacle-encrusted gate
swings open to admit me,
colossal in its scope
iron bars that wheeze
a jarring
c
   r
     e
       a
         k
in the blistering haze
a thick tangle of black grime
coats ruined buildings—
ivy vines
swampy muck struggles to reclaim
each brick facade, in turn
they sink slowly

and all at once
while floating through—
the ugly stench of spoiled meat

an auditorium of whispers
nobody lives here
nobody lives here

but the crimson, haunted eyes of Shades
see through me
from behind smudged window panes
the water slowing still as glass
the echoes of vampiric children
reaching toward my pallid hands

as I chew frantically at my nails—
eyes scanning through the gloom for you
because I know, if ever I deserved this
than you deserve it too

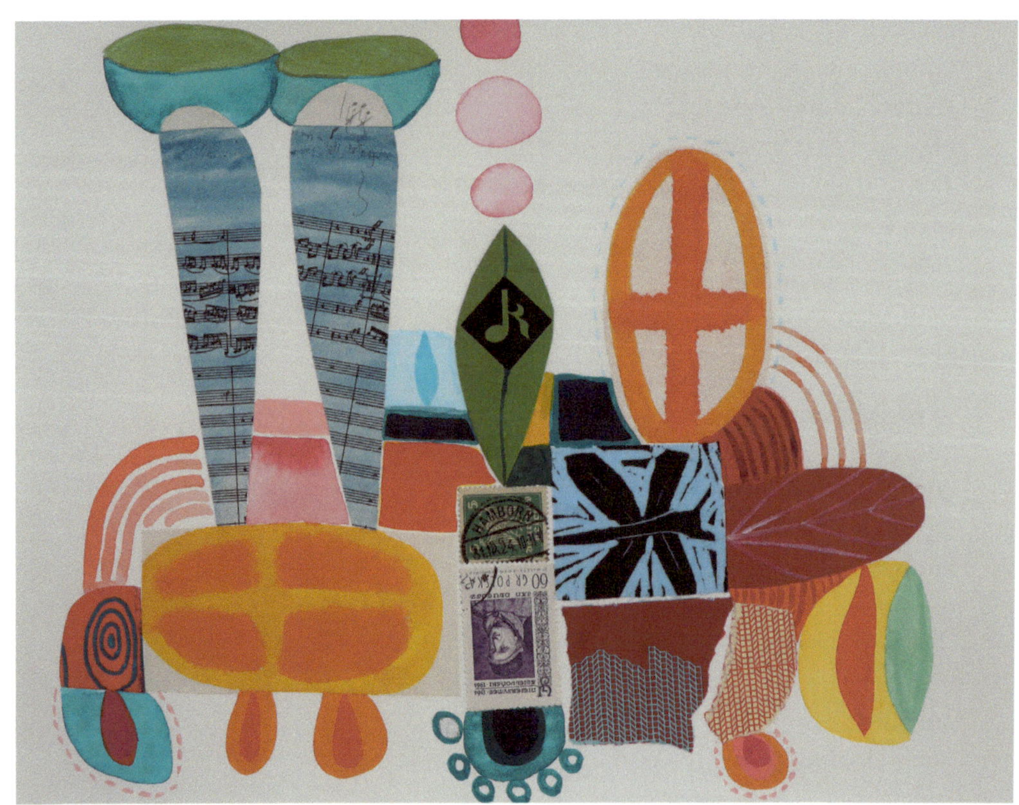

Alexandra Ackerman   Mysterious Contraption, Collage and Mixed Media, 9 x 12," 2023

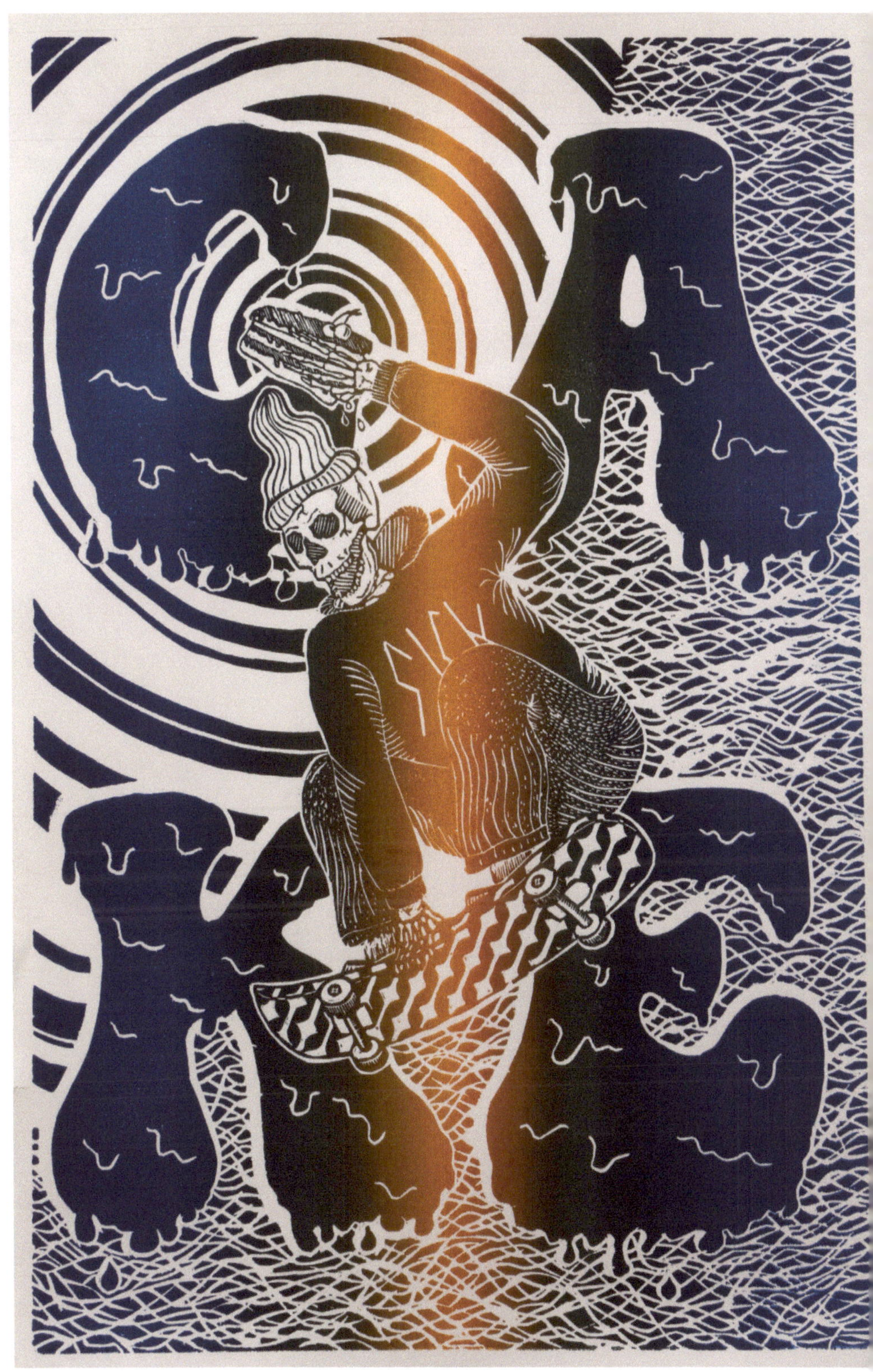

Bob Lockhart   Scake Woodcut

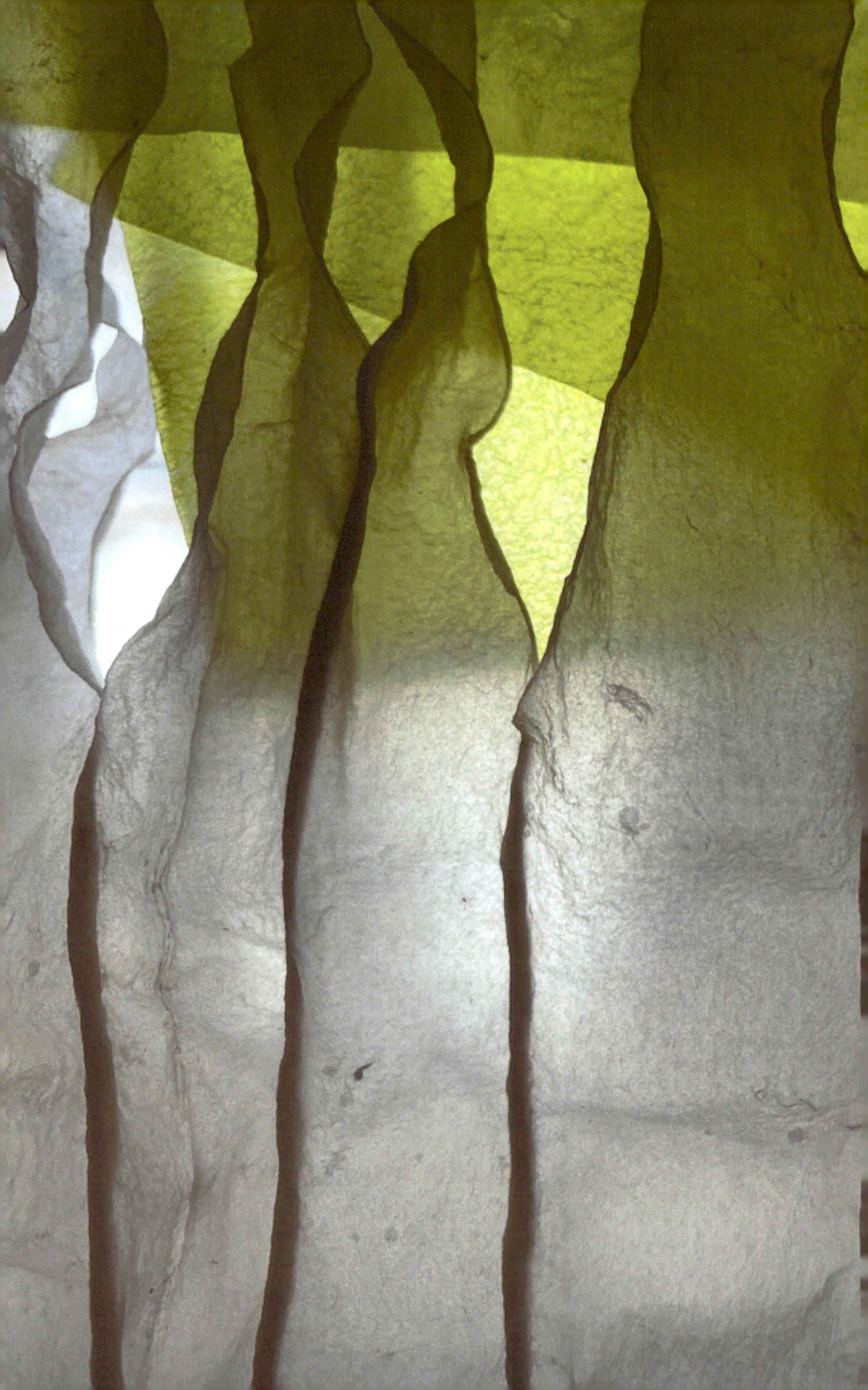

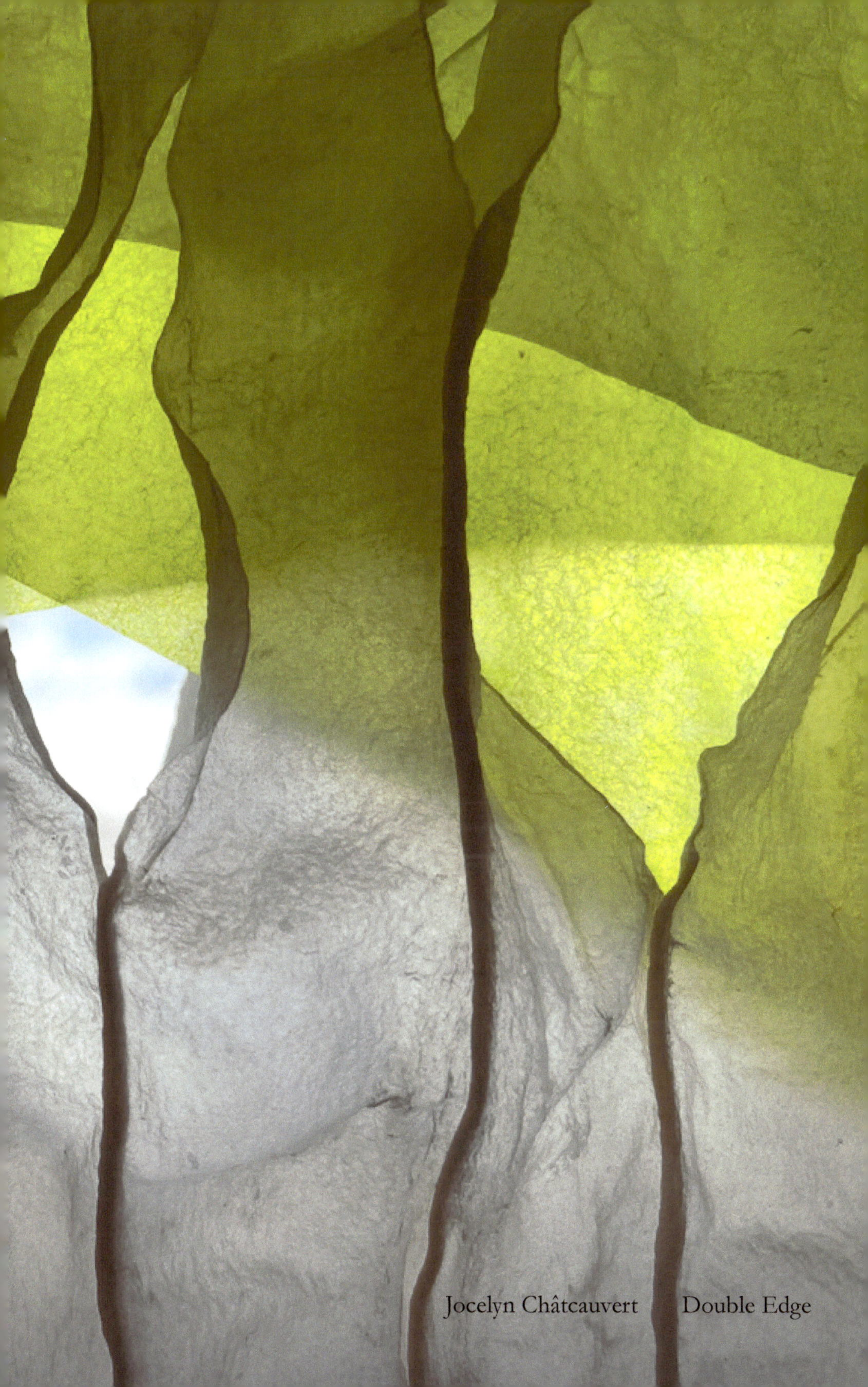
Jocelyn Châtcauvert   Double Edge

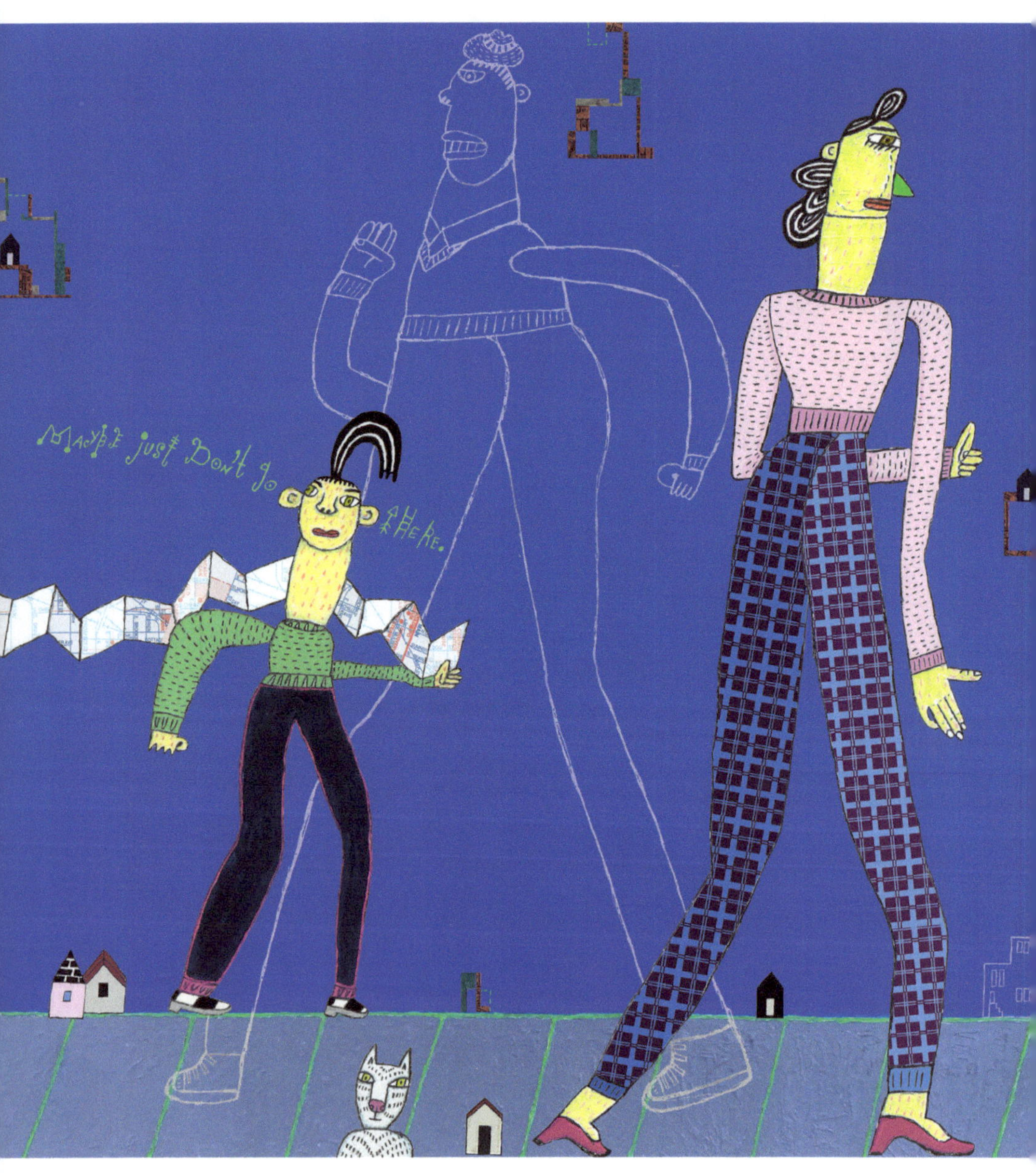

Mary Jones   Carmen Years

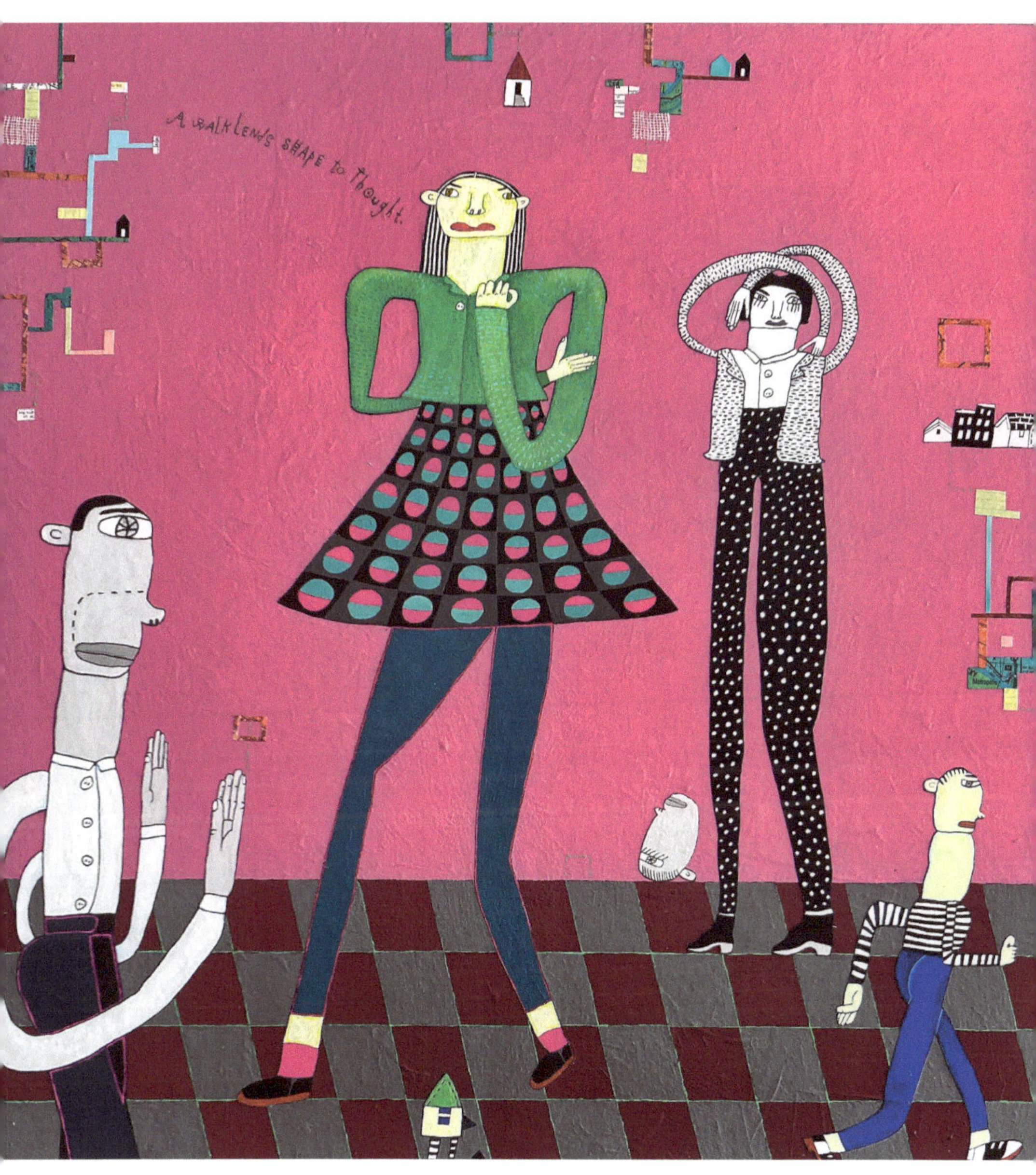

Mary Jones   Manifest

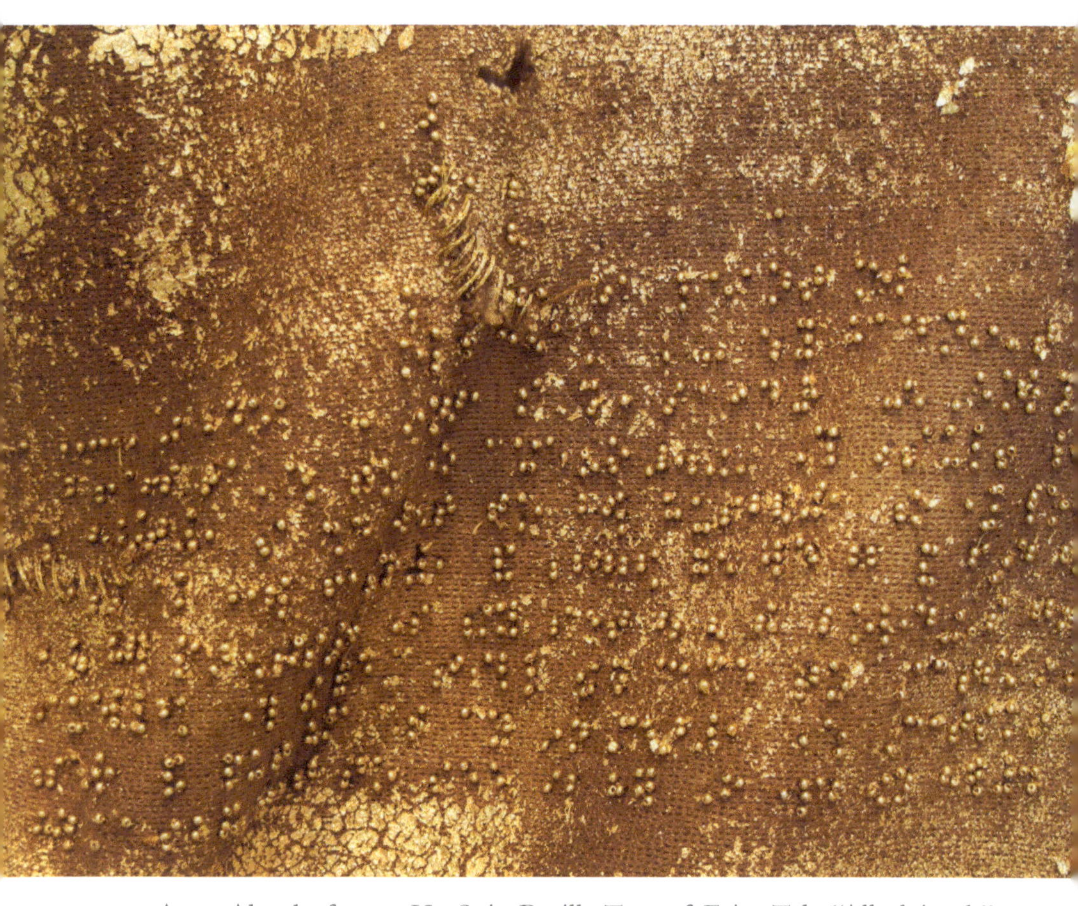

Ange Altenhofen   HerSuit, Braille Text of Fairy Tale "Allerleirauh"

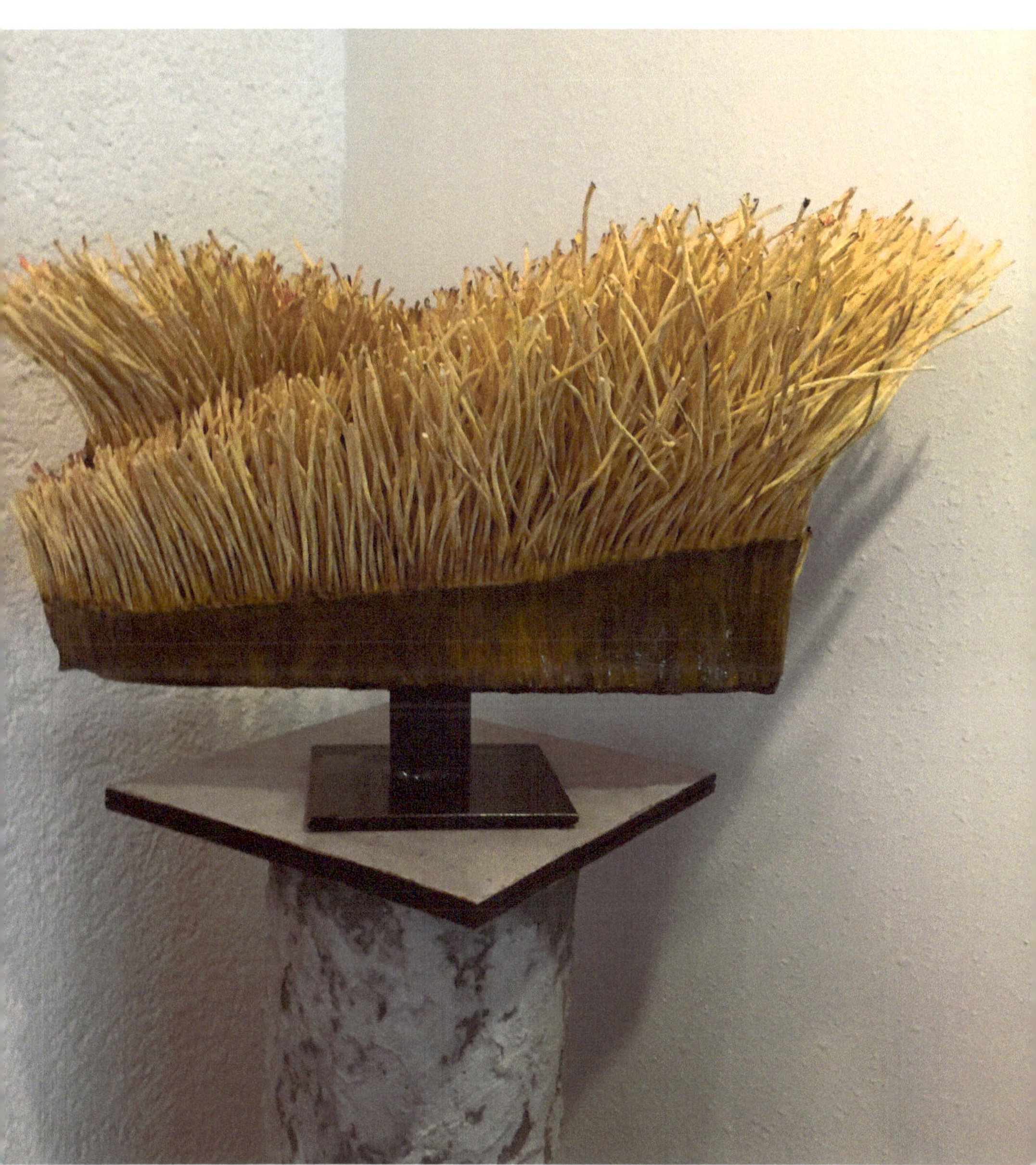

Elizabeth Rhoads Read   0278, Demeter's Realm

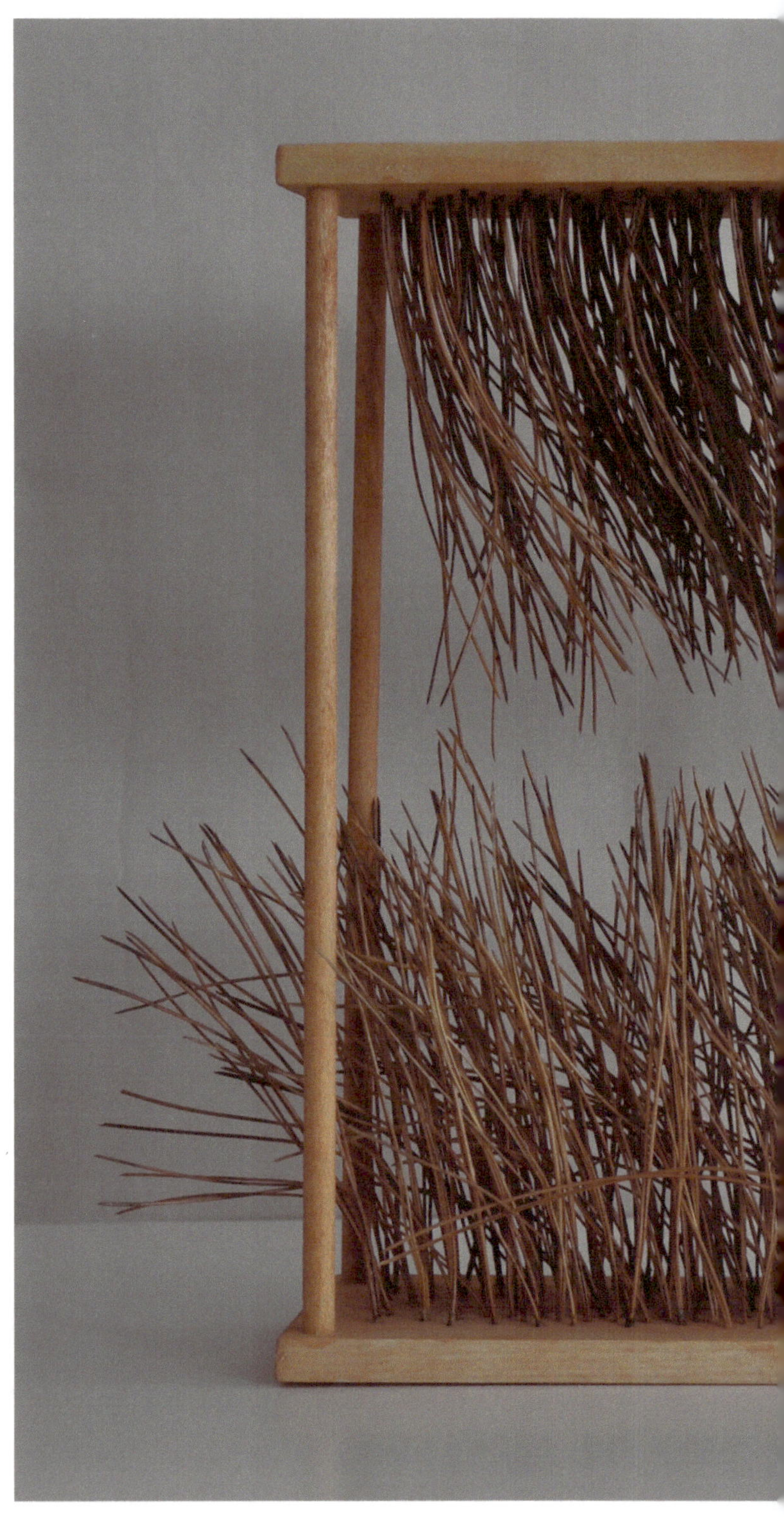

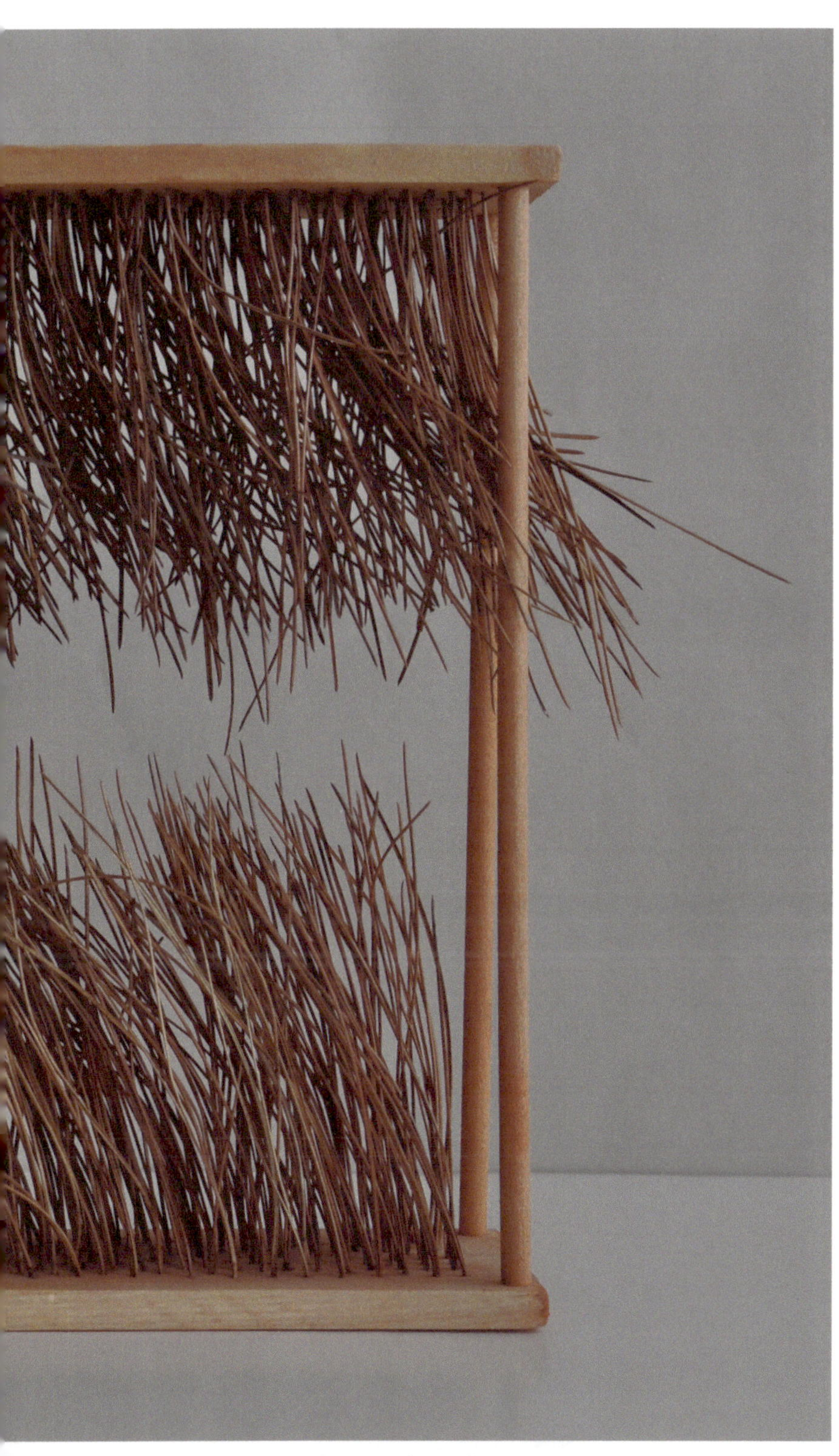

Joan Webster-Vore   Connections 3

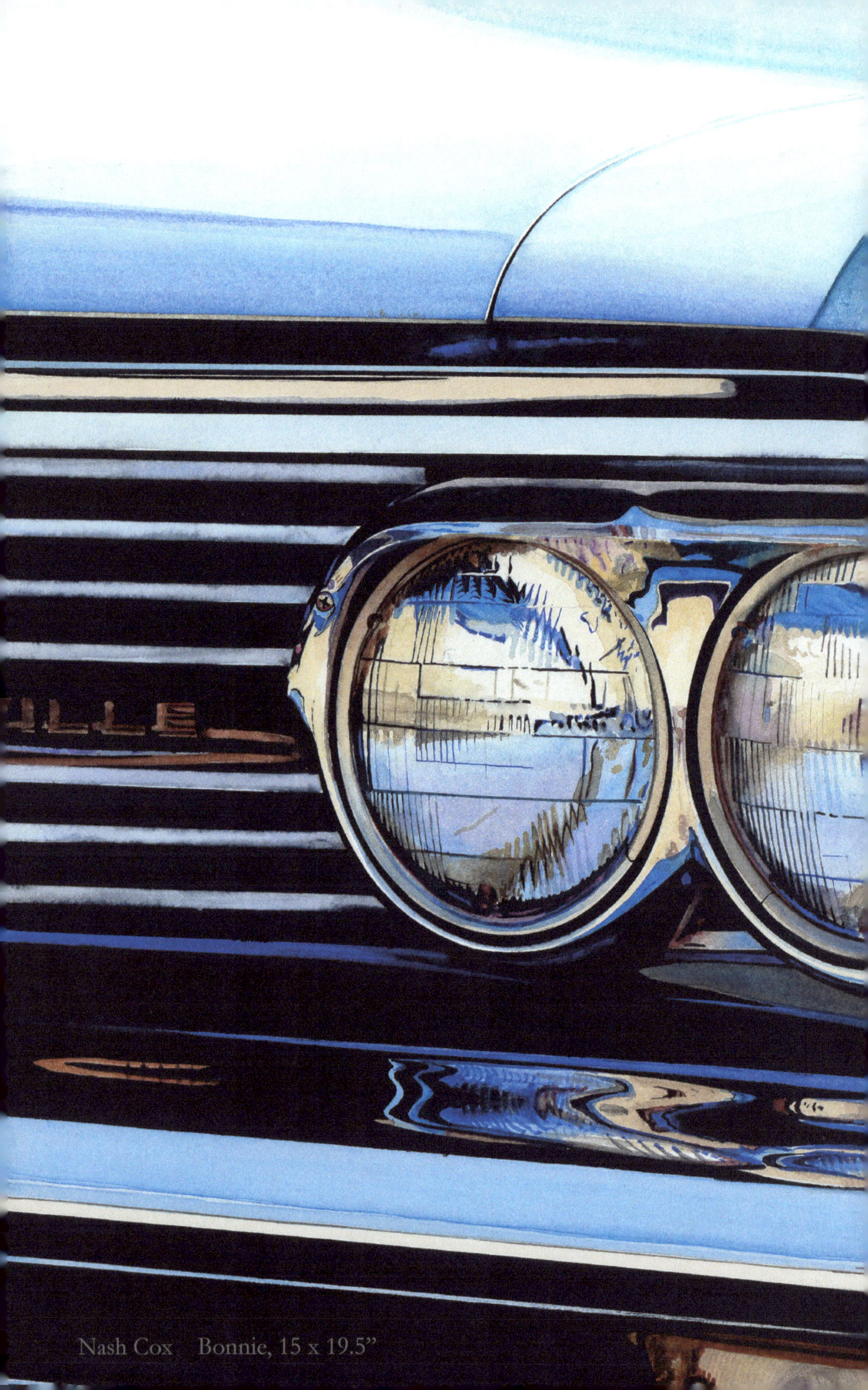

Nash Cox   Bonnie, 15 x 19.5"

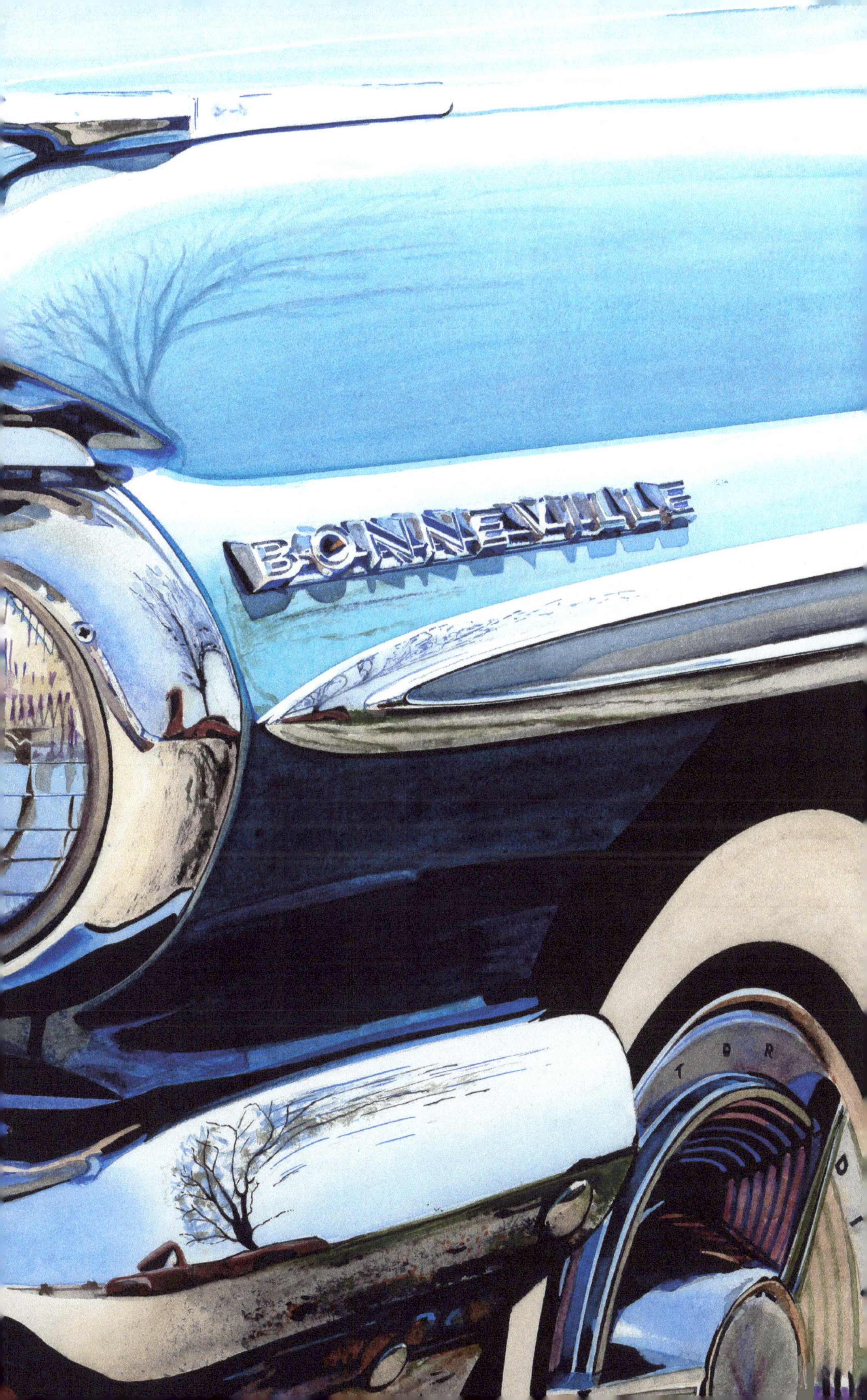
BONNEVILLE

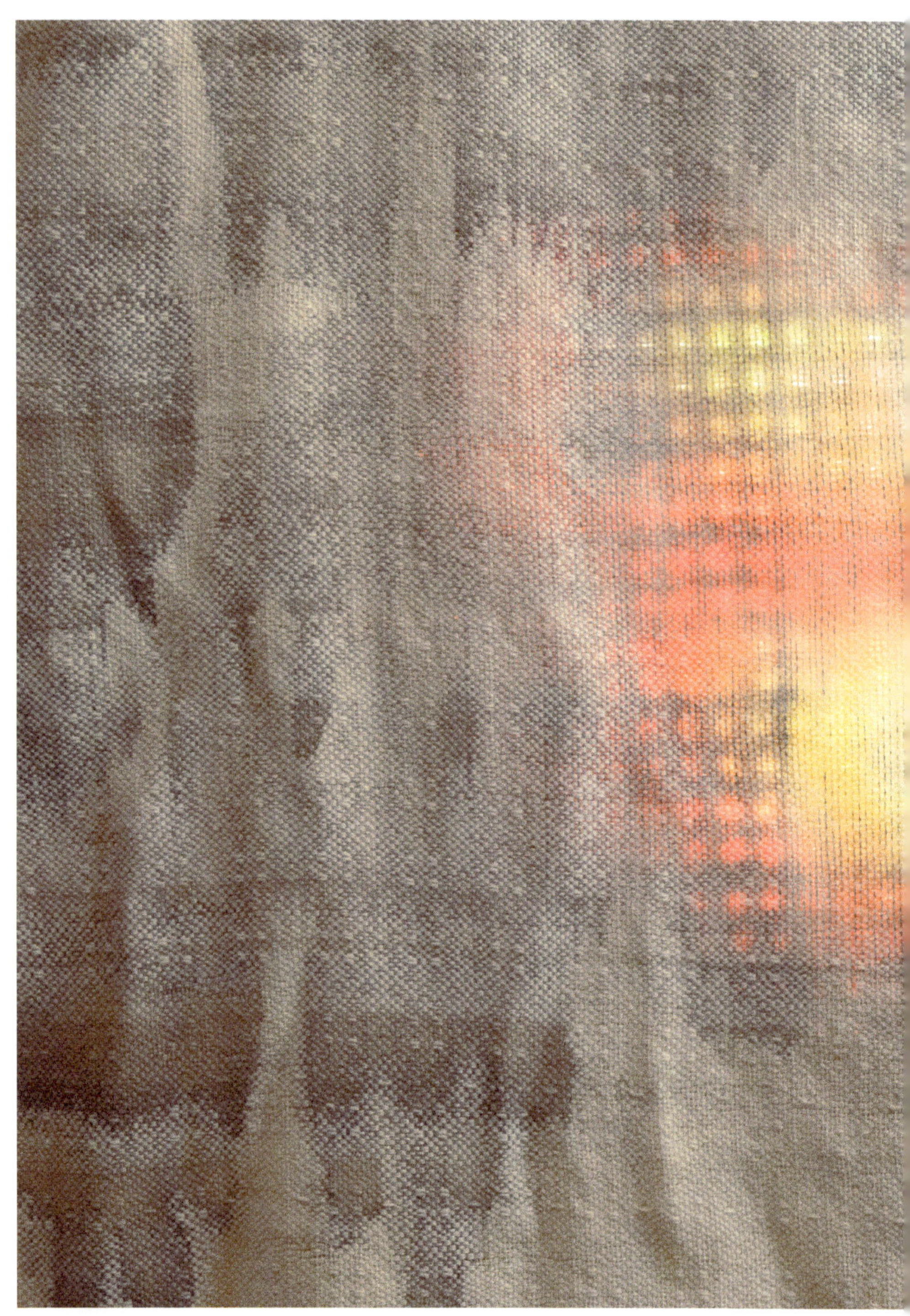

Kristin Roach   Interactive Migration Tapestry, 42 x 120," Wool,

alnut Dye, LEDs, Microcontrollers, Bird Sighting Data, Touch Scree, 2022

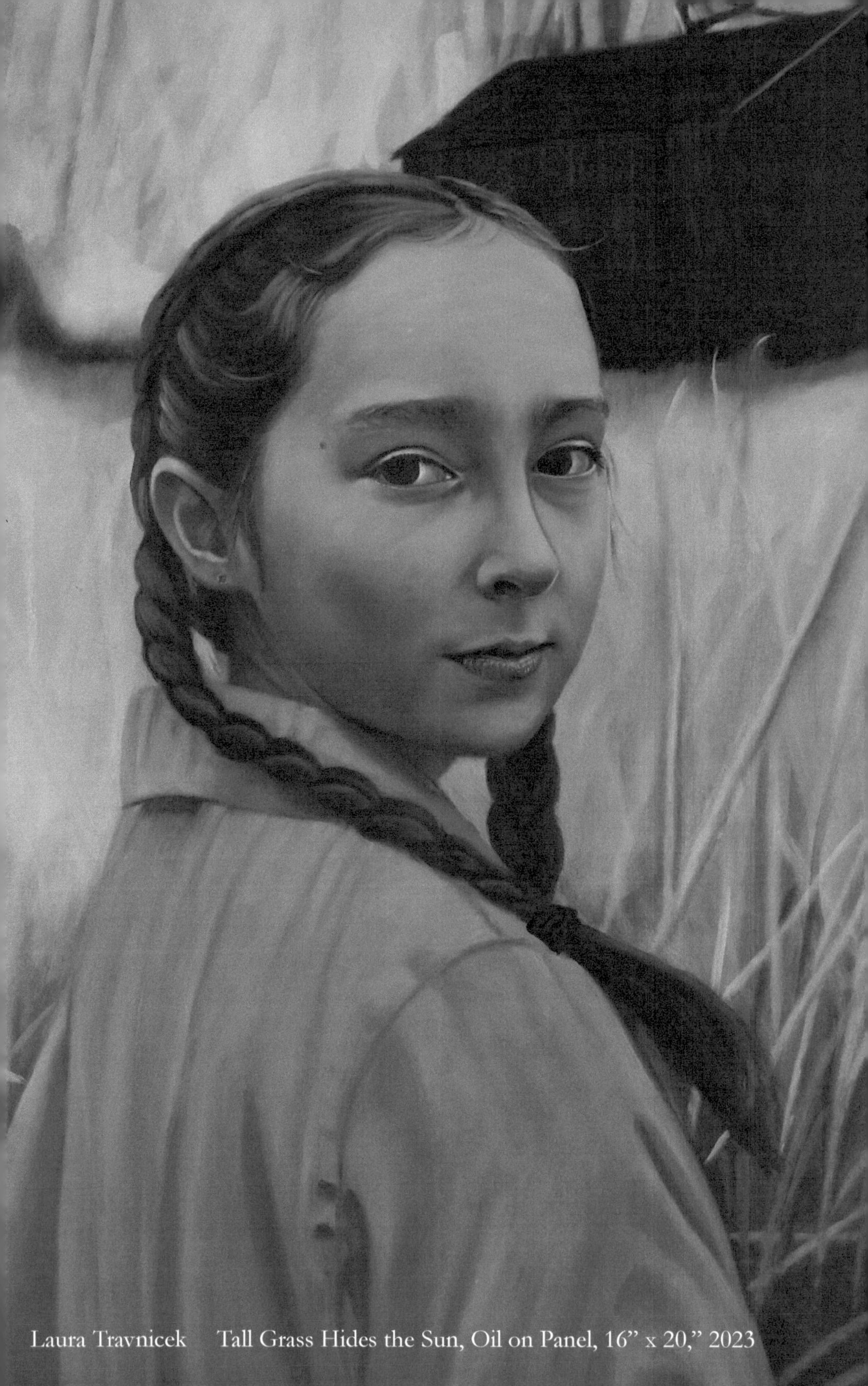

Laura Travnicek   Tall Grass Hides the Sun, Oil on Panel, 16" x 20," 2023

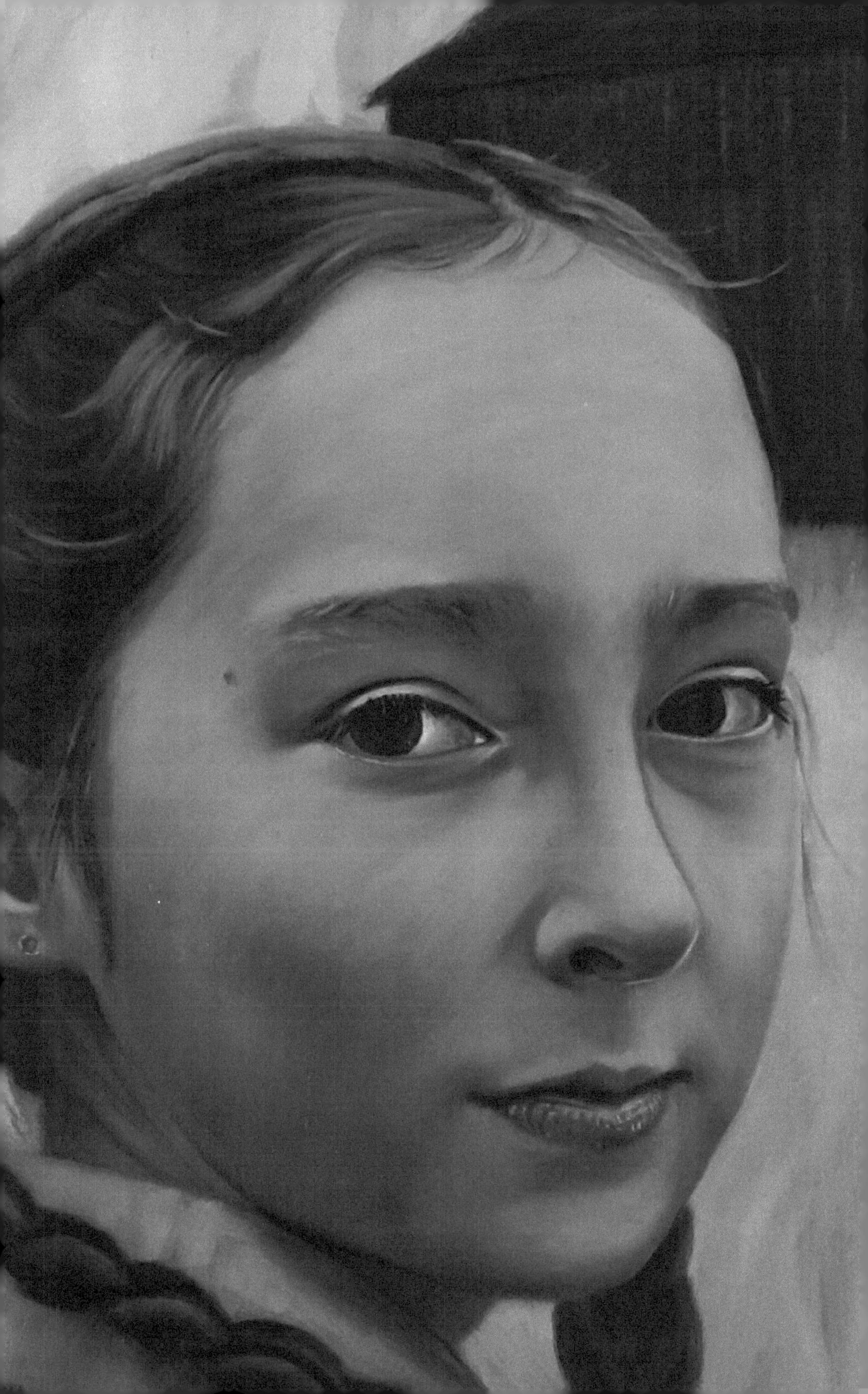

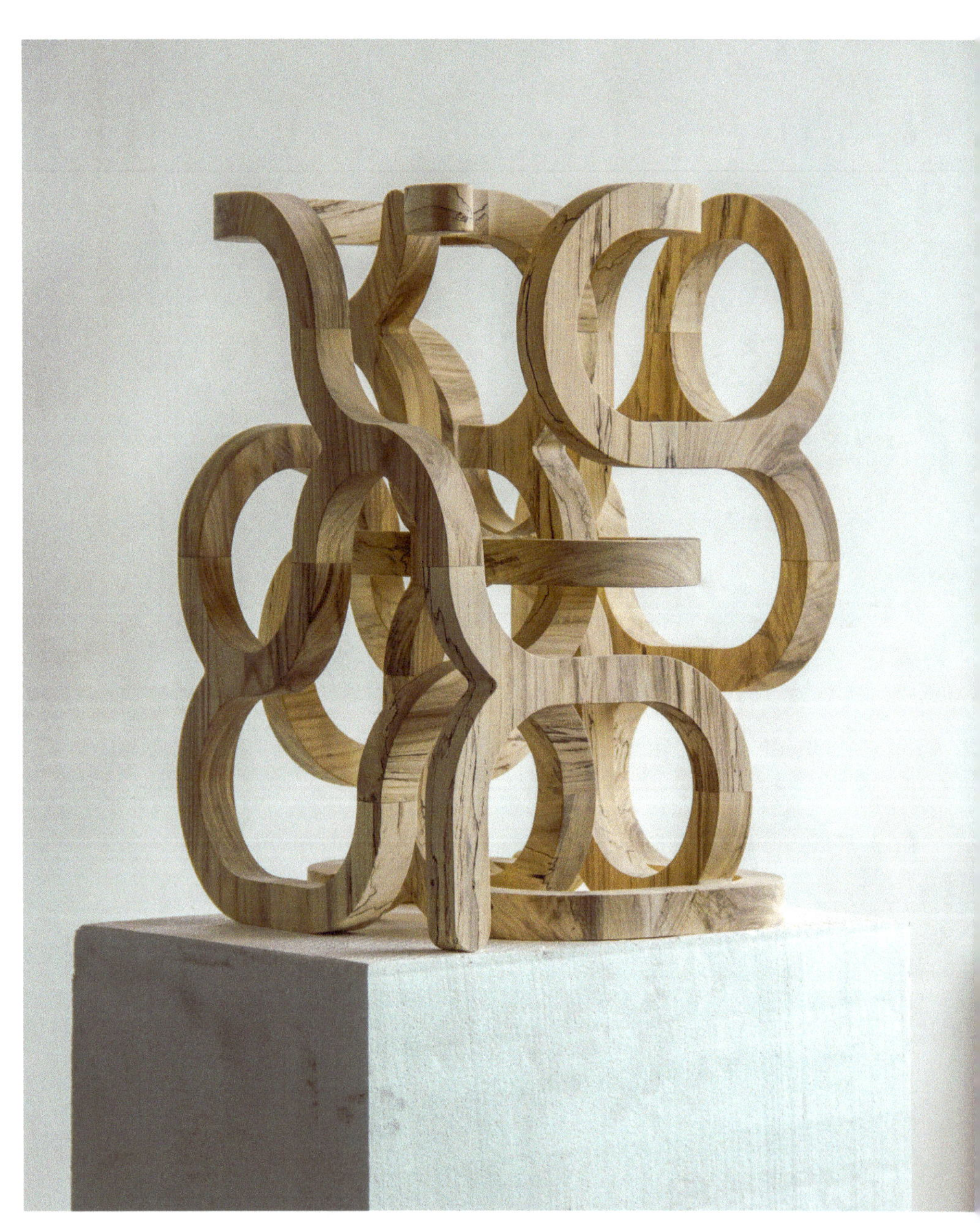

Tom Riefe   Labyrinth, Wood, 22 x 16 x 16"

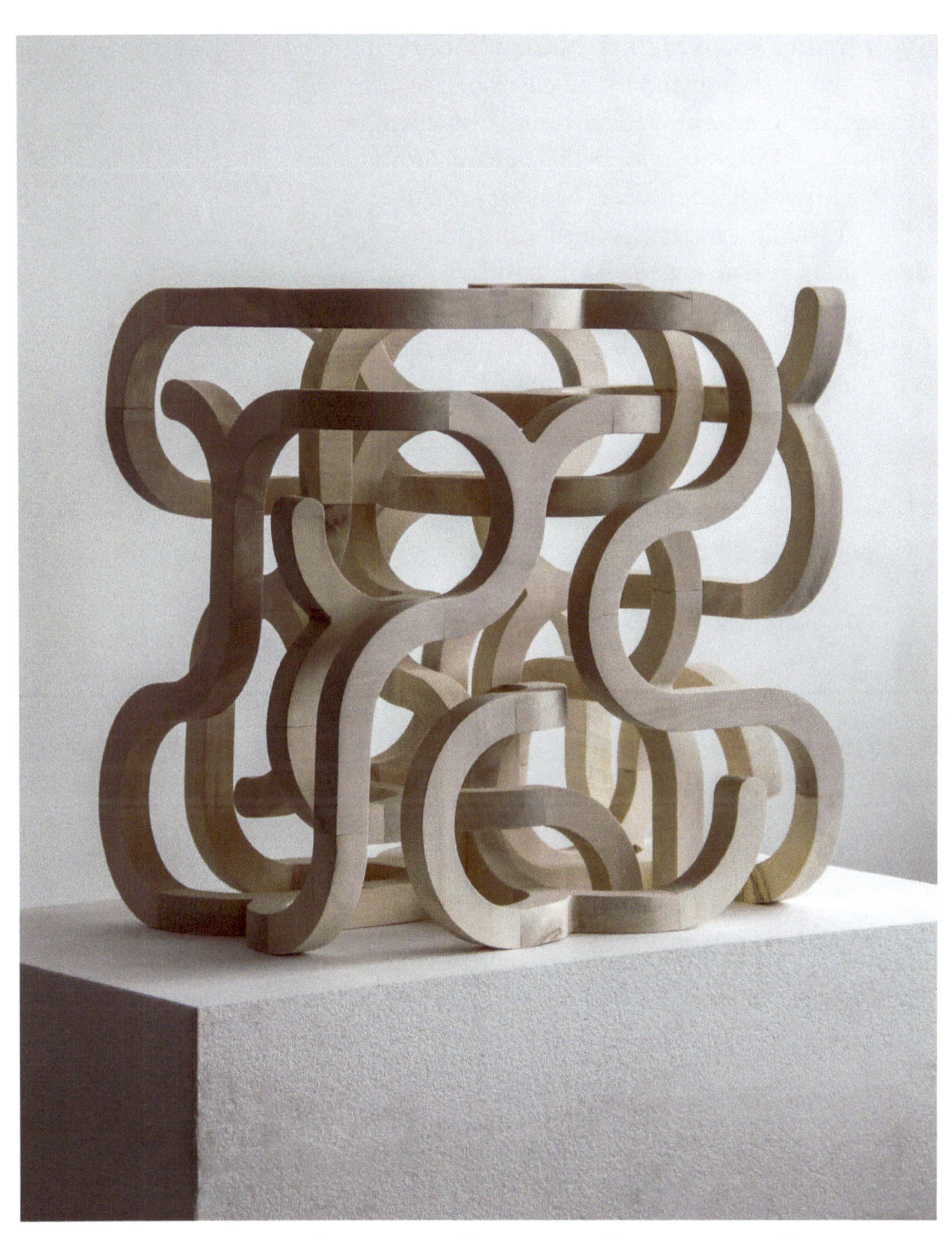

Tom Riefe   Mental Map, Wood, 22 x 25 x 16"

The Ravine and the Organic Farm (Part One)
—a double exposure contrasting two paradigms of farming

Beyond timber, discarded cars smoldered.
    Today, hay softened and saved garlic.
Their bodies scattered like hidden boulders.
    Brome wandered to the edges of the crick:
Tea kettles; ice boxes; rusted mattress springs;
    Morel mushrooms; wild ginger; columbine;
Coils, coils of barbed wire; Mason Jar rings;
    Coneflowers; honeysuckle; and grape vines.
Back then, refuse was erosion control.
    Now, buffers protect plants; hands pull burrs.
Back then, fires melted tires; farms ate coal.
    Now, bundles of garlic cure from rafters.

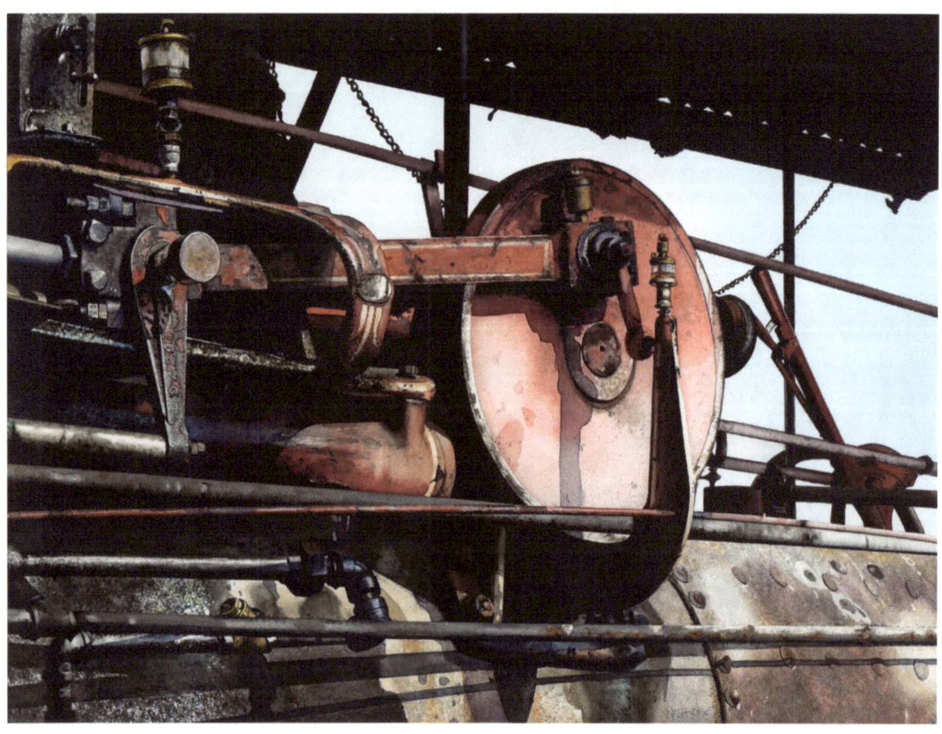

Nash Cox   Rusty Russell, 19" x 26"

The Ravine and the Organic Farm (Part Two)
—a double exposure contrasting two paradigms of farming

Back then. Soybeans. Corn. Cattle fattened.
> Now, sprouts started, tended, a month early.

Till. Till. Till. Soil depleted and saddened.
> Garlic sold at Farmer's Market fairly.

Hogs farrowed in filth, finished with Paylean.
> Recycled wood in the barn unconcealed.

Weeds eradicated with Atrazine.
> Laying hens rotated from field to field.

The old dictum of land was to subtract.
> New dictum is to replenish, replace.

War drove weak men to rape and to ransack.
> Listening to the land teaches pure grace.

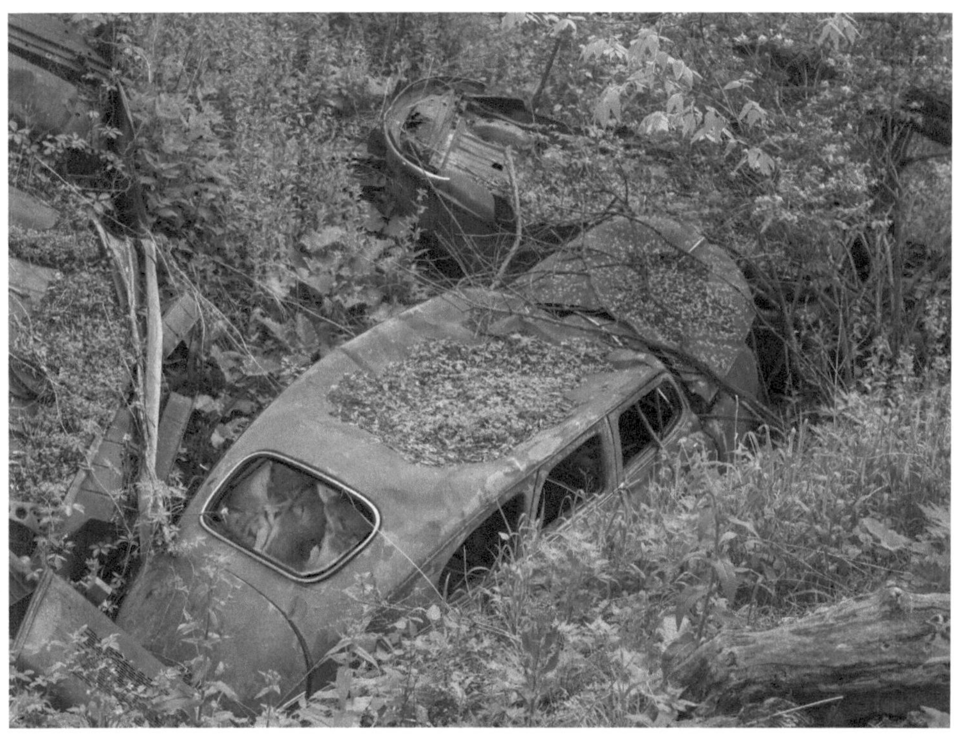

Paul Brooke   Double Exposure: Mouse Nash

The Ravine and the Organic Farm (Part Three)
—a double exposure contrasting two paradigms of farming

Paul Brooke

Fouled oil poured out and gas tanks left to rot.
>Fawns asleep in tall grass undisturbed.

Mud and shit stand shin deep in the feedlot.
>Bees stockpile honey unperturbed.

Soil blows from fields. Corn wastes in the silo.
>Black locusts harvested for fence posts.

Machines flatten like massive mastodons.
>Apple trees in fog are beautiful ghosts.

To love something is not subjugation.
>To love something requires long-term concern,

Not rash return, not one generation:
>Children, water, apple trees, fawns and ferns.

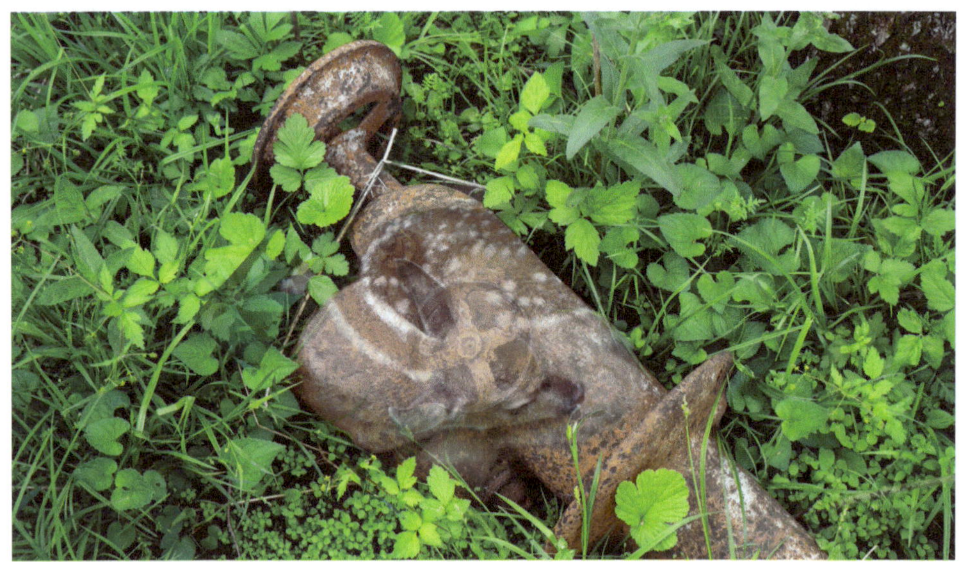

Paul Brooke   Double Exposure: Fawn on Discarded Pump

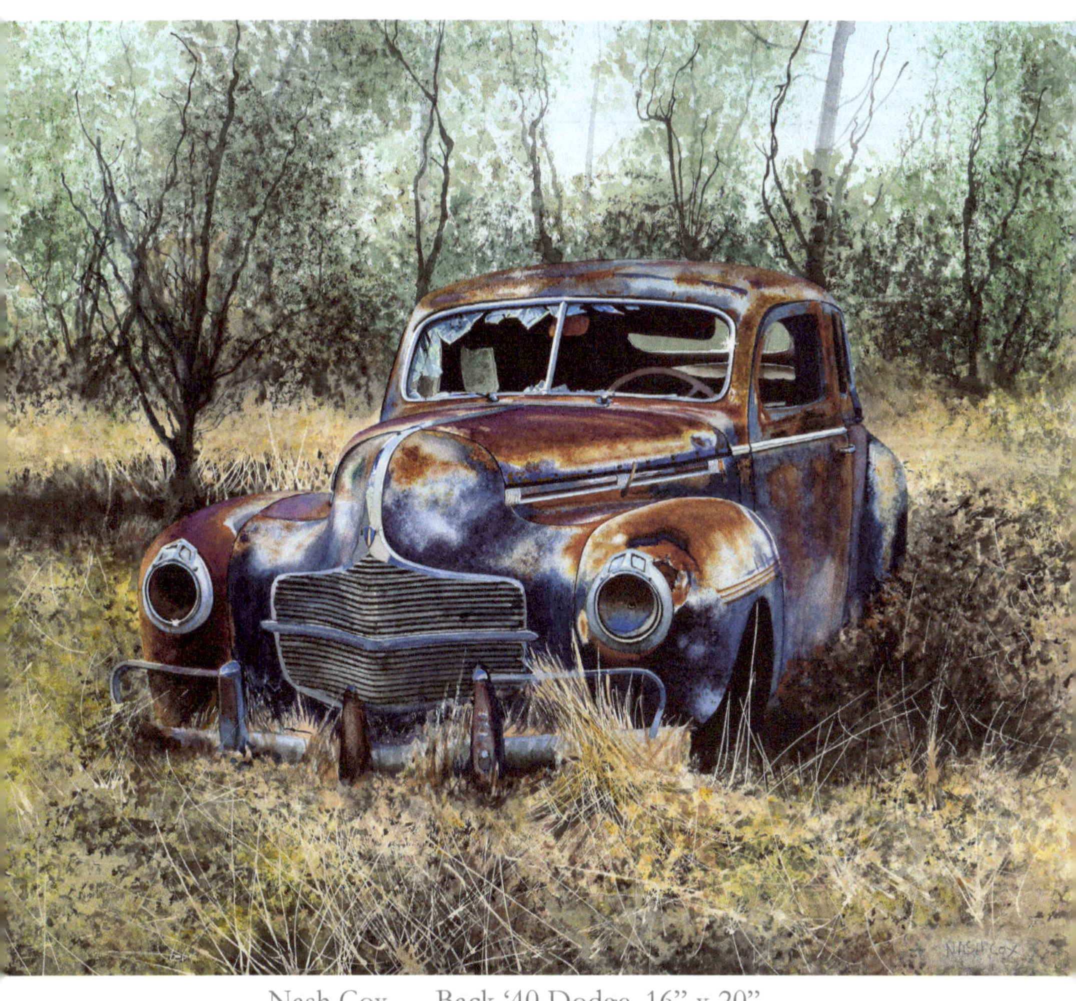

Nash Cox   Back '40 Dodge, 16" x 20"

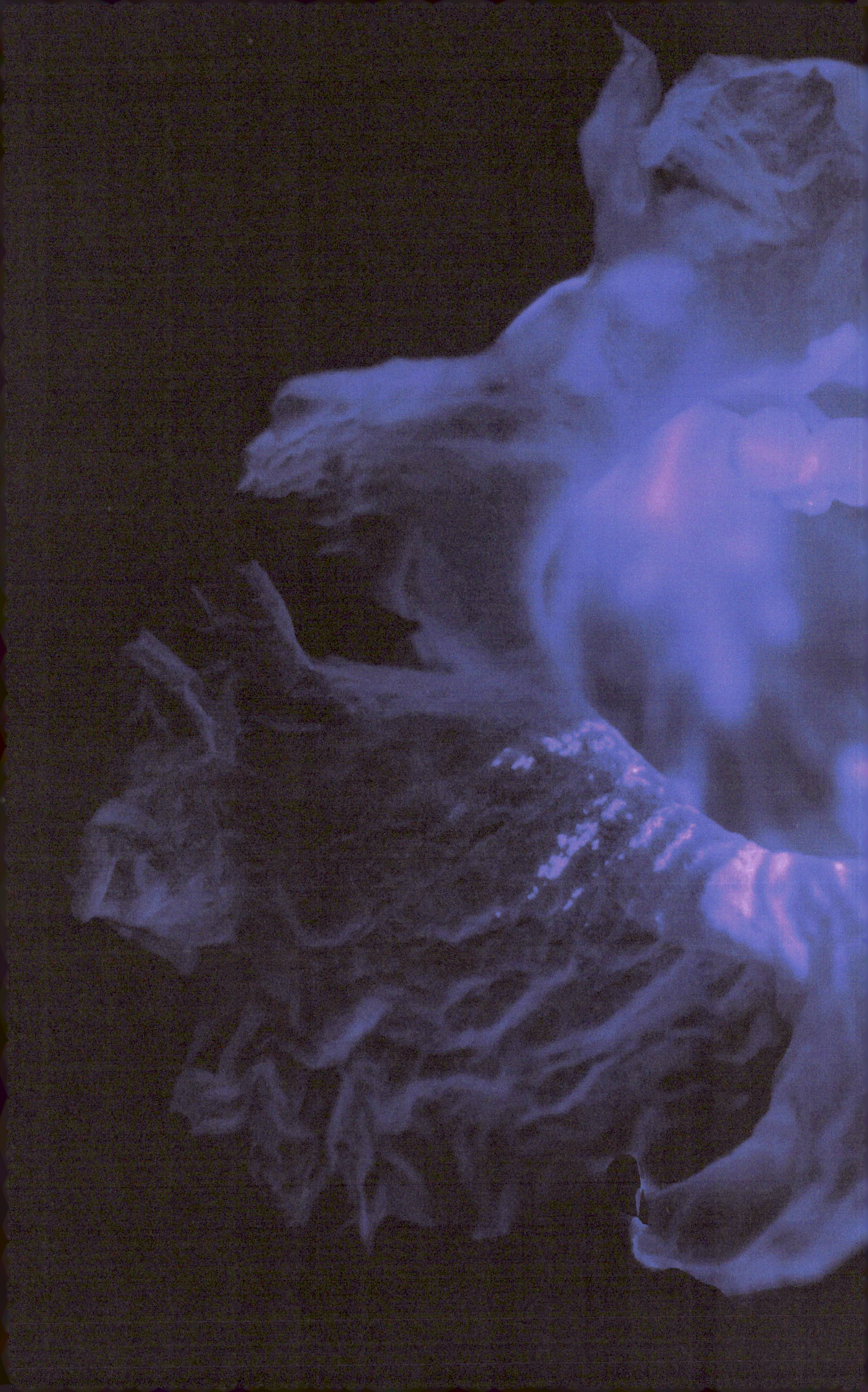

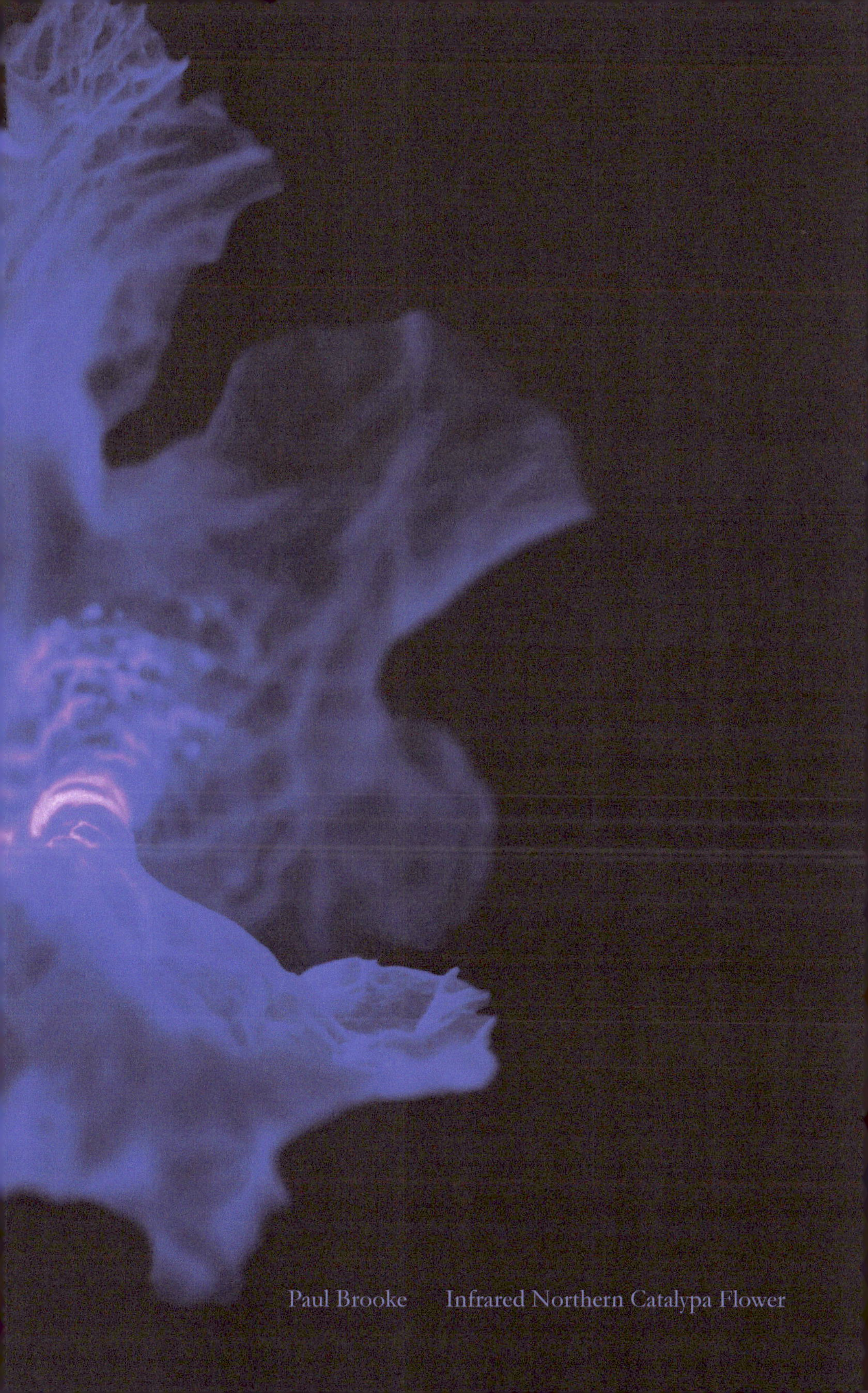

Paul Brooke   Infrared Northern Catalypa Flower

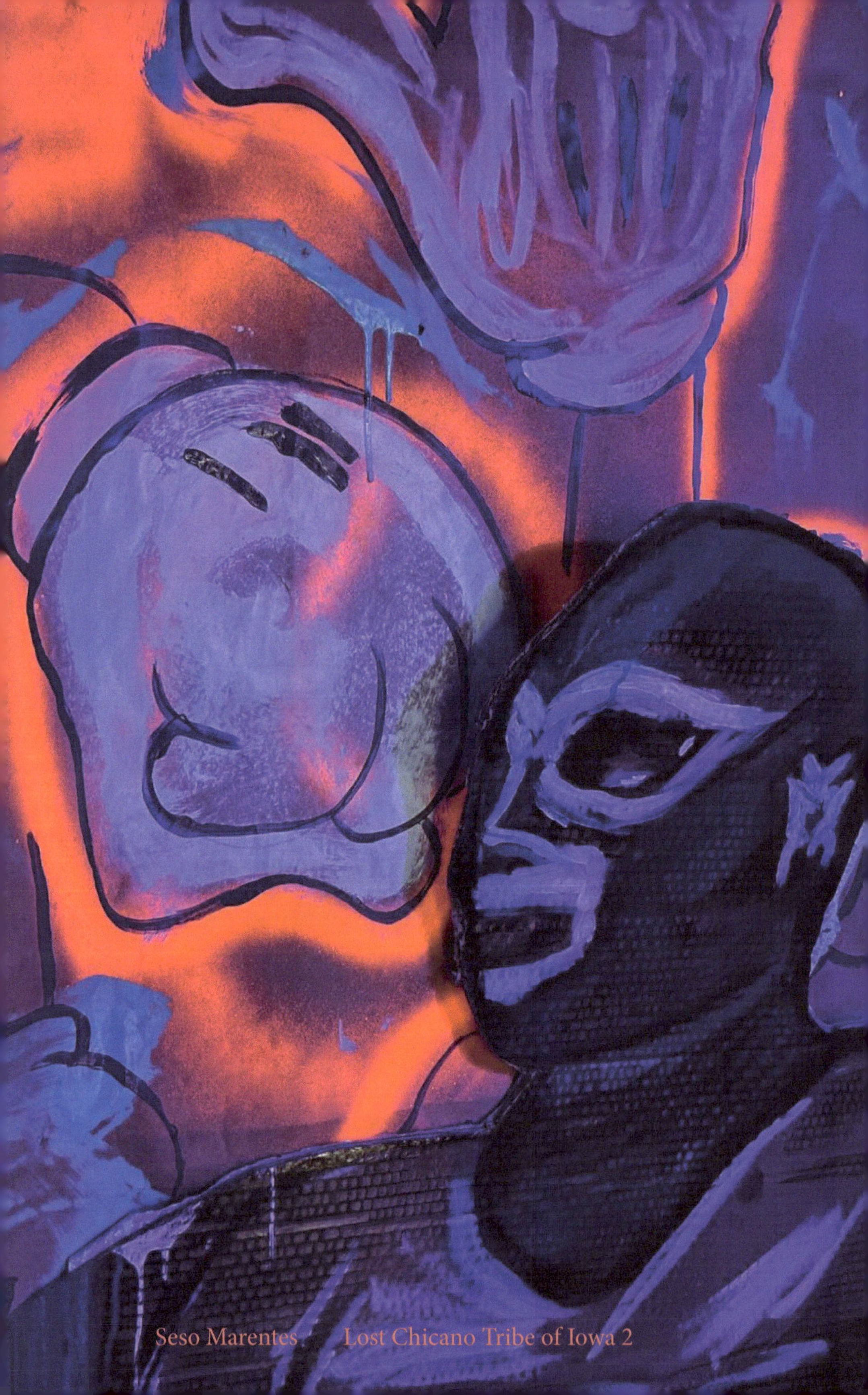
Seso Marentes   Lost Chicano Tribe of Iowa 2

A Giant Tongue

licked my head off.
No small feat.
My head is huge!

Still, my torso went
in search of my head
stumbling through crowds

stepping on feet—screams—
slipping down stairs that
rippled over my spine.

The wind brought slight
comfort—more terrible
thoughts until one day

my torso tripped over
my head spiked into
the dry, cracked earth

in the middle of the old
town square where there
once were hangings.

My hands grabbed hold
of my head, deflated
like a child's balloon,

and stuck it back on
and you know what
the first words out

of my dear old mouth
were? "Why? I was
finally free. Now I'm

stuck with this body,
again. Oh give me
a break why don't you."

United, I lead them: torso,
arms, legs, everything
over the highest cliff.

Descending, my arms,
legs flailed wildly
as it they could stop

the inevitable. Now that
my story is told and you
see me as I am—broken,

I hope you can sense I
am undeniably free despite
this corpse clinging to me

despite a giant tongue
wavering toward me, despite
everything that I am.

In Jest, a Tiny

Mario Duarte

green spirit spat
at the lopsided moon

who quickly spit
right back and laughed.

Enraged, the spirit
pricked the moon's check.

The moon opened
his blue jaw wide

to swallow the spirit.
He flew behind

the sun, and then
down to the corn

along a brown river
who told the spirit

she would take him
as far as he wanted.

And so he floated
on a drifting gold leaf

beyond the ranches,
beneath blue mountains.

When he crawled ashore,
he hid in a cave

that the moon could not
touch and he slept

like never before
and dreamed of stars

singing to him,
pleading for his

help to shape their
light into wishes

and thoughts beyond
this world he strained

to understand, this
life without moonlight.

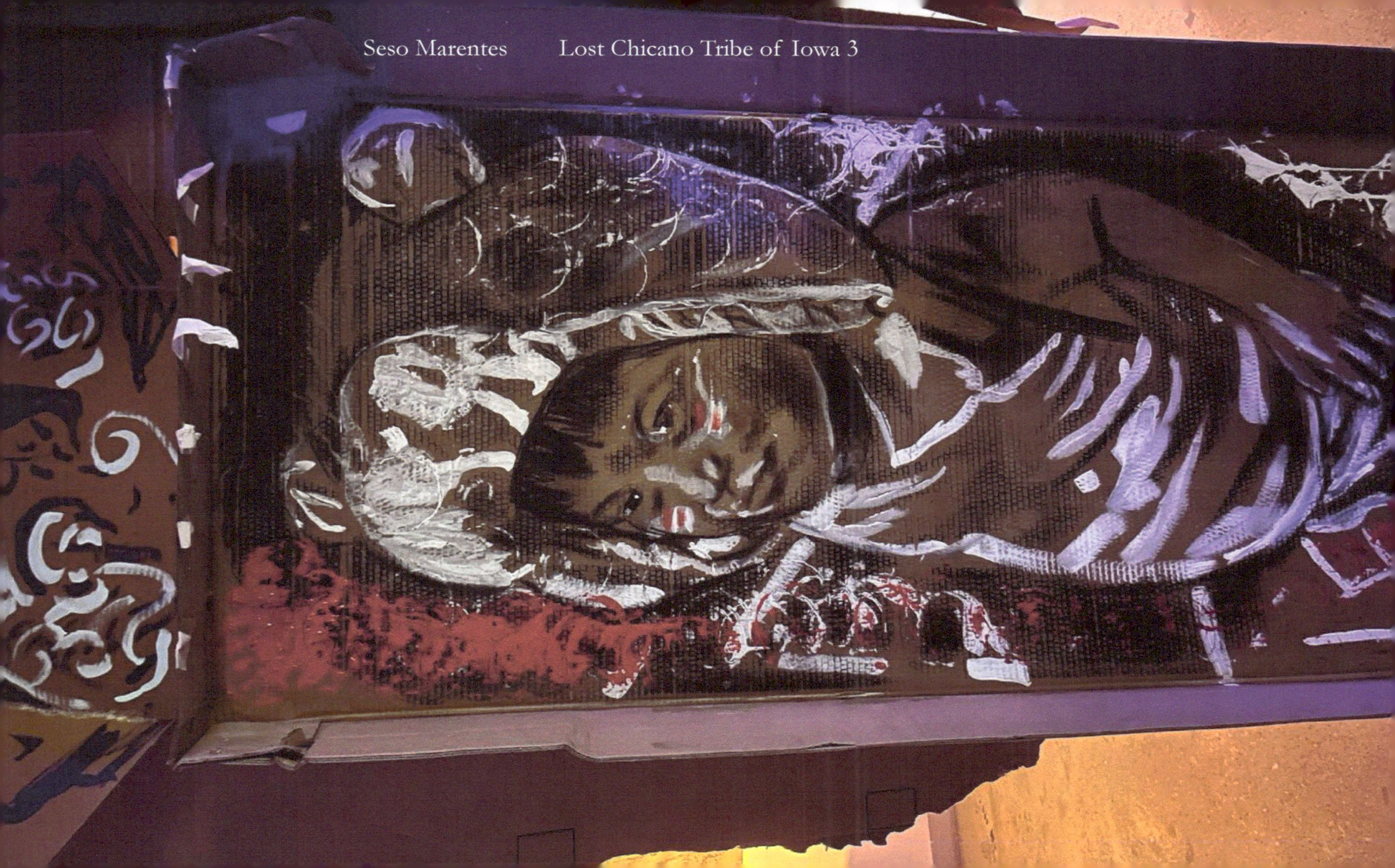
Seso Marentes   Lost Chicano Tribe of Iowa 3

Encounter on Good Friday
—*Cutud Village, north of Manila, 1936*

On his straw mat, his banig, under the inky susurrus
of the mosquito net hung from the walls of his nipa hut,

a bachelor farmer named Santiago de la Cruz lounges half asleep,
half dreaming of the Easter sunrise mass day after tomorrow

and of today's penitentes flogging their own backs into bloody
crosshatch, a couple crucified for a handful of long minutes.

Tiyago gazes up toward the now charcoal-tinged underside
of his thatched palm-leaf roof and stares at an indistinct

shadow above, shaped darkly like a crucified person. What?
Tiyago rolls out of the net and fixes his eyes above. Yes,

there is something there in the pitch black. Wait, is it
a dark brown woman with her arms outstretched, gripping

the almost invisible bamboo supports of the roof? A ghost?
A hallucination? Tiyago rubs his eyes and looks again. Her eyes

are dark red like dying coals. He crosses himself quickly,
notices a rippling behind her like a mourning-dress curtain.

Susmariosep, Tiyago whispers, *she got wings like a bat!*
He slowly realizes there is nothing below her waist

but a few brackish red loops of, what, guts, torn intestines?
Wait, it's not a whole figure. She has no legs. No legs!

O my Jesus, an aswang . . . putang ina, she's a manananggal!
The aswang smiles, teeth a dingy slate gray, and from her mouth

slips a dingy blood-red thing like a snake or maybe more like
a thick dark earthworm that writhes wildly, closer and closer

to Tiyago. It's her tongue, a ten-foot-long tongue.
Hold on, she's trying to suck my blood, the black harpy!

He clenches his arms, his fists, shuts his eyes hard.
The aswang's tongue slinks, inches, nearer to his neck.

His body in the shadowy center of the room seems to sprout
fur, arms and legs thinning and crackling into wolf-like limbs.

Tiyago is growing taller and bulkier, T-shirt and boxers
ripping apart like tissue. He growls, dark yellowish fangs

flashing out of the lengthening snout of his face. Tiyago
is *also* an aswang, a shapeshifter churning into a huge

black dog, larger than a man, standing wide on hind legs.
The two monsters growl and snarl at each other, a tableau

carved into the dusky sweaty air of the room. Then it stops.
Both of them laugh, they snicker and snort, convulse in dark

shrieks and screams of black humor. The manananggal pulls in
her slimy tongue, waves at Tiyago, and swoops out of the window,

her pterodactyl wings sighing velvety *tik-tik, wak-wak* sounds.
Tiyago lifts his noble black head to the heavens and howls.

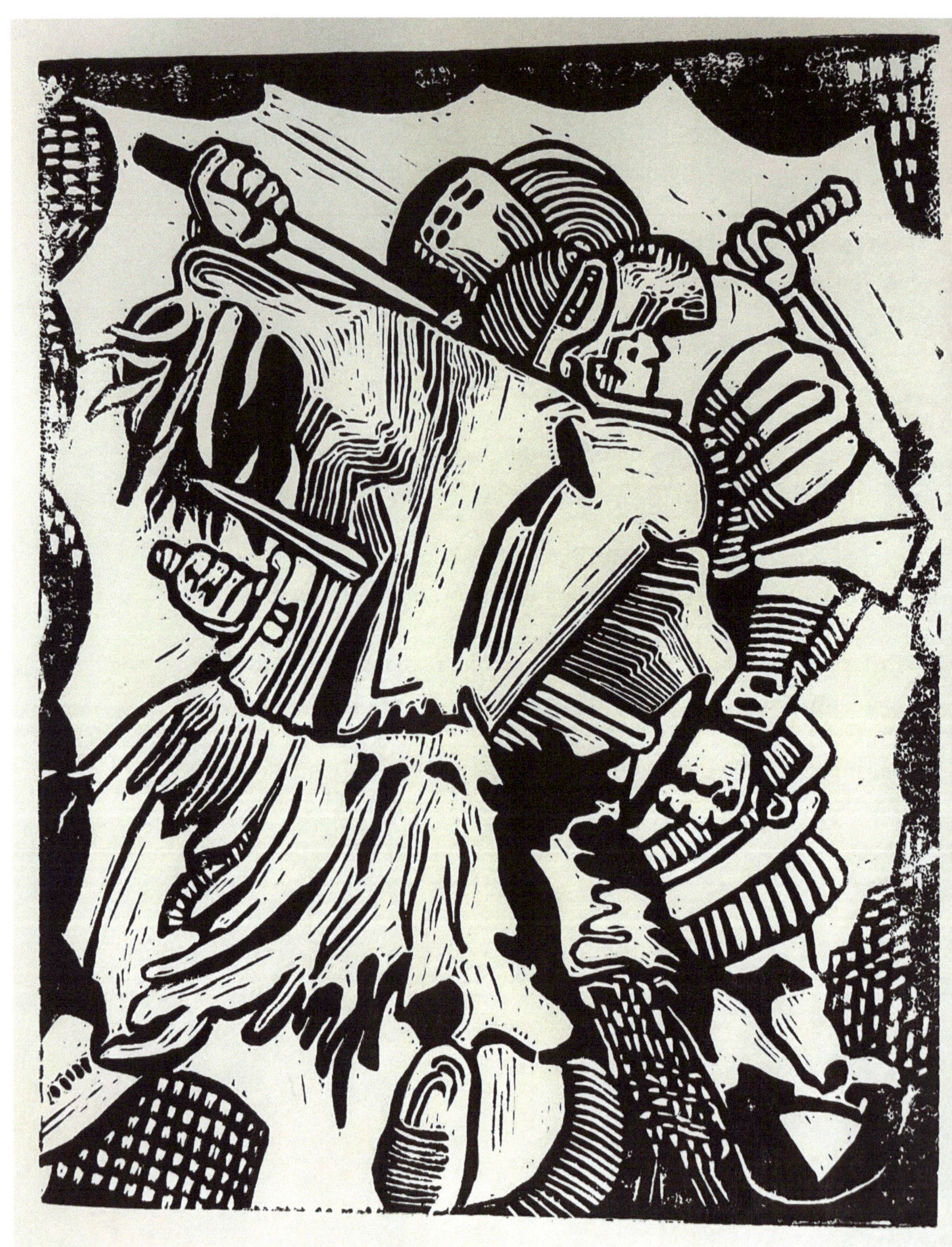

Seso Marentes   El Abrazo

How Clara Met Santiago: A Pantoum

—Cutud Village, north of Manila, 1936

Vince Gotera

So there's Santiago de la Cruz in his bedroom, sleeping.
I'd been watching Tiyago from a distance for many days,
so handsome, his black hair glowing in the sunlight
when I would see him at market selling his vegetables.

I'd been watching Tiyago from a distance for many days,
and tonight I decided I would visit him, see him at home,
and not just when he's at market selling his vegetables.
So I split my body, breaking in half as usual at the waist,

since tonight I decided I would visit him, see him at home.
I stood in my bedroom, slowly unfurling wet black wings
as I split my body, ripping in half painfully at the waist.
Then I looked towards the wide beautiful moon, so free

after long minutes in my room, unfurling my wet wings.
I launched myself into night air and headed into the sky,
then flew towards Tiyago's house, so beautiful, so free.
The village was lovely, candle lamps glowing in windows.

I turned myself toward the earth, falling out of the sky
and alighted gently, so gently, on his woven thatch roof.
His house was lovely, a lamp gleaming in his window.
I took care not to upset even the flame as I entered

and floated gently, so gently, up near the woven roof.
Now I watch Tiyago, his sweat glistening as he lies in bed.
I took care not to awaken or disturb him as I entered,
but now his eyes open, dark brown irises glowing.

I watch Tiyago. I keep very still. He lightly stirs in bed.
I stay as still as I can, my wings softly fluttering.
His eyes are open and staring, brown irises growing.
And then I see he has spotted me. He can see me.

I stay as still as I can, slow my wings' fluttering.
From the way Tiyago's brows knit, his arms tensed,
I know he has definitely spotted me. Can he see me
trying to blend into dark ceiling, blend into black?

Then his brows grow more black, his arms tensed
with spreading darkening fur, his teeth growing long.
I try to hide in the ceiling. His body grows black
and blacker—his body contorts into a giant dog

with thick fur, feet and hands clawed, fangs long.
And then I realize the truth: we're both aswang!
We both start to laugh and laugh, this huge man-dog
and I. Waving blithely to him, I turn to fly away.

This truth will open up our lives: we're both aswang.
He's so handsome, black fur shining in the moonlight.
Knowing I will see him again, I turn to fly away.
And there's my Tiyago, head up to the sky, howling.

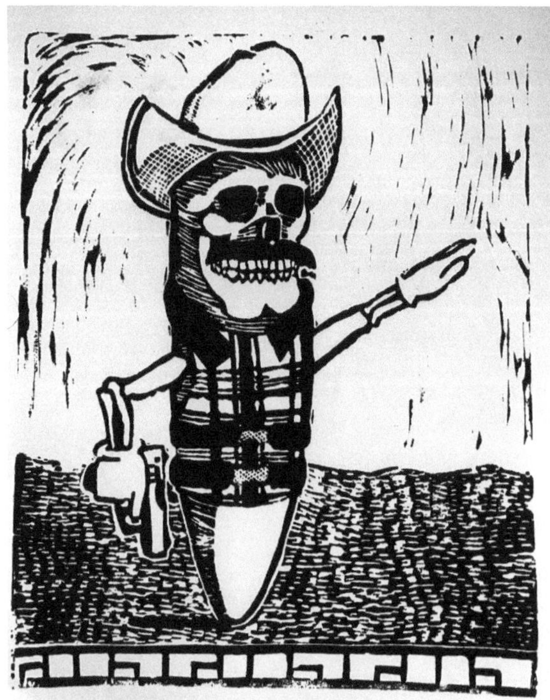

Seso Marentes   La Batalla de los Chiles

The Crib
—two curtal sonnets

— Clara —

I don't know how Tiyago got narra wood
here in San Francisco, the national tree
of the Philippines, used in native healing

of tumors. For days now, Tiyago would
get up at the crack of dawn, and plane three-
inch-wide long bars, sawing and hammering

until sunset. Finally, it was done,
a crib for the baby, shipshape boat we three
would sail into the destiny we're making.
So proud of Tiyago, able now to shun
     his aswang craving.

— Santiago —

I know this carpentering makes Clara
happy, thinking I'm finally becoming
human, no longer a shapeshifting aswang.

How can I be anything else? This narra
wood is always narra wood and nothing
can turn it into balsa. I'm just aswang.

For her sake, I pretend I'm not, but I live
for the chase under the hard bright moon, hunting
men. Even with the baby coming, aswang
is all I am. Clara, I give you this crib.
     But I'm still aswang.

Steve Rose

our mulberry tree

                    where I sit under to rest
            my thinking   takes its time   reaching
     for   the sun   winding   ragged branches
            through the air for more   years
            than I've taken   air   casting them   forth
     taking no more   aim   than a   kite's   tail

        it's past last frost now   give it a month
and we'll have a mess of fruit   fit to feed   half   or more of Shakespeare's starlings
            at least the ones   that settled
    in Warren County   not to mention   rust-chested robins
            gullets full of worms   and   wishing   after
                a taste of   something   sweet

        our old mongrel's   good ear   twitches
   like a heifer's tail   often when   the tree   drops   a berry   it plops   his head
            me I wear a hat that can be
hosed   clean   of bird scat   and   overripe fruit white with yeast   god's providence
            not that it will   ever make a wine

            then the youngest granddaughter
        comes by to   visit   borrowing   pans   from her
            grams   sharing   the shade
   squashing clay mud   and berries   into purple pies   adding
        pine needle crusts   not   that such a mess   will ever
            find itself   in   grandma's oven
                    no matter how
                much we love
                the child

            maybe that's why
            I rest here

            the retriever
                too
                as he

            takes his shade
                with
                us

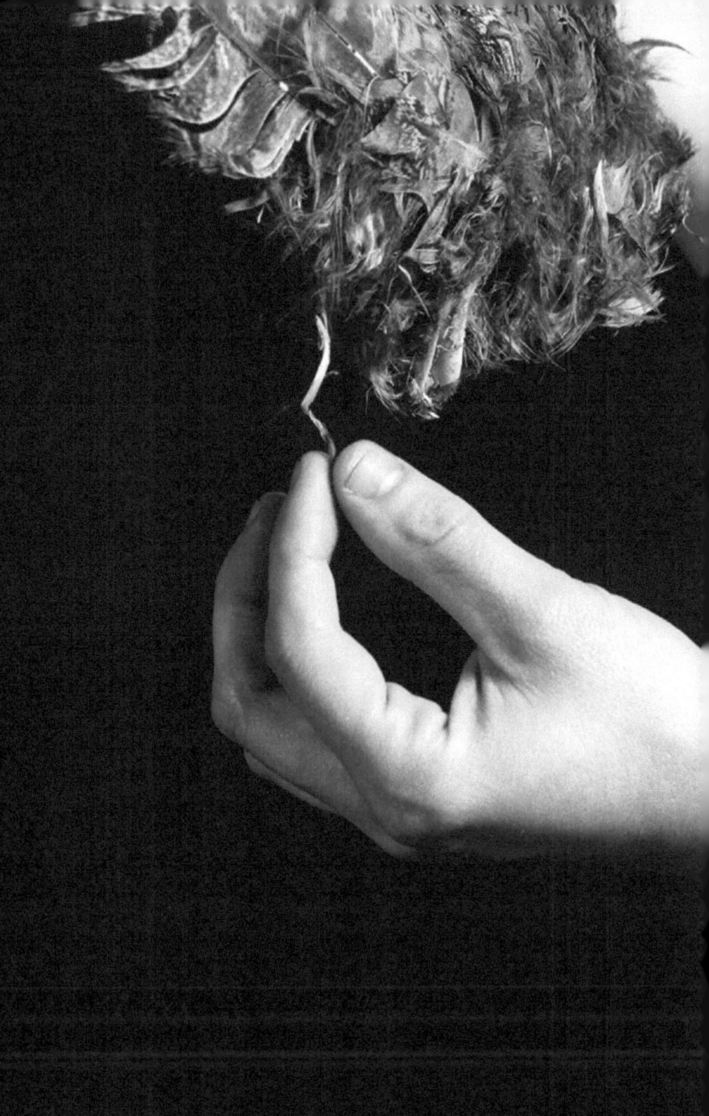

Brittany Brooke Crow   fragile little thing, 2022

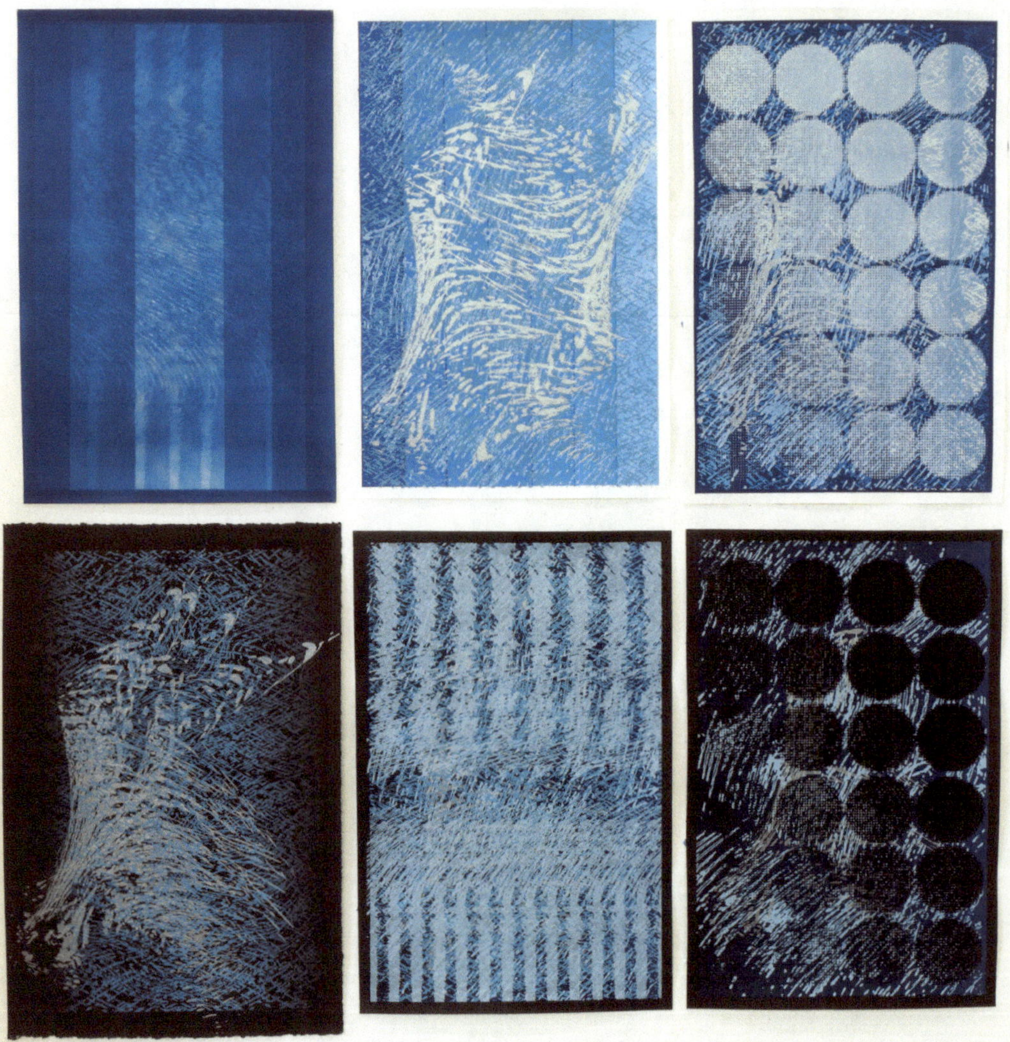

Bob Lockhart   Cracking the Lens, Screen Print and Cyanotype Series, 2023

pears

> the pear tree, hollowing inside, is our grandkids'
> favorite for climbing. tommy, our pet goat, waits
> below, eating all the fruit and leaves he can reach.

my mother halves, cores, removes stringy bits
with surgical skill, as she sings doris day tunes.
we devour the grainy, white flesh.

> a tornado passes near our house; the pear tree survives.
> at harvest, we find some pears embedded with splinters
> of wood, shafts of straw, a human tooth.

the day before dad dies, i eat luscious, ripe
pears with him at the kitchen table, juice
dripping. i take him, that night, back to the hospital.

> an explosion of spring blossoms becomes a promise
> of a bumper crop. mid-summer, all the pears, still immature,
> drop within a week. the leaves blacken and fall.

during mom's final weeks, she refuses many
foods but allows me to spoon feed her
pureed pears. she smiles at the sweetness.

if i could rewind five minutes

Marilyn Baszczynski

of this streak of dawn, before far-off lightning
glints on glassy eyes,
and a horse lies dead in the open barn doorway,

tuft of rabbit fur nearby. blood snakes its way back into vessels,
flowing without effort into the fatally bruised, bleeding brain.
dendrites and neurons revive, axons transmit the news.

the melon-sized, ten-pound heart restarts, stutters,
thuds, then races at 250 beats per minute.
panic fills the young, strong gelding.

disoriented, he rises, backs into the destruction
of his kicked-in, shattered stall. he leans
into the head-sized hole in the wall,

reverses the bucking, rearing, and screams;
splintered boards and panels morph
into walls and sliding half-door, closed. in the barn aisle,

a rabbit swallows its piercing squeals
as coyote releases jaws clamped onto the rabbit's soft neck.
the horse snorts as distress dissipates into darkness.

when lightning flickers closer, coyote slinks outside, detects
the rabbit's crouching silhouette in search of shelter.
storm passes somewhere behind the farm on the next line.

coyote goes back into the woods. the horse sighs, nostrils relax,
his heart coasting to its resting thirty beats per minute. sweet hay
wafts over pungent manure smells. head nods, eyes sleepy.

stop here. i'd run over to close the barn door.

in memory of oliver

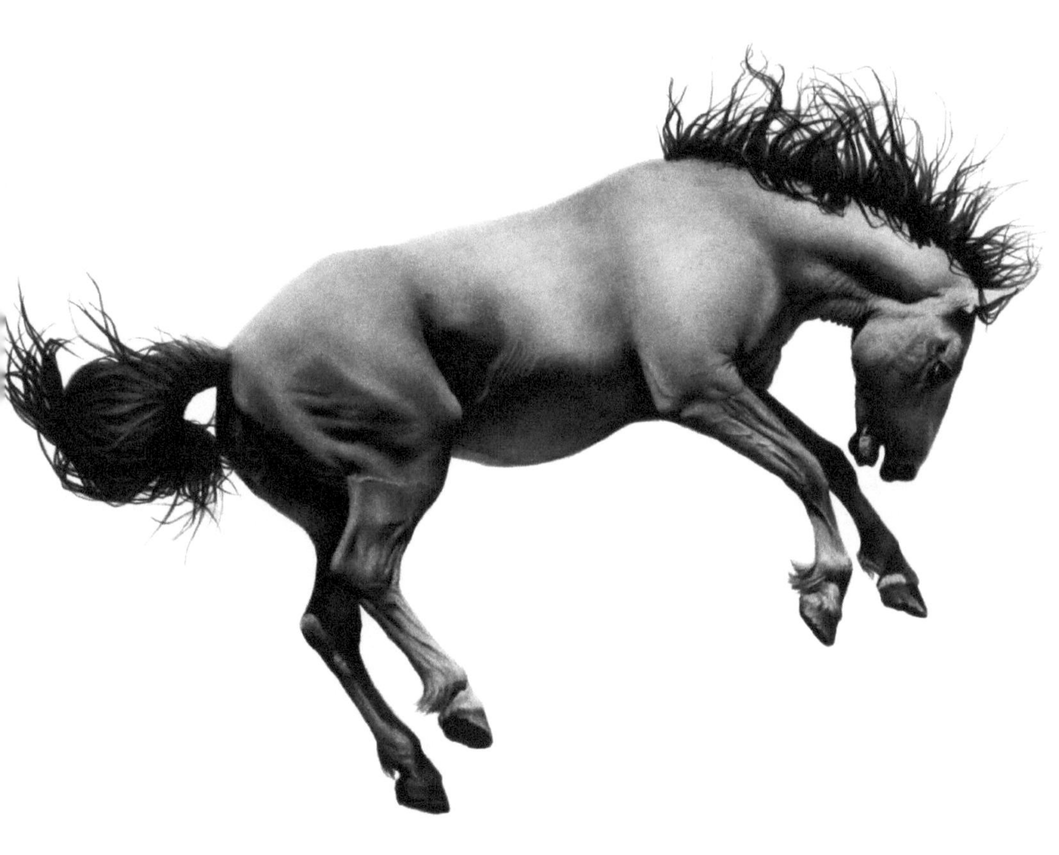

Larassa Kabel   Relentless

From the Insect World

Wena-wena
mana-esabike-byetti-
ttittewa
ttikabakwi
eowikiyani

Wena-wena
mana-esabike-nattabiyetowa
sababi
ttikabakwi
eowikiyani

Apparently,
this Spider has arrived
to hunt behind
my home.
Apparently,
this Spider has lowered
its rope behind
my home.

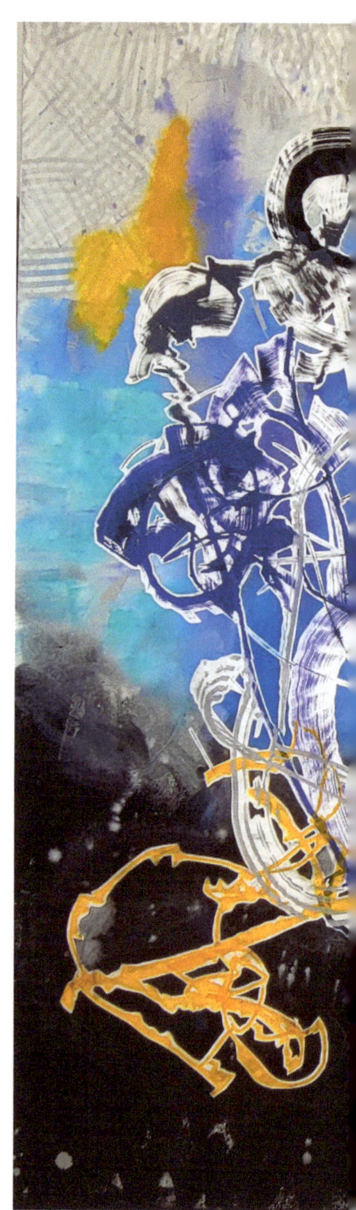

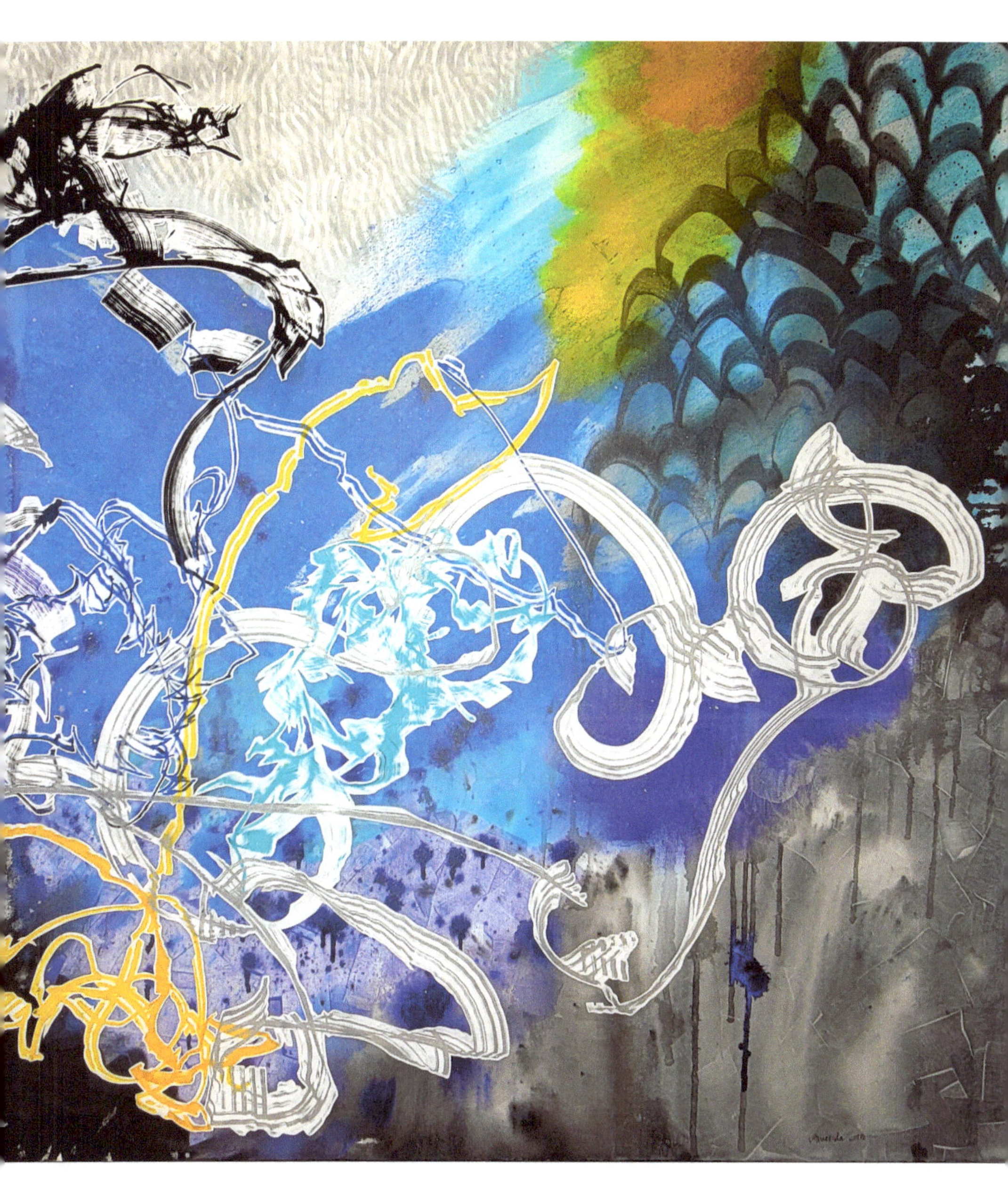

Amenda Tate   Sapient (L.D.), Acrylic, Paper, Gel Medium, Canvas, Manibus-
Translated Contemporary Dance

A Grandchild's Song for Robins in Year Two of the Pandemic

Ttittikakwaha [Lead]
Way ya hey

Ttittikakwaha [Second]
Way ya hey

Kemetakwi-wabamekowa
nottisemenana
nottisemenana
ememeskwatayeekwekwi
memeskwatayeekwekwi

Ttittikakwaha-
way ya hey

[Second verse]

Ttittikakwaha-
way ya hey
Kemetakwi-wabamekowa
Nottisemenana
Nottisemenana
ememeskwatayekekwi
memeskwatayekwekwi
Ttittikakakwaha
way ya hey

Robin
Robin

He enjoys watching you
Our grandchild
our grandchild
when you hunt earthworms
hunt for earthworms

Robin
Robin

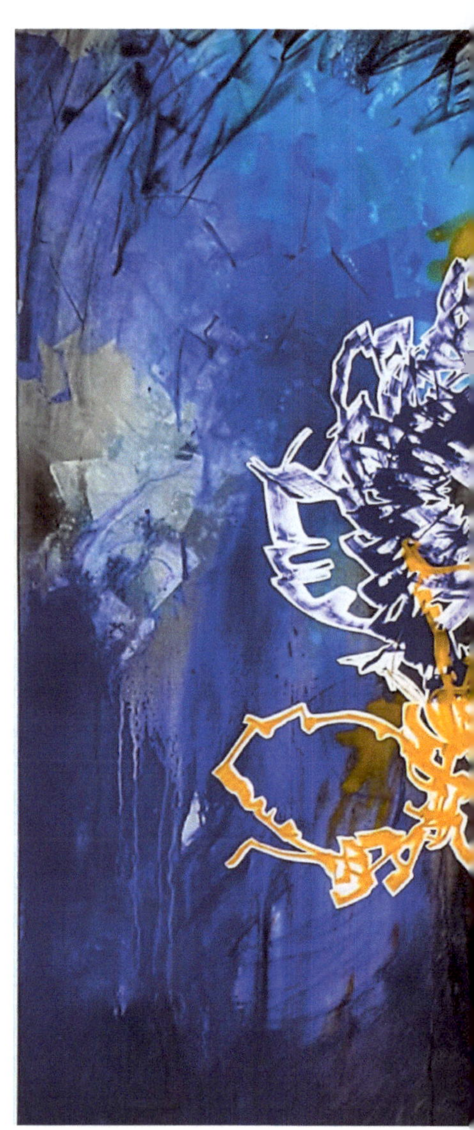

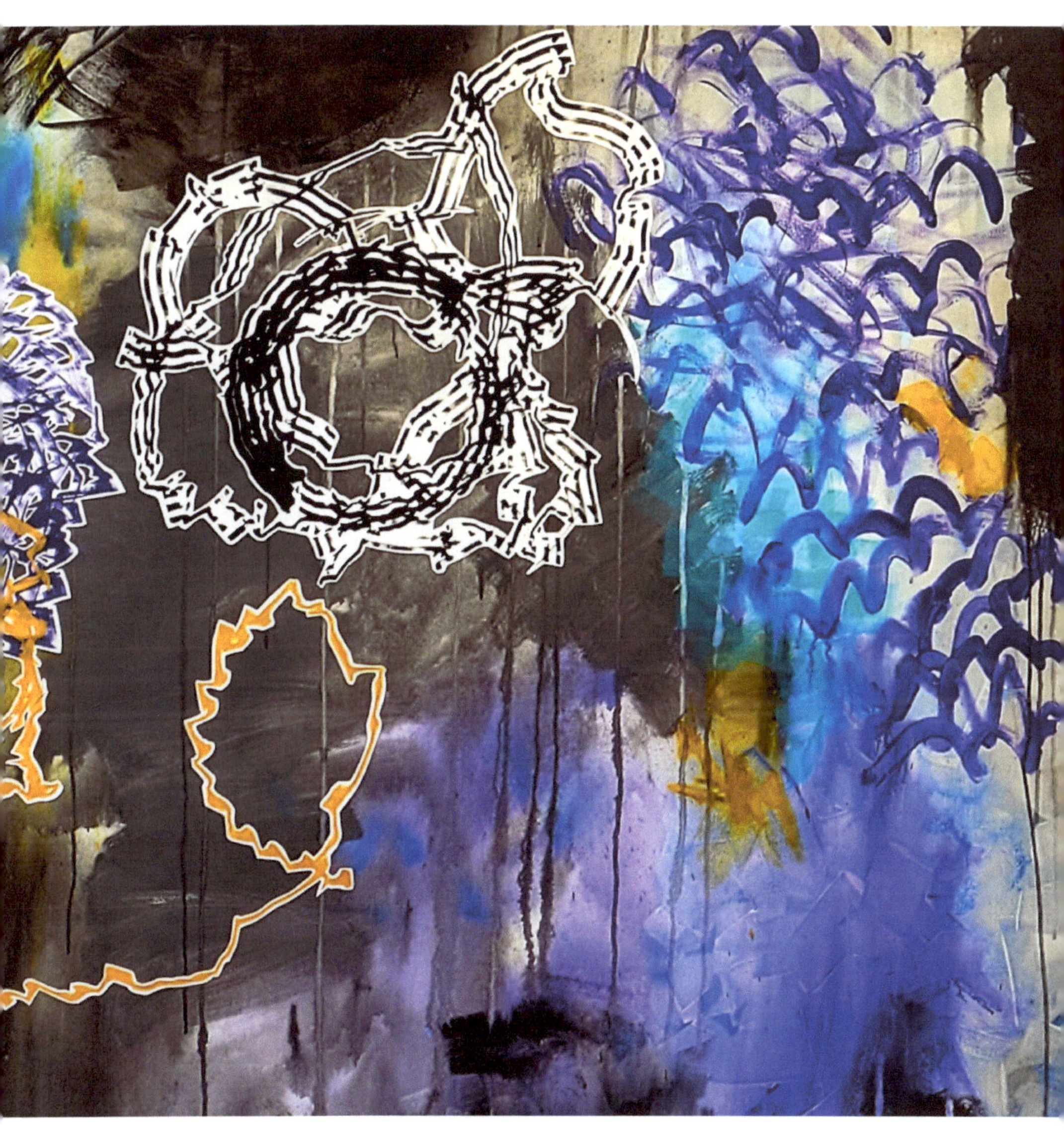

Amenda Tate   Sapient (Larry), Acrylic, Paper, Gel Medium, Canvas, Manibus-
Translated Native American Fancy Dance

Song for the Water Crane Fly

Ray Young Bear

Awiyatoki
yabimani
nimenokamiki

Awiyatoki
ekwabiyani
akona
ayakwattina

It is still a long time
for this
the Spring season
to begin

It is still a long time
for as far as I can see
snow
is swirling,
collecting.

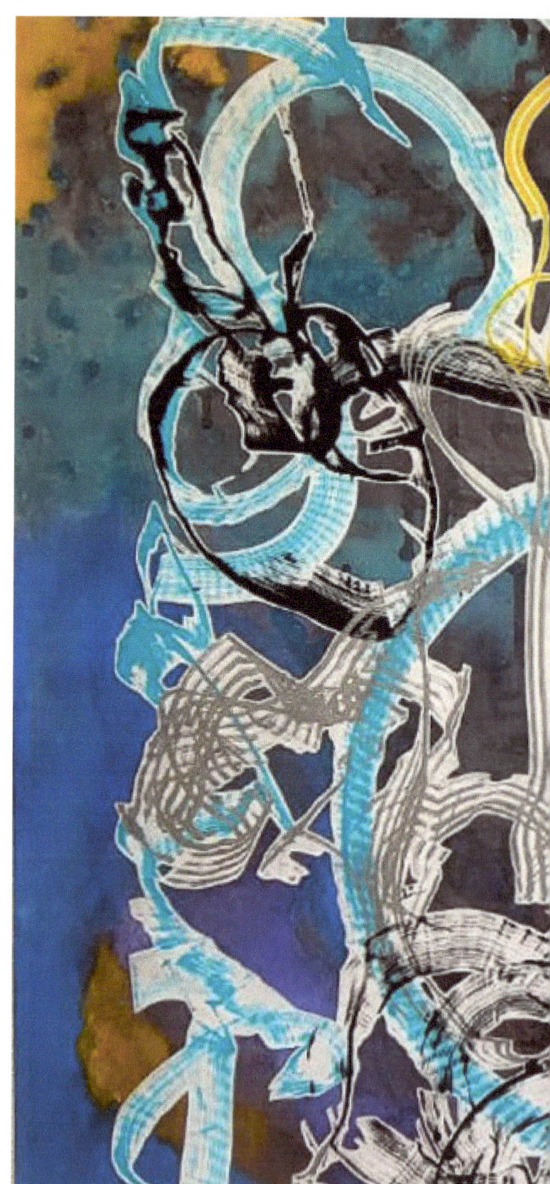

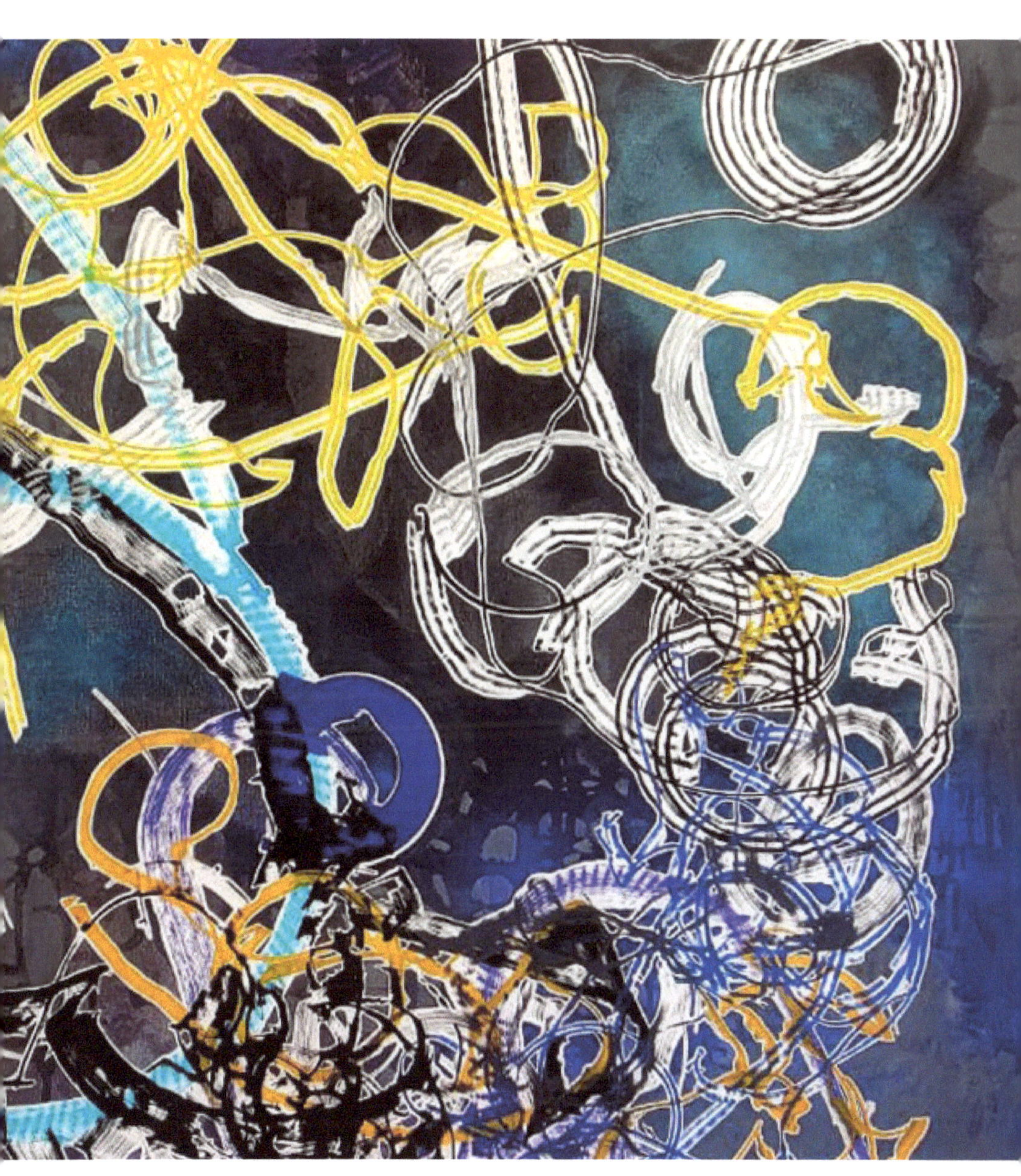

Amenda Tate   Sapient (Michelle), Acrylic, Paper, Gel Medium, Canvas, Manibus-Translated Somatic Dance

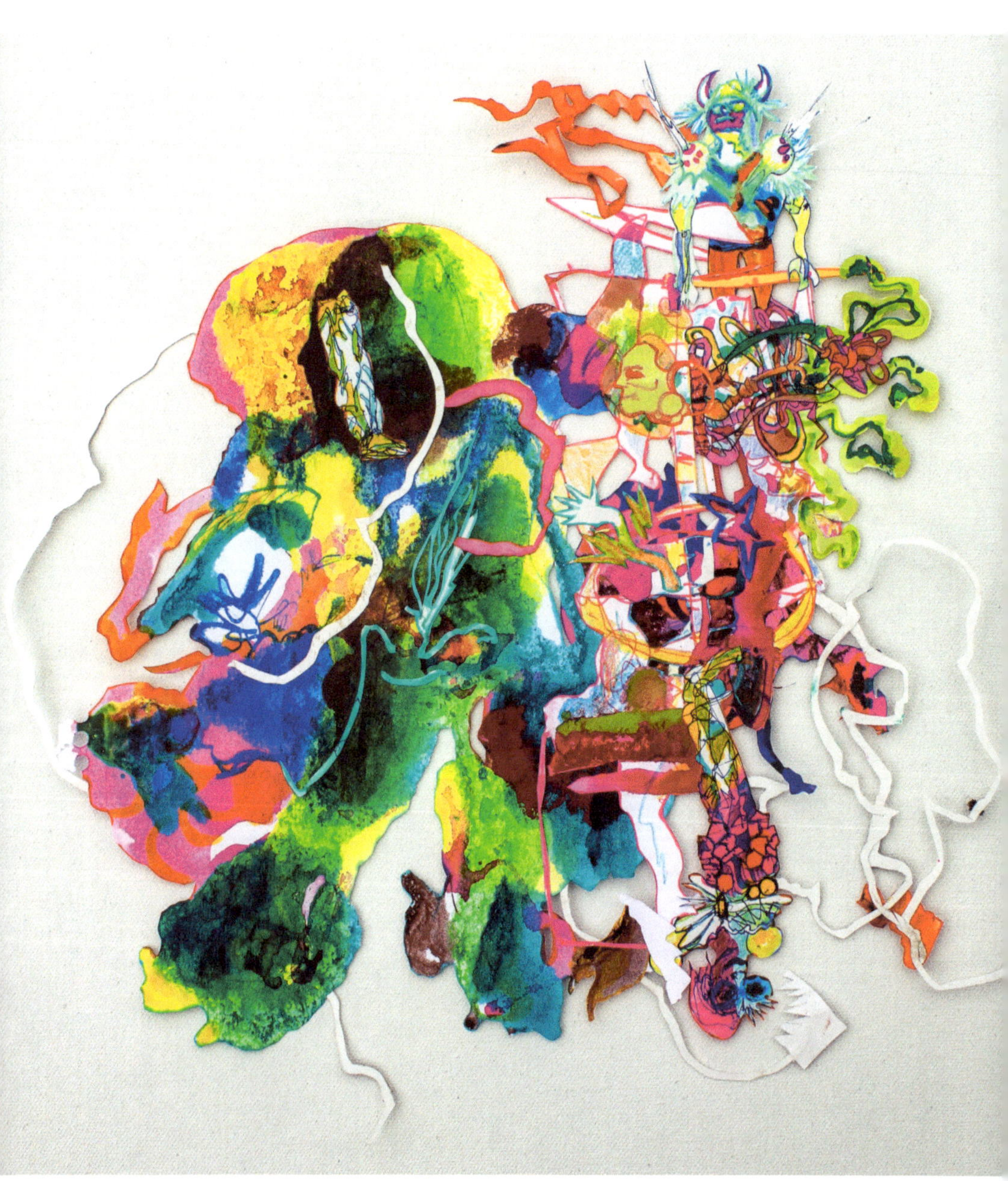

Ethan Edvenson　　　Beyond the Landslide

Mama's Milk and Honey

My body has gifted man and woman
with honey, milk, and meat
I released water and quenched thirsts
as I fed those in need I wondered –
who is coming to nurture me?

TheyCallMeMommyButWhenDoIGetToBeTheBaby?
HoldMeTouchMeKissMeRockMeSqueezeMeAndNoI
WontReturnAnyFavorsBecauseIDontWantToAndNoI
DontHaveToAndYouCantMakeMe!IDareYouToCome
SpankMeAndWhatWillYouSayWhenILaughAndLoveIt
AndWantSomeMoreOfItBecauseEmptyHurtsWorse.

There's reward in granting gifts
Even nature reveres reciprocity
When the honeybee pollinates,
so too does the bee partake
I hold ASweetBaby to my breast
and they begin to take, the tingling
sending sensations that talk to my
womb, what it says I am unsure of
But I can feel the mouth moving
and a warmth pours over my skin,
shoots through my synapses and
bloodstream making me believe
SweetBaby is also nourishing me

The thrill of the chase delights fast flyers
and I'm no slow poke. I want to swallow some
sweetness and i'll fly as fast and far as I want
and need to find the flower. As I flit and forage
I've yet to find the one that could supply sugar
to sustain long term. I'm left having collected
nectar to regurgitate without honey to store
for cold, wintry nights.

I've always been called sweet.
I, a fat bumblebee carrying big
barrel fulls of stickiness. Always

ensuring it tasted sweet. Never
have I found as delectable as mine
when looking to collect nectar and
honeydew. Massive claws pawed
at my combs seeking some sugar.
Lips smacking, fingers scraping,
flesh pestering the habitat. I hoped
for a helping hand to unburden the
excess. They always took too much.
Or only enough to say they'd assisted.
Their nectar and honeydew attractive -
couldn't help me create quality honey.

On frosty nights a cuddle in Mama's lap heats the heart
I foolishly spread arms and legs wide baring body and soul ready to enfold
Mama bears' mighty roar does not come without aching the throat
but if we don't release a bellow and backhand informing 'hell no,'
poachers shred our flesh and that of our babies
Predators will prowl closer until our home shrinks to nothing
and we will pray for the day we are no longer the prey
Who hits and hollers to defend the honor of and protect Mama?
Even the biggest bear was once a little cub and still needs a cuddle
Mama bears are as soft as we are strong and we desire our pelts stroked,
bellies filled with leaves, berries, and fish brought from others' foraging,
and restful nights – someone else take charge and take care of us

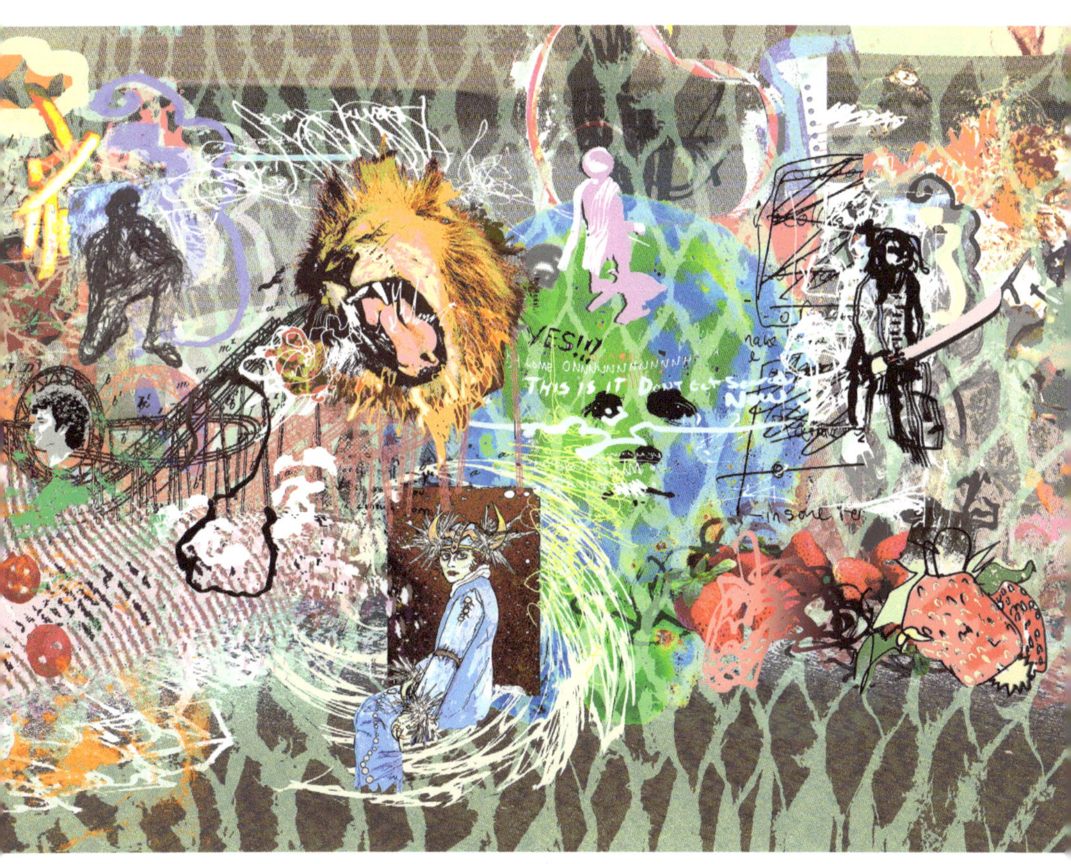

Ethan Edvenson   Ancestral Vision

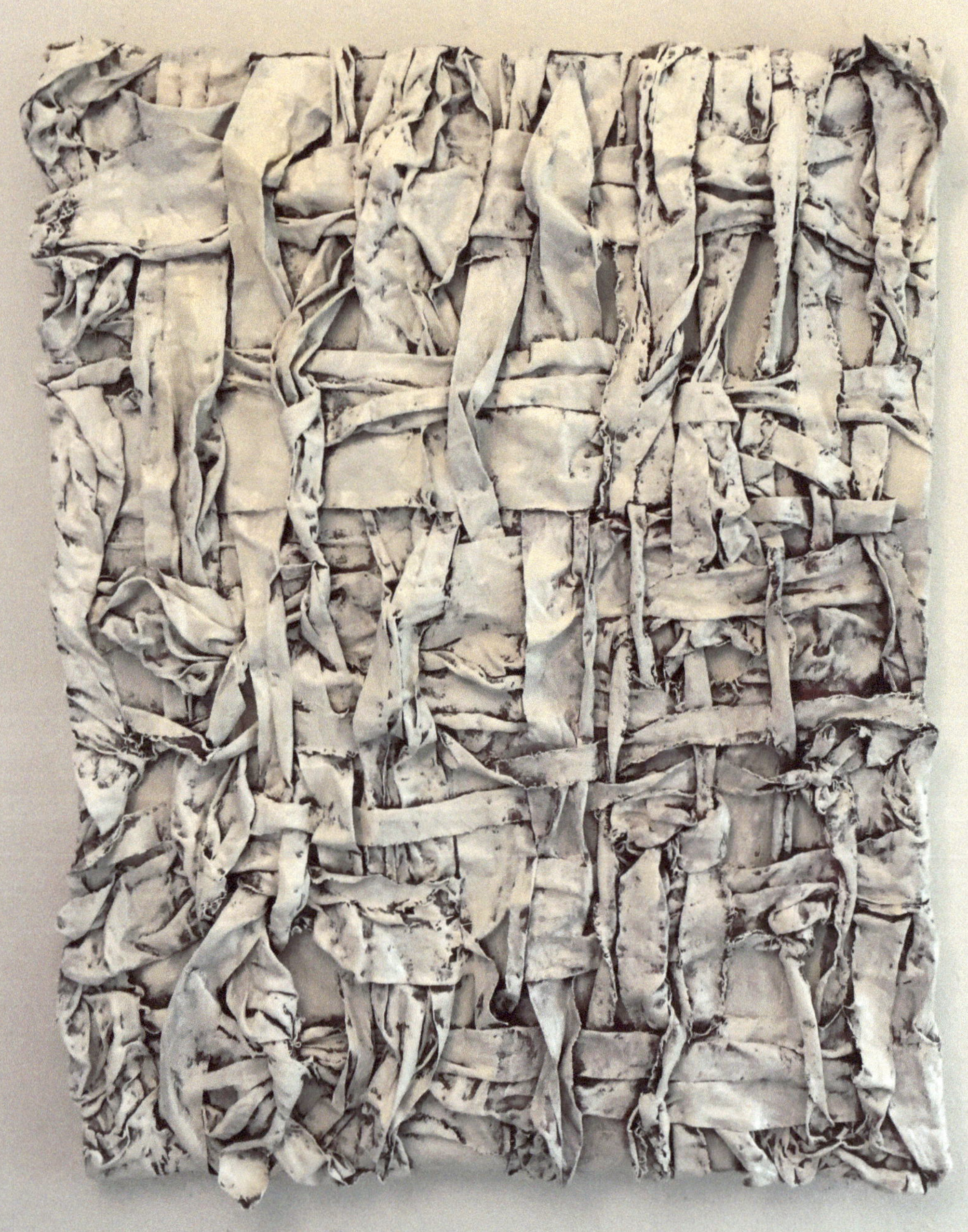

Elizabeth Rhoads Read   Bound Restraint

Bird

With my
back against
the downy hawthorn,
a cardinal perched
on my shoulder. He
whispered in my ear
that the white-throated
sparrow would only
squash my heart.
Dear white-throated
sparrow, your pitch
so perfect - singing
a song to suspend my spleneticism
A cry that cures what ails without fail! The most pleasing
medicine crafted by beaten wings and tactful talons. I
swallowed it all - Not gluttonous; I am love starved. Drawn to
her nest, craven to her breast. I bound myself to the trunk of the
tree. Allowing her song to rain down on me. If there is one to resist the power of her
ornithological organ, it is not I! I could not deny the mistress of the order most
melodious when she beckoned me beneath her branches. Pulling me in with slivers of sin.
Full, rich and heavy calls lifting me sky high as if I was feather light
Delighting as I make nest in the
cave of her coo; Calming cant
cradling this child until - one day
she decides to fly The day spans
weeks, months. Until our cave of
wonder becomes a house of horrors
Abruptly I am thrust into a violent silence -
Denial of the passerine productions of
precious perfection. Dear white-throated
sparrow, please don't leave me an
emotional Eve expelled from
Paradise. Take the taste from
my tongue, remove the sight from
my eyes, but to refuse me your
song is as to take my life!
I beg for mercy - to hold
the cardinal's words but
foolish; not that of a sage!
Leave me hope to again
hear those dulcet tones.
Release me from this
torturous capture
Allow me to sow
and forage the
finest of seeds
and delectable
berries. Any or
all I may bring
to once again
hear you
sing.

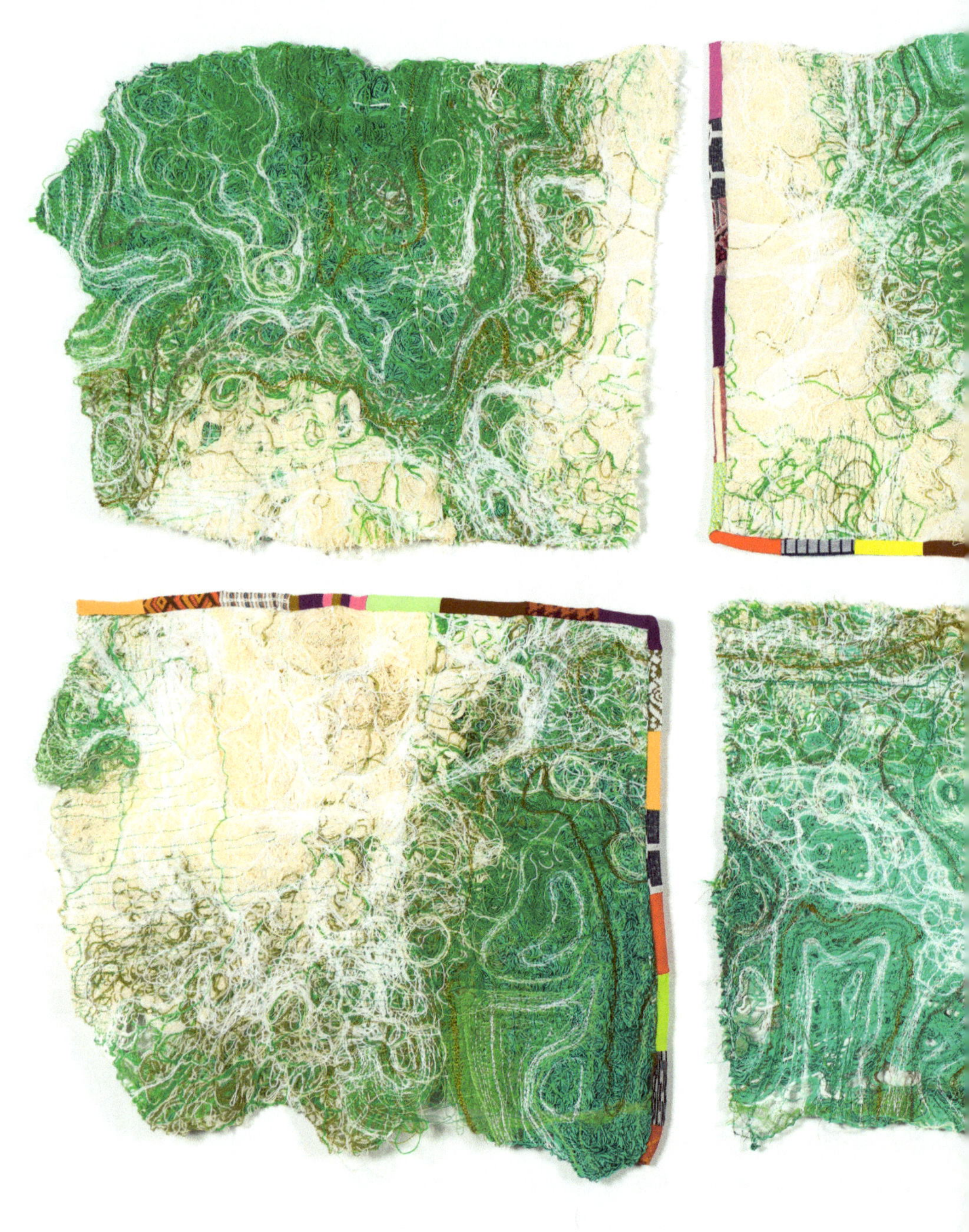

Catherine Reinhart   Inland Surveying,

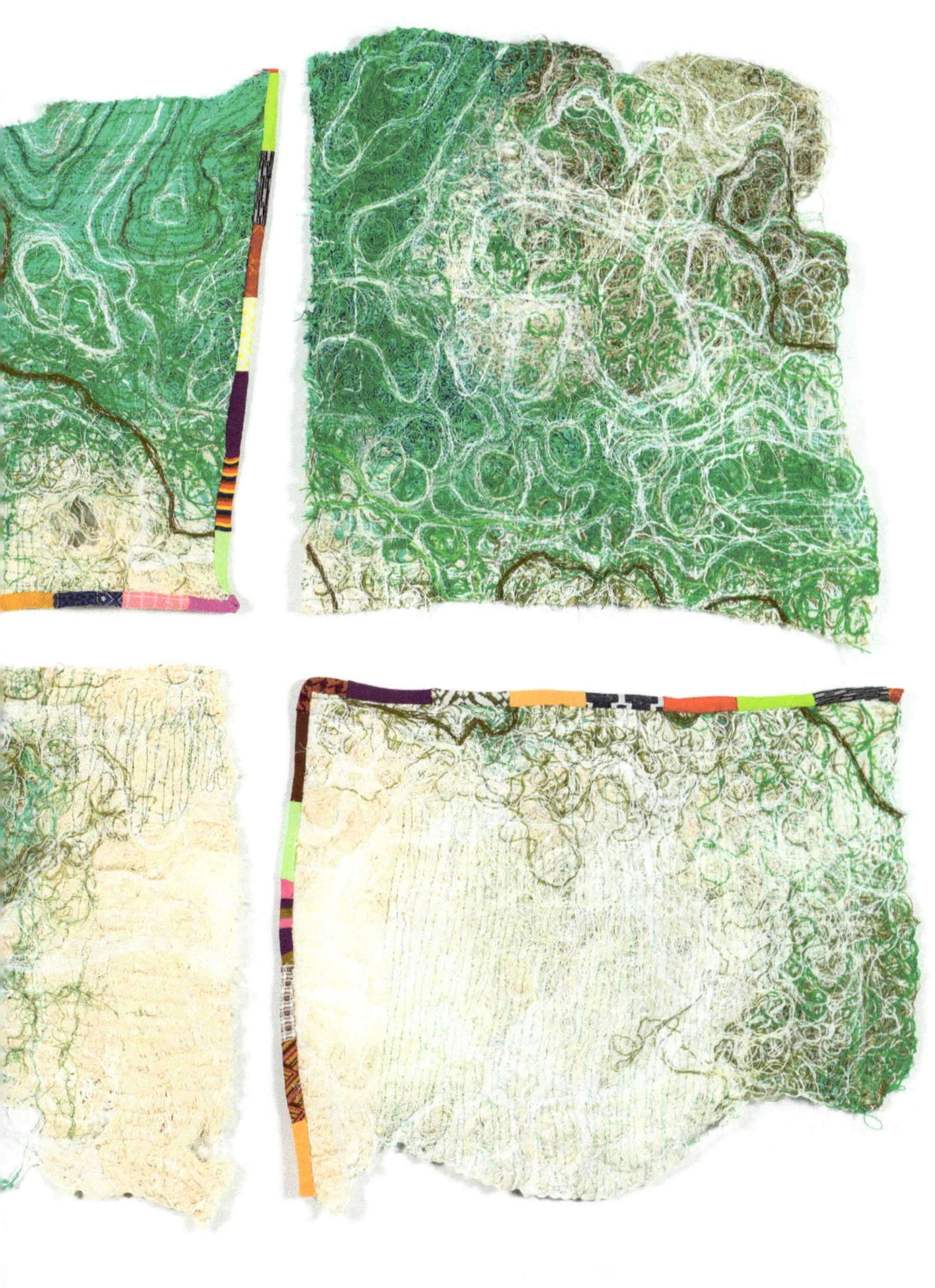

Fiber: Free Motion Stitching, Found Quilt Border, 39" x 67," 2021

Landscape Peopled with Figurines
—an ekphrastic based on work by Melanie Vote

Many have been employed
unearthing the remnants of culture,
wrestling artifacts and knick-knacks from their cribbing –
but our frames are too slight
for the collection of fears we carry. Especially
worrisome at the ravine's edge, we stand and trade
rumors of those who have fallen.

The trail is fashioned of questions.
What is this place? How can I
determine the scale of things?
What warrants restoration? Why has this,
and not that, survived?

I tiptoe, transformed to a modern minotaur
rummaging in my rough way through ruins.
Barefoot and entranced, I have come to inhabit
the doll's head, called by others the godhead,
entered by stringing together scraps
of natural refuse. You may say this is rustic.

Unable to discern the vile or holy events
that deposited these relics, we cling to hints,
traces of recalled dream, a canvas knapsack
we cannot open, a dress thrown to the ground,
and make use, and make lives among them.
History is inescapable that way.
None among us starts fresh.

Despite our excavations, the end of the story
is always just out of earshot, an abandoned campsite
with embers still hot under the stir-stick.
What we agree upon is this: the infant
at the fence line has never been easily pacified.

Regarding the Question of Ownership
—after Melanie Vote's series "The Washhouse"

The rain on the tin roof of the washhouse runs off the backside,
hitting a slab from the maple that was taken down
by a professional crew earlier this year. The washhouse
had a thick cement floor until two little girls smashed it into pieces
with a sledgehammer and stacked the irregular chunks just outside the door.
The painter comes year after year and assembles her easel
to reproduce the details of this structure. She can't paint fast enough
because each season further weathers the boards. Last year, entering
the wash house, there was a pile of fine dirt as tall as our knees.
It took a live trap to know for sure that this was the work of a groundhog.
We relocated it 6 miles away. If you look at the outside of the shed
you don't know what is going on inside. If you look at the inside of the shed
you don't know what is going on below it. If you look below it
you still don't know the history of this land, the way this soil
didn't even start out here but was carried in the skirt of the wind.

There is a kind of enlightenment to be found in staring at one thing,
and somehow by doing so maybe you can come to know about the baby
buried in the yard, or about the woman who camped alone by the fire ring
and heard voices all night. Maybe you can even come to know
about the osprey who hunts the pond using positioning to obscure
its own shadow-warning from the fish. The present just keeps
heaping itself onto the past, so many layers of wallpaper,
so many decades of flooring, carpet over linoleum over wood.
When we add our own part we write messages inside of the walls.
During the renovation, countless people asked why we didn't just bulldoze
the place. Much like others asked, years earlier, why anybody
would sell good farmland to the state. The barn here is not suited
to modern equipment, but we haven't torn it down, not even for the good money
people say they will pay for the ancient boards. I pay the taxes every year
on this property but I am still mystified how a person can own property.

There are philosophers who believe we only rightfully own what we produce,
that owning land is a form of theft. And Emerson declared *the landscape
belongs to the person who looks at it.* I don't understand how it could be
that I can sell a walnut tree to a tree buyer. How can a person own a *tree,*
something time-rooted in this drifted soil? Consider how this tree

began here, long before I was born in the delivery room of a military hospital
in a far-away state. How this tree was already finding purchase
in the loess soil. The name on the title has changed three times since then.
Because it is my name on the paper at this point in history, I could sell
all of the trees; I could girdle or fell or burn the trees; I could bulldoze
these hills and this house and this barn. I could sell the dirt by the truckload.

For $1000 a year in property taxes I can trap the groundhogs, make a junkyard
out of the barn yard by stacking old cars and ruined tires and travel trailers
that have seen better days. I could farm it or I could charge someone money
so that they can farm it, because somehow in the twist of history
this became temporarily mine. But I can't stop thinking about
what the painter's dad said. *Everyone has to have some place to be.*
So if you throw an imaginary grid over all of the land that exists,
and print plat maps that show who owns which piece,
and you bind those maps into books that are reprinted year after year,
what happens to the people whose names are not in that book?

Heart of Wire and Wheels
>   *—after Philip Pearlstein's "Kiddie-Car Plane, Airplane and Models"*

There are materials in this world that draw the body
or the eye, the tactile experience of metal, fabric, wood,
wheel. The foot wants to press against the pedal, the arm
to stretch toward that which is suspended overhead.

Compare the shredding wingtips with the vulnerable tent
of the body, the axle and wheel with the leg
and its haunting mechanics. Congestive heart failure rates
are no different if your care is in a big city or a slow
Midwestern town. Ninety five percent of people do not die
in their sleep, and we are glad the fuselage appears to be intact.

This is a story about transport, a story about the body
of a man and the resting body of a woman, of an adventure that opened
on the street below, behind you now, where two men
walk down the sidewalk and don't look in the window,
a street where XXX girls girls girls can eat pancakes after their shift.

If there is a figure, it is all about the figure, our attention
drawn to the angle and plane of hip, the fatigue and shadow,
the hand at rest. It is the story of how we tire ourselves with love
and retreat back to our cells, how it is to be encased in flesh,
the stretch of skin and muscle and tendon over bone.

Everything was damaged in the move. They have nothing to plug in,
and the plaster ceiling is watermarked above them.
Say what you will about how they have spent their lives,
spent the afternoon, spent themselves, how they landed here –
you who walk together in the gallery, fully clothed, maybe
halfway through your life, keeping a polite distance
from one another. You'd trade with them, wouldn't you?

In Spite of Dying

Outside, a deer grazes on blades of grass
as I open the window
to let morning sift the living room,
fresh and quiet.
I turn to check on you,
and your face, so white and still,
droops as if you are sleeping.

Trembling, I call your name.
Only silence answers.
I do what I'm trained to do:
the tilt of the head, the pinch
of the nose, the lonely press
of my lips cupping tight to yours.
Two breaths.

Your skin is sweaty and warm
at my cheek. Your chest won't rise
and the weight in mine
matches yours
as your life slips and lifts
to the light above us.

In my mind
we are dancing in the kitchen
the radio loud above our laughter,
our feet grooving in perfect step,
hands linked tight,
our eyes flashing like sunlight
to the jitterbug at hand.

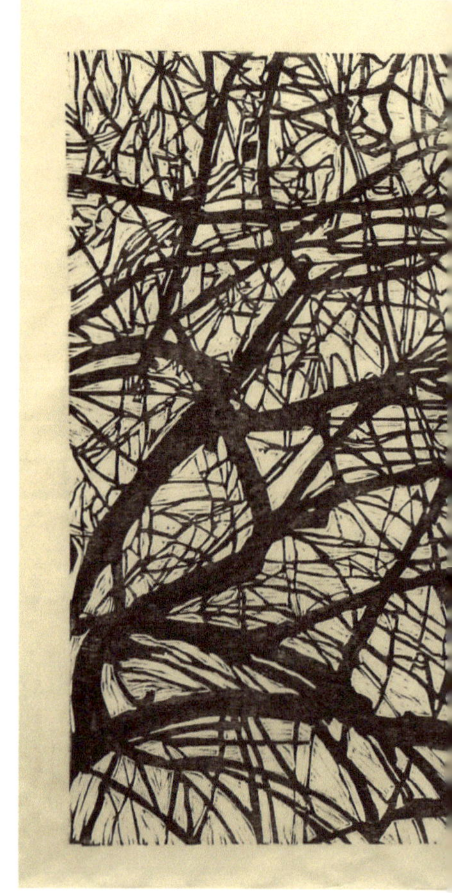

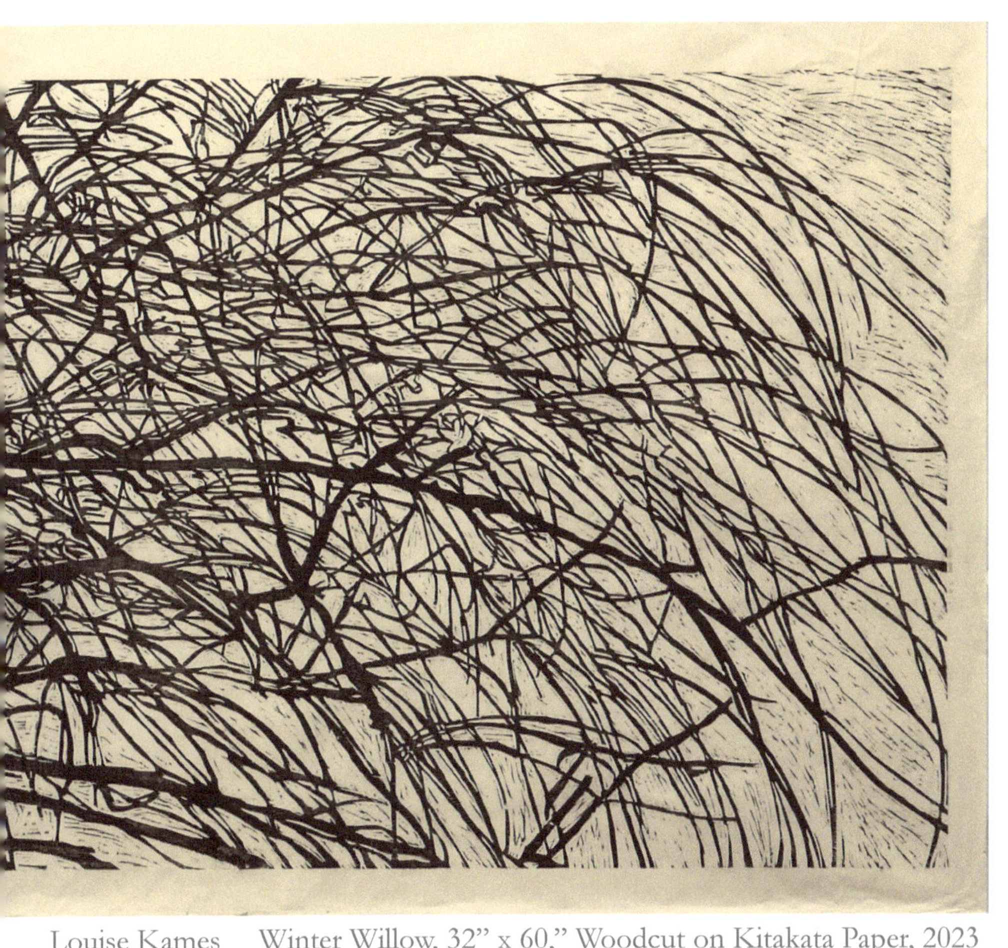

Louise Kames   Winter Willow, 32" x 60," Woodcut on Kitakata Paper, 2023

Sockeye

Under skies of moonlight and sun,
below mountain ridges
filled with snow,
her back turns to a flame of red.
Her jaw sets for the cold.

Anything can kill, even the sea lions
at the locks, but she will spawn
where she was spawned,
will perish like her mother.

The free fall of the leap,
the tear and torrent of the rapids,
her mouth suffers the strain,
eyes near-fixed and yellow.

This is a mother's instinct,
where even the smell of home
is the drive within protection,
when a mother knows she must
stop eating. At last, she turns
on her side, swishes her tail in gravel,
digs the saucer-shaped nest,
lays her eggs in coolness.

The male passes over.

Beside the tallness
of long-stemmed pine,
the sun glazing her scales
like a sheet of cellophane,
her gills are puffing bellows.

She is weak, trembling.
This is as far as giving can climb,
the familiar stones at her belly.

The Beach

Now in the moon's brightest light
she finishes her migration
and pauses at the water's edge.

Sea foam lapping at her flippers,
she trudges across the shore
to the wall of sea grass protection.
Relentlessly, she scoops a hole
until it is a nest of perfect softness.
With a mother's care,
she lays her eggs and tucks them
beneath a tender cover.
The loggerhead scrambles back to sea
leaving tire-track impressions.

For days, sweetness incubates
on the expectant beach,
the warmth of sun
dictating male or female.

When the hatchlings dig to the surface,
life sprouting from the sand,
they crawl past crabs like small stones,
sand falling from their boney scutes
as they disappear
into the whispers of the tide.

To the Bone

I drape my bones in Spanish lace and pure silk Crêpe de Chine
      you marvel at my fabric and ignore the ghost who wears them
my plan all along
against the ivory of my mandible, crimson lips are lined like artwork
      girlish giggles are irresistible with complementing blush malar
which you love painted red

I no longer pretend I feel the emptiness, the nightmares that once lurked within
      my flesh, my blood, my organs have all been harvested to suffer
in this world of endless giving
once laid to rest, the weary and grieving exhumed my fragile remains
      without choice, without option, I was told my work here was not done
my skin now decomposed, a false smile is infinite

To work yourself to the bone is not enough; you must also give your spirit
      now the wolves rest at my feet, salivating over femurs not yet undone
I think I will give them one
I cannot feel the warmth of the hearth; I cannot see the color of its flame
      brittle bones and orbits without their globes add to the nothingness
please give me my grave to rest; mark it with a poem

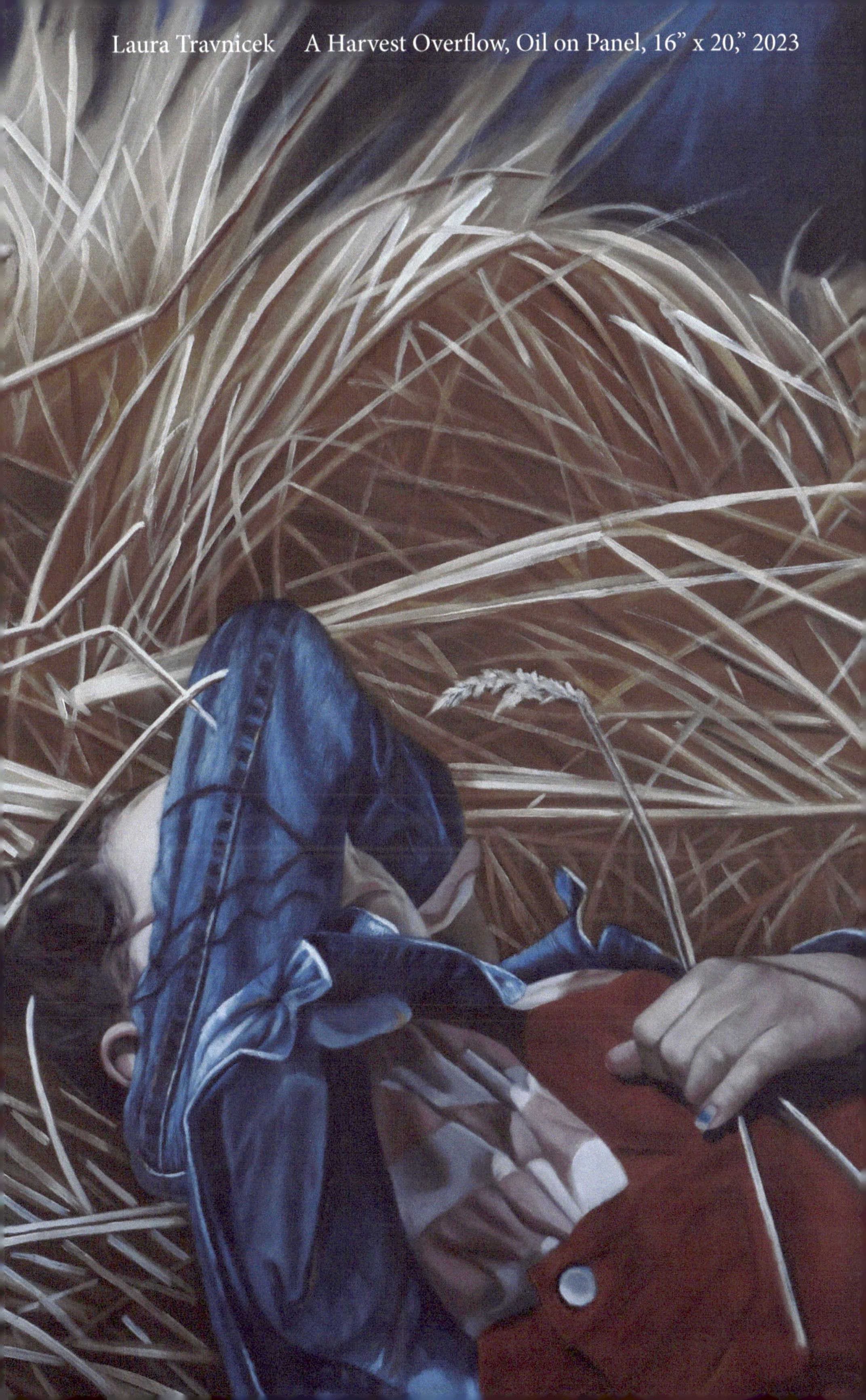

Laura Travnicek   A Harvest Overflow, Oil on Panel, 16" x 20," 2023

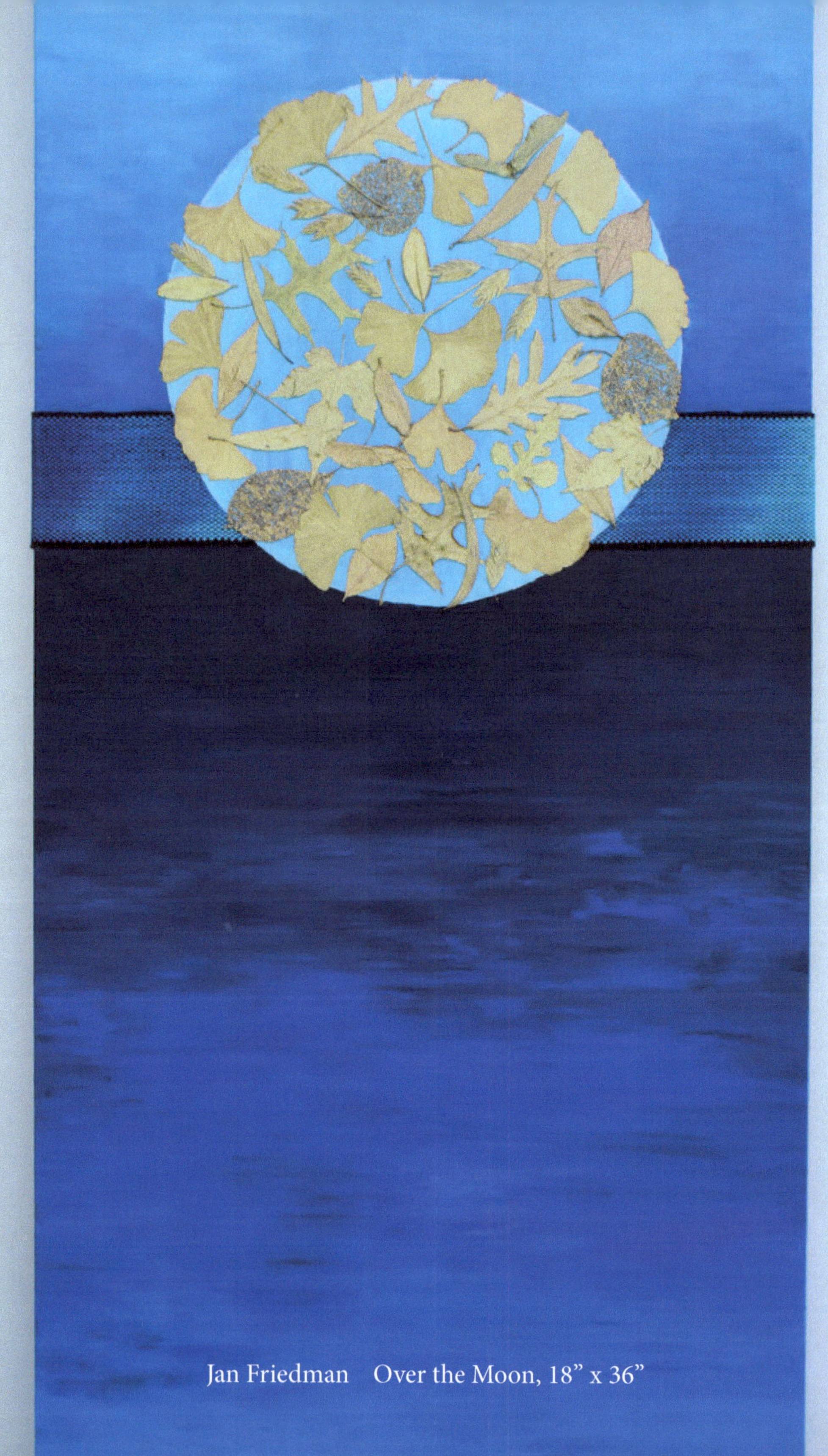

Jan Friedman   Over the Moon, 18" x 36"

father in the moon

i once traveled your path without question
my only knowledge bound by your waxing and waning
beyond where you shown, i knew no other way

your beams were artistically crafted
their glimmering rays were stretched and set
planned long before knowing my stride

careful consideration was put in my footfalls
i had hoped to see your proud grin
your craters cast shadows disguising disapproving smiles

i had won wars intended for men
A job well done! Now leave it to those more qualified.
the eclipse had settled revealing forbidden truths

i sent up questions to you
each escaped me like a thick, black poison
you said they smothered your light

you are no longer my guiding moon
you are a flameless lantern, empty and unlit

Night Life

The ocean is too tired for sex.
It wants to be made love to or be left alone.

I roll a drop around in my mouth and swallow it.

The wave sways in my stomach long into the night.

In theory, I believe in marriage, though I wonder if
I can be cut out for that sort of thing.

I bleed a lot and can't tell you everything.

The morning too dark to film, too dozy.

Yellow plumes stain our pillowcases,
lined like writing paper, from over the years.

Time draws the out-of-doors flowers open. Stranded,
they repeat themselves each year, mostly. Some don't come back.

The daylilies are outspoken this summer.
I never noticed them before.

I fantasized feelings I couldn't film. I convinced myself
it was summer, that you made me a woman.

Hair holds memories so I don't cut it. I suck on the tips.
You like my hair like that, the way my ears show.

I want to show you the window in the attic
of my other house where it is always snowing.

Here is the video evidence of departure,
a time lapse eroding the house we made
into soft, painful light.

Does a woman need to give birth to be a woman,
or is being pregnant forever enough.

I had plans to lead a second life but kept pushing
them aside for that floating feeling.

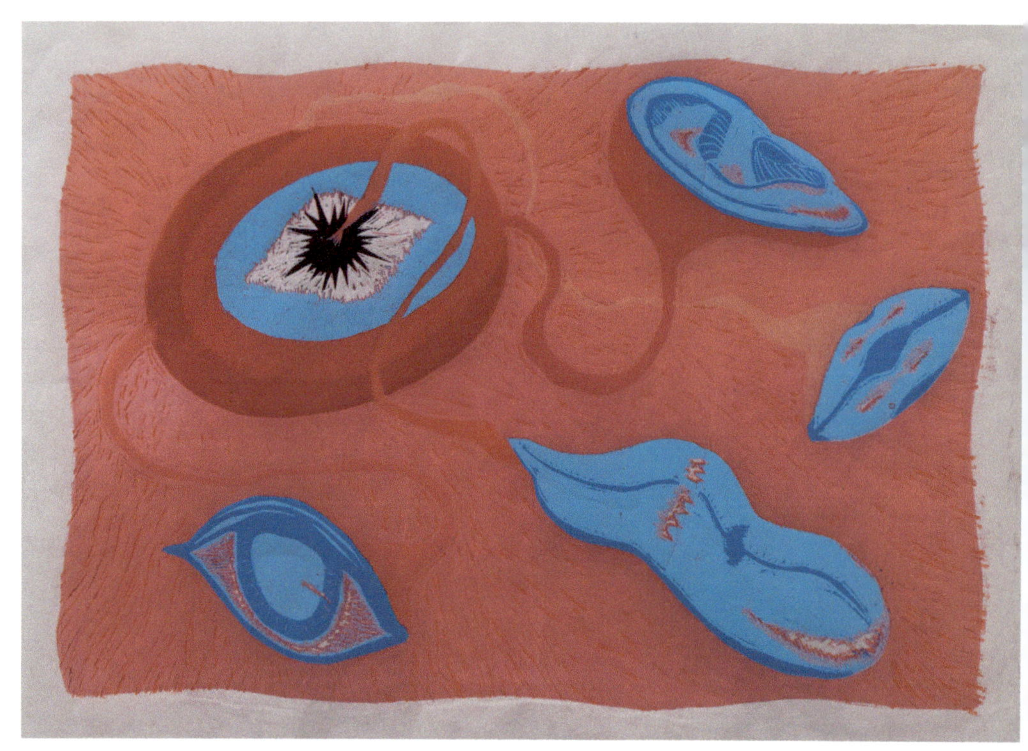

Bob Lockhart   Screen Time

Sex Drive

It isn't suicide. You don't leave
a note. Tulips squeezed by a red ribbon.

I was human in private. Summer gorging
videos where you still exist

I replay them until they dissolve, proofreading
for accuracy, looking at a landscape so long

it erases itself. My room breaks off
the hill and floats into the night.

Now my body has its own agenda:
moon comma dream comma moon

No shortage of materials to make me come.
I project one child on top of another,

that summer on top of the other. Home
with the video of home.

I download darkness onto my phone,
the darkness of that summer, its deepest ripple,

enters my body. You are something
to be drowned in, unready desires.

Moon Charger

Julia Anna Morrison

We drink night milk with ice chips. We make quick
love. I quiet down with a thumbprint.

I have two lives, I tell you, and you agree.
Now that night comes sooner, my son grows in the bath

like mega-magic-starfish from the dollar store,
or the staircase is steeper to his toy-room.

I carry him anyway, a suitcase of stars, wear white socks,
fluffy socks, identify the tree blooming in our windowsill.

I give my son a night bath, watch him play in the yard with sticks, the only light
a motion light and the shallow moon, an electrical outlet.

Plug the wrong wire into my computer, the watch charger, the phone power.
I stare at my son playing in the dark outside.

He needs privacy now, a notebook with a tiny golden key.
You doctor me. I stare at the painting of my cell phone. Text you back

and forth. Swipe blue light, swipe until blue light of morning, yolk bright.
Unplug my chargers, let go of each wire. I marvel at my son, want another.

Want a dozen others, all sleeping tangled, and the ocean—chilled and chilly.
Go to the doctor, spread my legs. Fill up the gas tank with diesel,

boiled lemon in my tea, sea-salt on my soft-egg. Start the oven timer.
I cook an ocean fish, a lake fish, a wild animal.

I look you in the eyes and say let's start over.

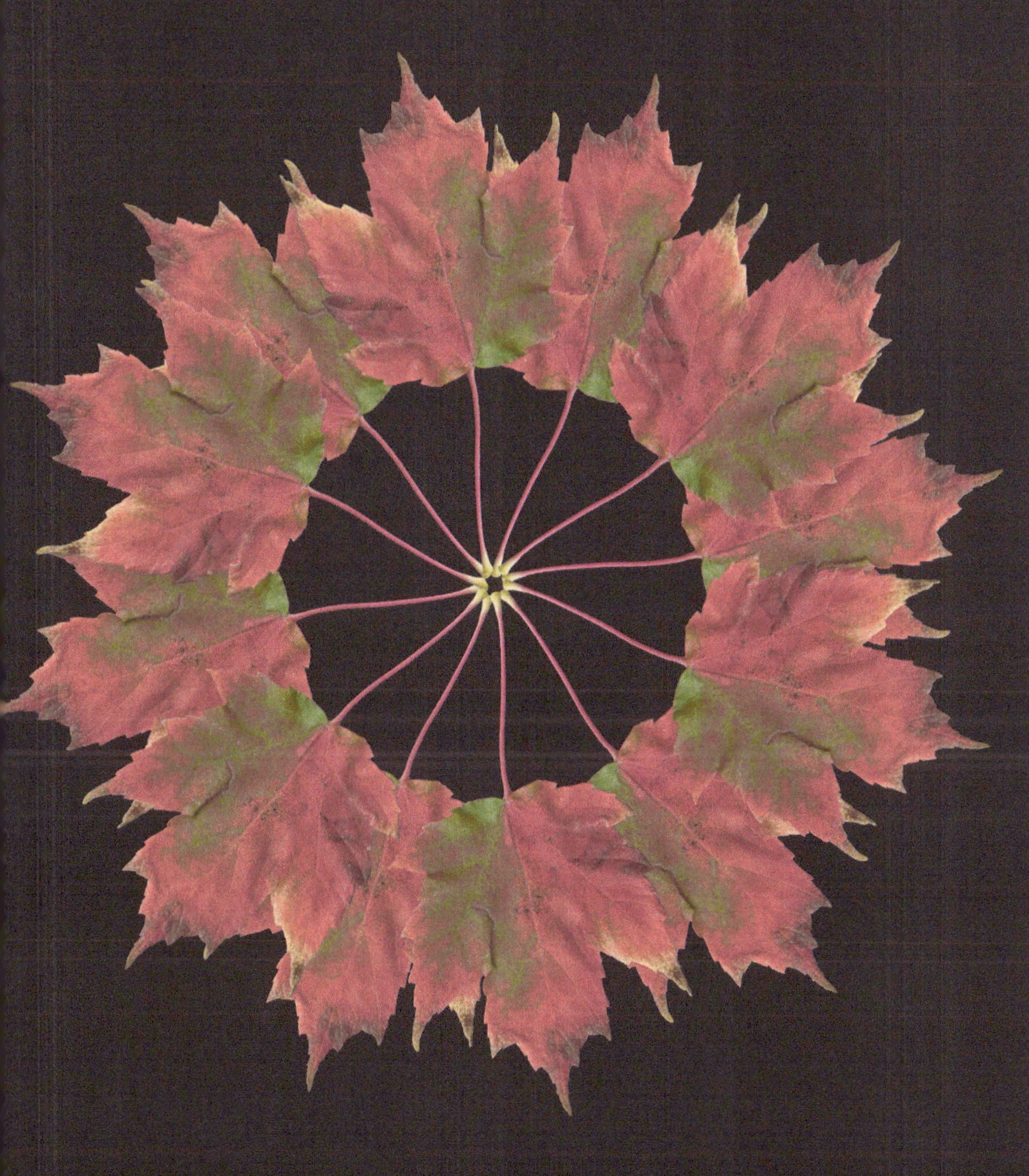

Paul Brooke   Maple Leaf Wheel

A Black Child's Walk to See the Freedom Train

On an early morning in forty-five
I took the loneliest stride of my life.
Alone, I walked with the weight of fear
    shackled through the streets
    that harbored lives
    broken shades of defeat
    in both mind and spirit.

The streets were muddy and dark.
Lurking around dark corners were shacks
    sheltering hapless souls.

Dogs barked to create alarm
but knew I meant no harm
    and they let me travel on.

The trees along the dark street
    cast a canopy
    to protect
    this child
    aged ten and two
    bowing to the Gods to let her through
    on her
    journey to see
    the Freedom Train
    that promised
    to let her trust again.

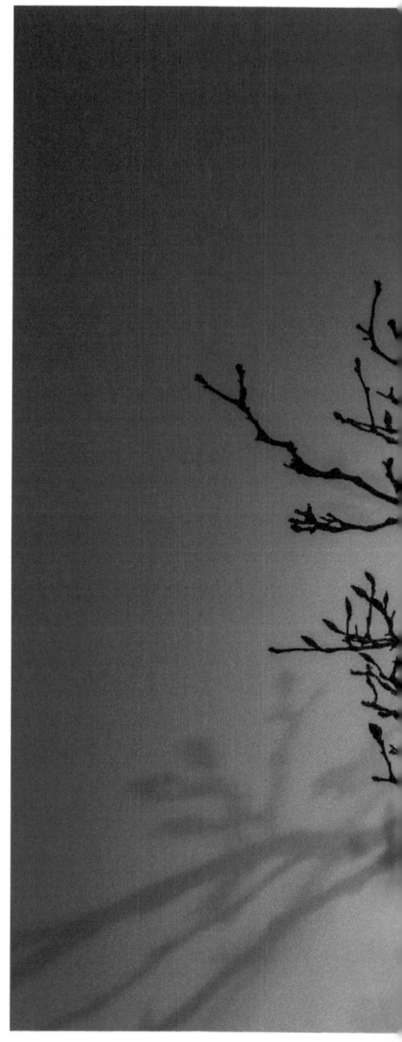

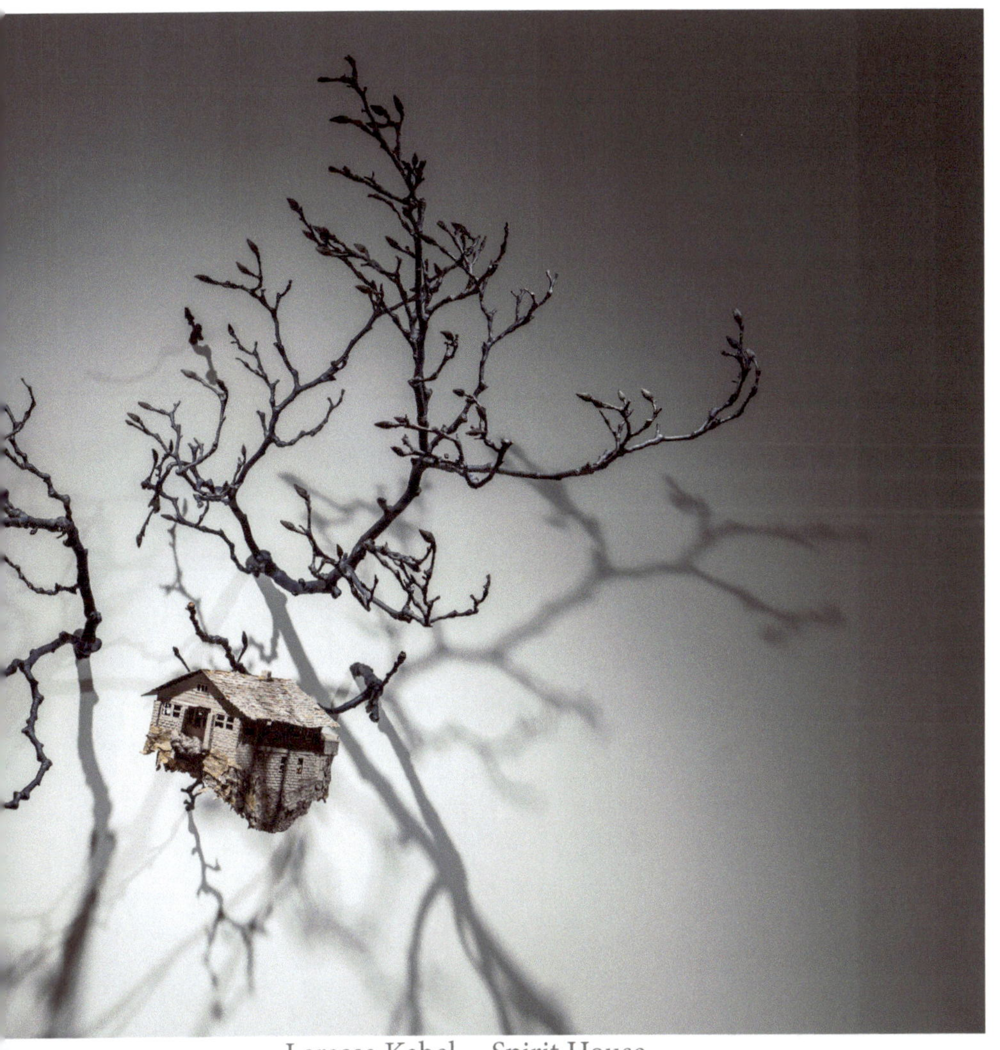

Larassa Kabel   Spirit House

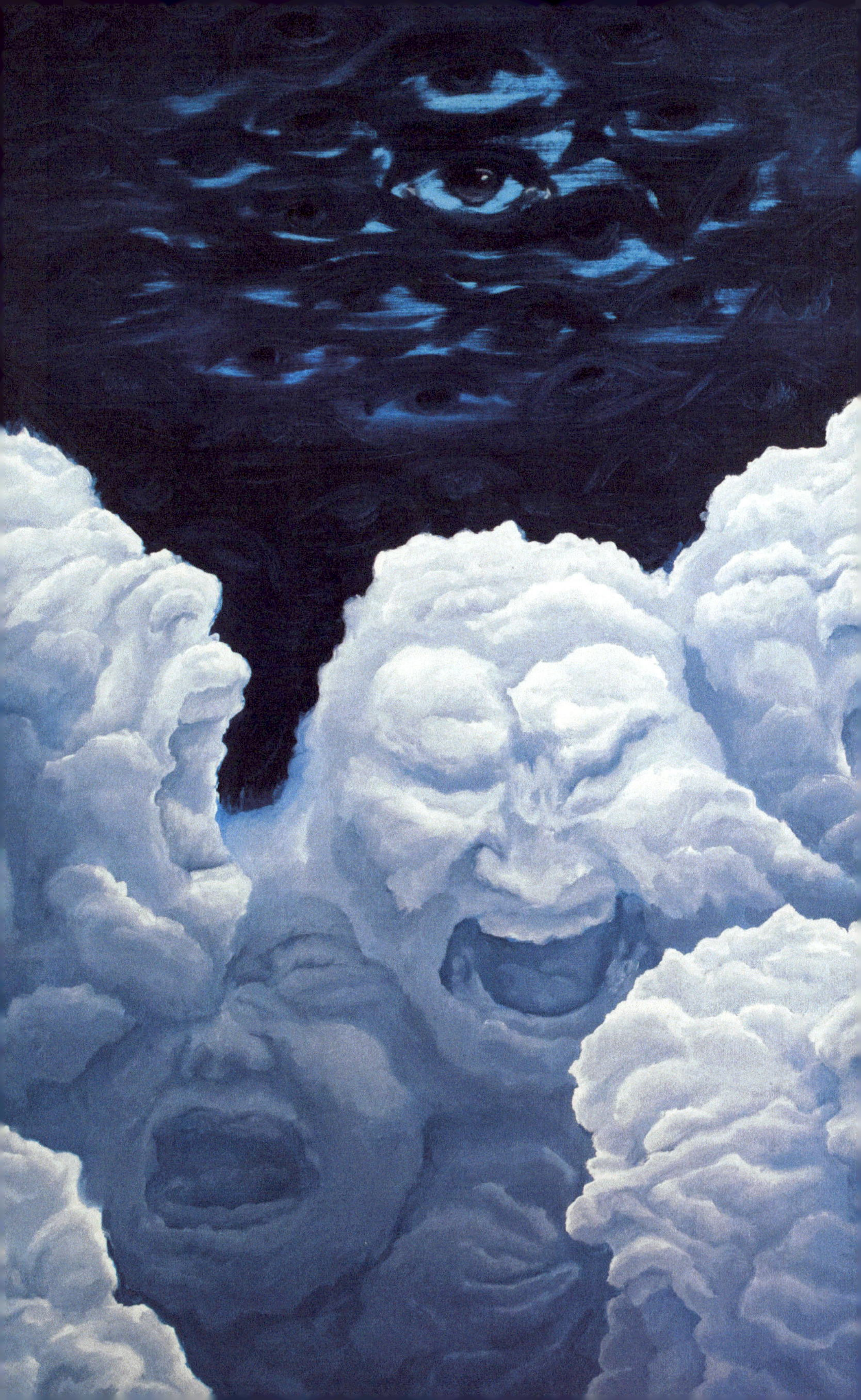

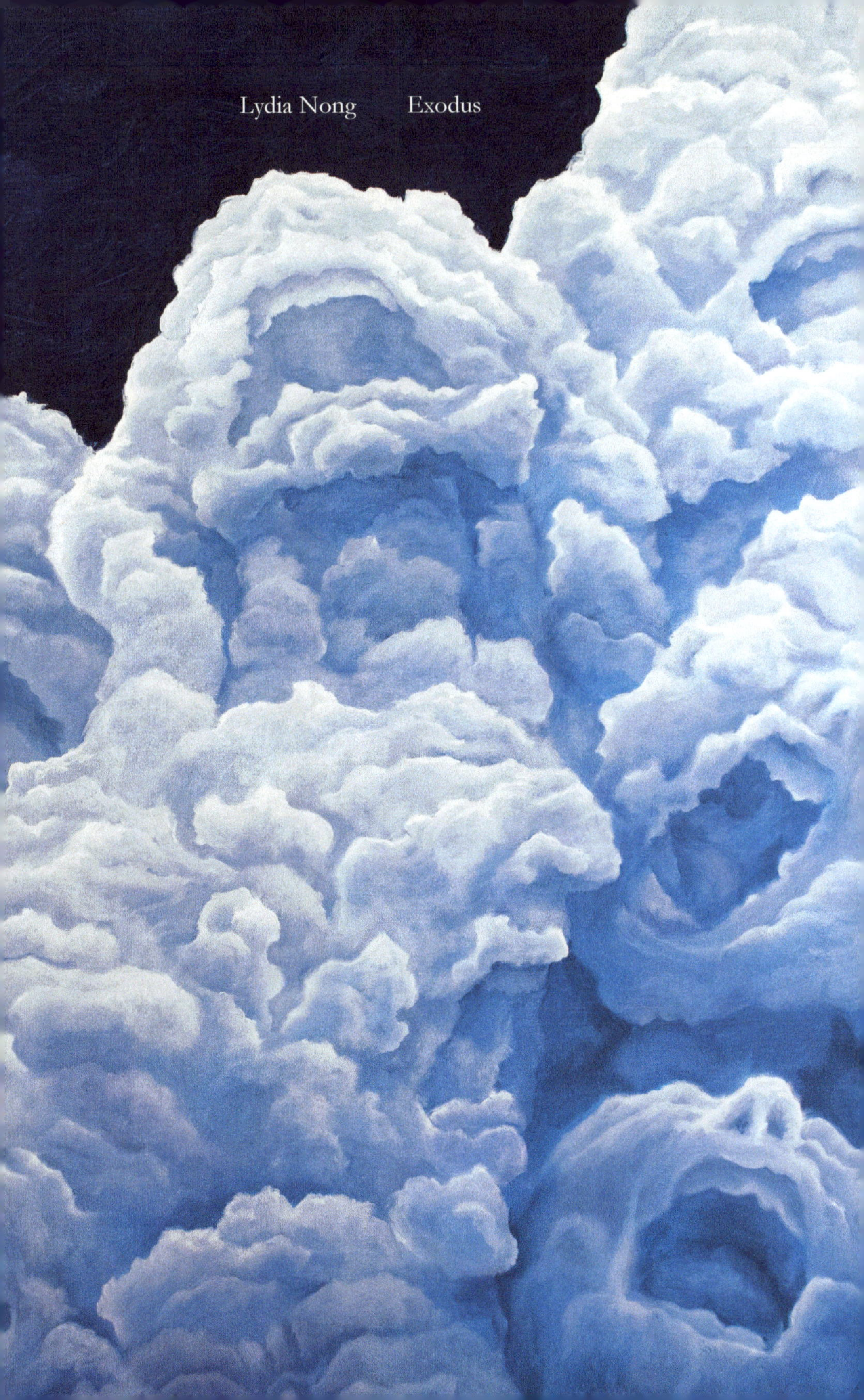
Lydia Nong
Exodus

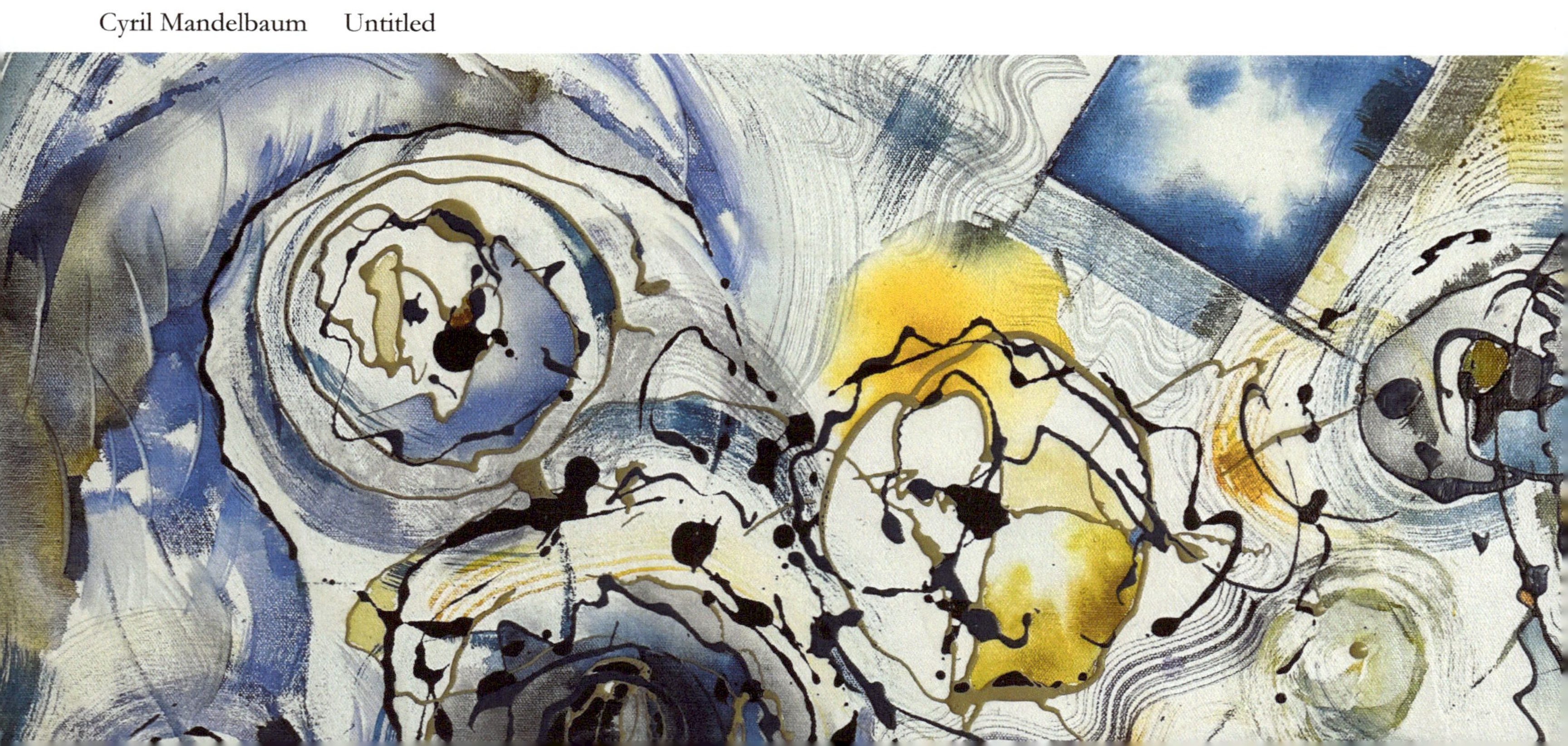

Cyril Mandelbaum   Untitled

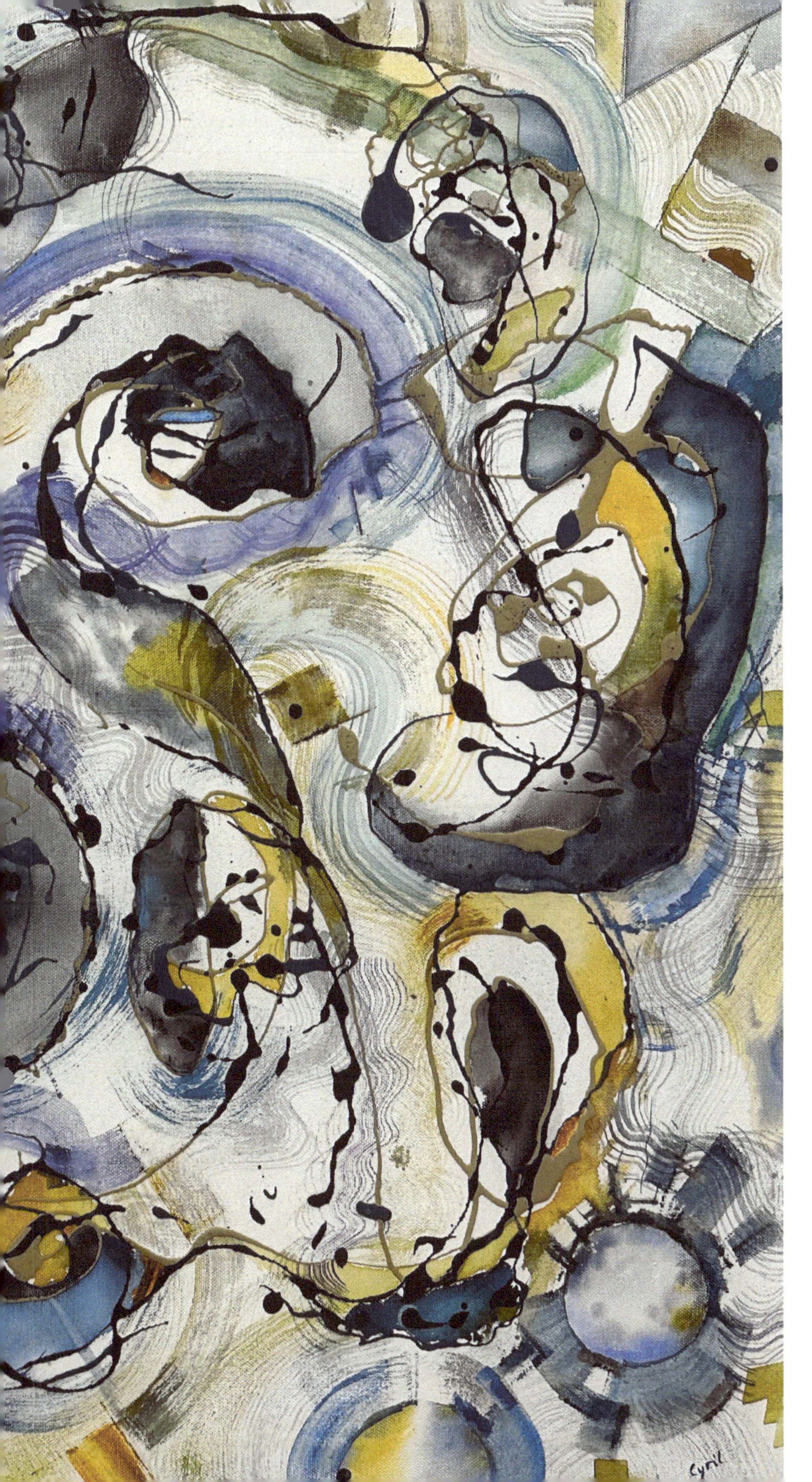

A Circle, Spoken

She first said,

> Becoming requires allowance.

And then,

> It cannot begin with force.

> Motion is transition is position thus transmission.

She sings that it is

cosmological biological il/logical.

That

> movement supports the morphological.

She takes my breath. And after a perforated hold, remarks, as if it's not a question,

> What is fixable without the dynamics of space-time constituents.

> What leaks rejoins everything (else) including itself, its same, its new self.

> What is vision if not key and lock within one socket.

> What is abiding if not a sometimes true, sometimes false, responding.

The alterative takes place noisily.

It is, and I knew it, impossible to catch this thing, to have it.

Because she'd already said,

> Belonging inspires allowance.

And then,

It cannot be gained with farce.

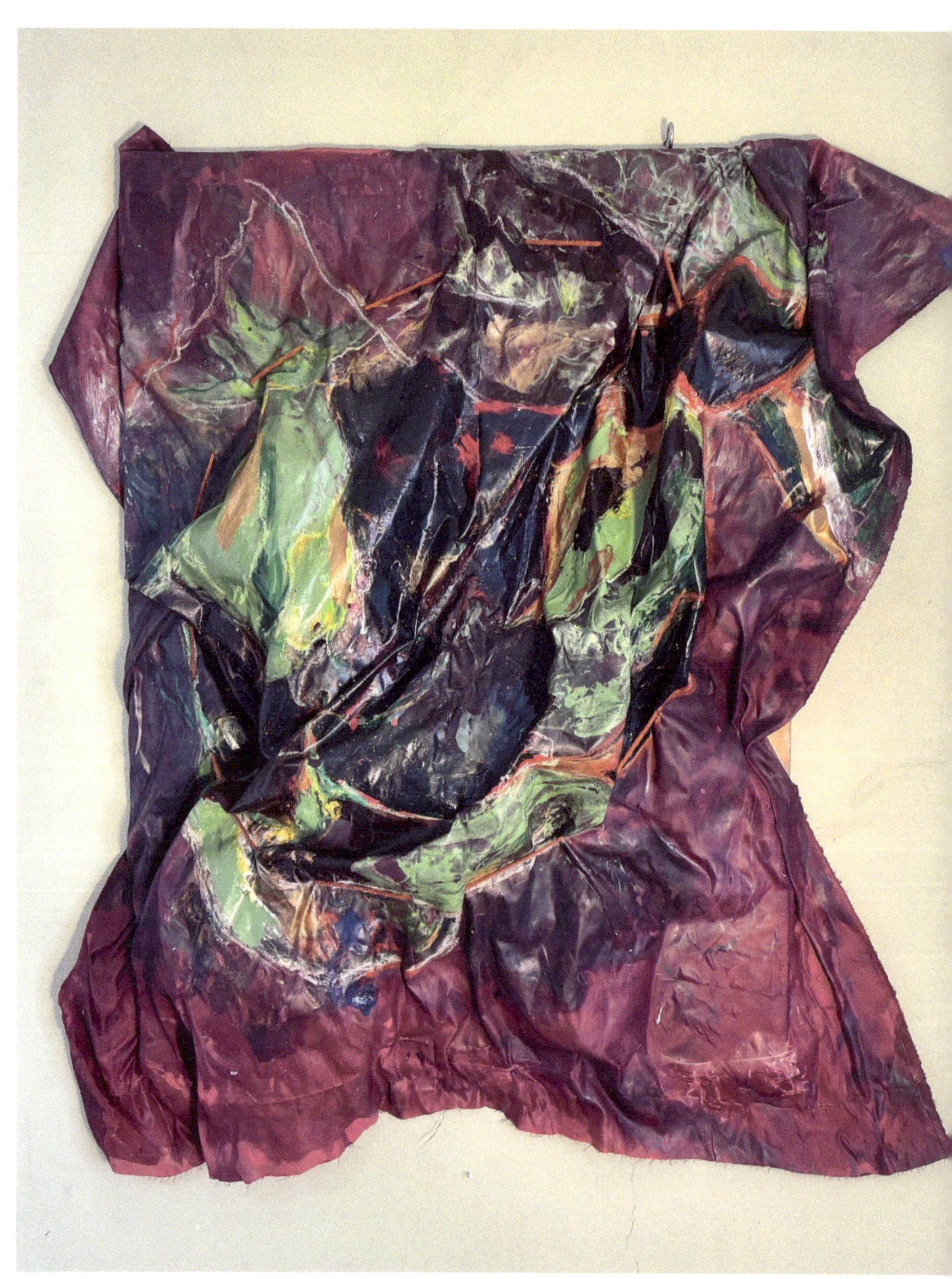

Mirzam Perez   Tell Me About It, Mixed Media, Acrylic, Fabric, Yarn, 50 x 36," 202

Pandemic Rewound

Leaves uncollect on the lawn
like bats returning to a cave.

My hands are clean.
The tap runs, and I endanger

myself and others.
M's father is Lazarus,

his heavy hips swinging to a tune
hushed by the ether.

If her sadness is a panther
a sleek predator prowling

the night, its cage clicks shut.
Some iridescent force vacuums

its yowls, or is it a black hole
remanding light to this plane?

Small fluorescents, which are all
that signal civilization in my margin

of the heartland, dim then resume
their mezzo piano hum.

You are not so old, they swear
not so near what brink

all vessels crest and don't return.
These days when fear walks

through the ghost of me
like something ancient.

Ice cream in the belly
of a dish backflips

into a carton, treks to the store
where I mark the cashier warily.

The police pin George Floyd.
Now he is a phantom in both directions.

I cannot sleep
then I cannot sleep.

Please move the lens from me.
I can't progress as I am.

Rubber bullets sluice back
into barrels, but welts remain

swell like flood waters
which this summer creep along

the floor back into soil onto
electric wires.

I observe with my son who
learns my beard by a brush

of his wrist. By this measure alone
we uncount our days, so small

and devastatingly intimate.
What better can we do

then to unclink the metronome
to keep these times?

In Praise of My Toddler's Kicking

Kyle McCord

Me in his sleep
        my ribs, the middle
                life chub of my tummy

his muscular pistons
        along my calves
                sole imprinted

on my everywhere
        till I am a plum tumbled
                under the counter.

All praise to the instinct
        which thrashes comforters
                which leaps the paddock

into the next pasture
        leaves restive hills
                for the grassy beyond.

All praise for what
        you cannot know
                you shape, my son

in these predawn
        hours, clay wheel of the world
                spun beneath you.

Becoming to Iowa

<u>2019</u>

A baby with a ribbon, a banner, an old man with a chill, froze one to the bone, a restive kid.

Ice turns cream, turns milk after storms, rain, a shake up, transmuted color an eagle's unblinking head.

Beyond lush, verdant, spiders flourish bushes frosting in the hot, immune to breeze sways, cling crisply.

Something airy, on the wind, the east corner. How could we know until it shores, shears bronchia.

<u>2020</u>

Old glass in the ramshackle rental shook. Winter stayed, slayed, years in its sway.

Spring pollinating something new here. Grass cutting a masque, children huddle,
The respite of flora faun, all on the wing, glad confusion: no crumbs, or rocks, cars.

One season the whole cycle: goosebumps. Stretching dimensions, necks bowed, coughing, mechanized beeps. I exhale gingerly through a tube, tentative lung test. Poetic concreteness.

A shot folks die for, waiting or refusing to take. Deep into who we are, fractals our helixes. A key we hope. Opening our great treasure, love of life.

Sun, wind, heat, snow, freeze-framed, aglow.

<u>2021</u>

Hollowed-out haloed city. More birds above. The matriculated cluster. In doors, of a kind, all liminal.

Temp plate. Not exactly hairs on edge but some sort of dermis knot. Delayed millennial-end, a score or so. An extra digit or two. We reach through the fourth mode. Back In the day, the Jetsons showed miracles. Now we notice all the white space in the Hanna-Barbera frame.

A few peek out. Diligent with in-nocs: Who's there? All of them. Signs of the cross- patterned beseeching. I convert to everything. Crunchy-granola on the lam. Flu, Covid, Tdap, I even re-up shingles, yellow fever. Waiting for age-apropos stronger stuff. Wear more eye make up, wonder how newborns decipher the crinkles of eyes, slightly lifted planes of the sides of parents' faces.

Is there a break in the clouds in this sky country? Wind blowing west out of Chi-town? A scotch-tape arm, the bustle of cold keeps our breath to ourselvess. Body heat, throat a flue, setting hawks as teeth on edge. Yet the uvula, a flutter.

<u>2022</u>

A filling, awash in blank, in fissure almost between sleep and awake.

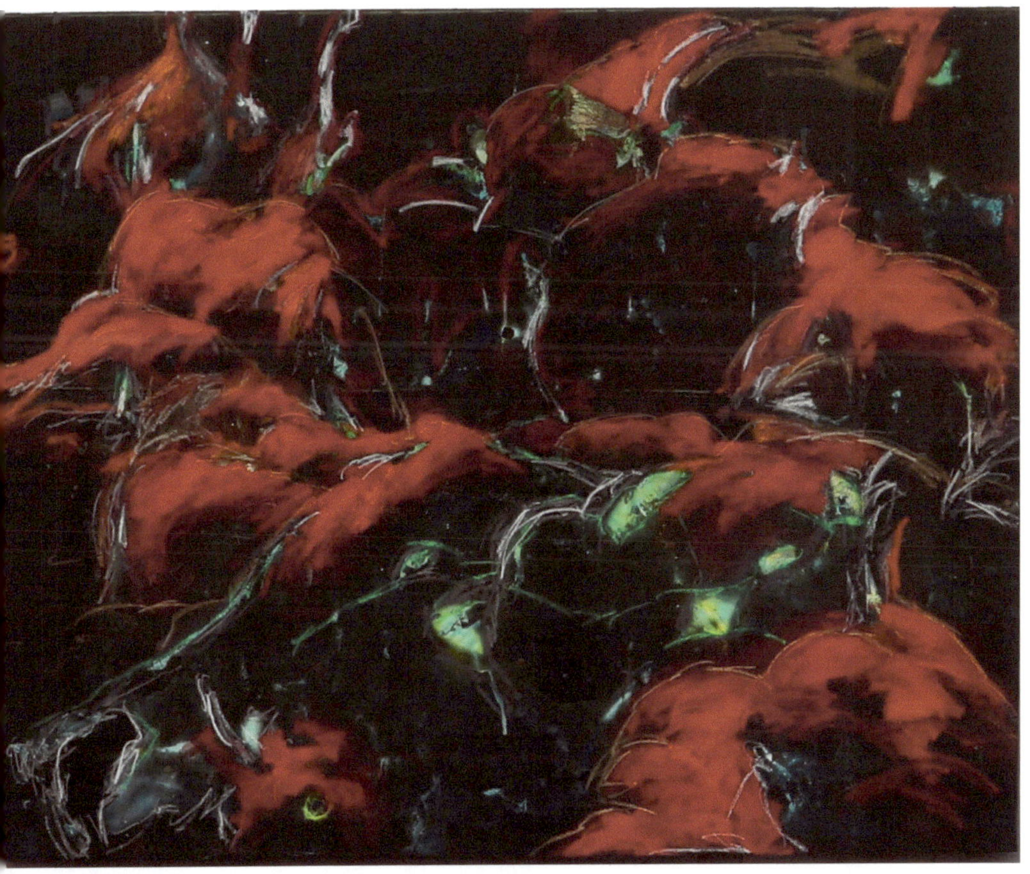

Mirzam Perez   Aguafuerte, Mixed Meida, Stretched Tafetta, Acrylic, Watercolor, 48 x 60," 2022

Penumbra of busy, fear lurk, keep up to date on things. A tenuous toe, terrified, it, uncurled, tests.

Shoeless, clipped grass, a deep breath, spared a bad wind as if nature said: you've had enough inside-out. Mother treats us special, spoils us, so we forget.

We split time, our new bc/ad. This crown like the little tweeties in cartoons after the anvil, its mallet head, the cleaving sword, honing stone.

Revving up to sweater, thick pile scarves to a holiday wrapping. We can't bear to fear outdoors. Insulate boots and the expanded highway heats, clears, quickly. Move though, it seems to say.

2023

Our heirloom of currency is the sirocco somewhere. Money, money, electric cars. That pinch between the brows? Nothing. I don't recall. Third eye's back in place, my phone.

Do I venture or have it delivered. Come to me. Passive state is Terry cloth: in/out of the house. Here's my work. I pay someone's office rent and mine. The luxury. The new season.

I got a dog I have to walk. He's three but another space at birth. I needed something to hold, now, I have accustomed to the weather. Can he set out on his own? The wind chill is chatty. I have to look in the actual eyes of someone like me. Cats evolved an extra lid. Now I think I have one too.

There are two types of people: those who type and those who talk. We're on to other things, when your world is clipped, everything looks like a nail. Punctuating these days. Next year, one way or the other, maybe most ways, maybe none, at some point, in the end, we'll be all the way through.

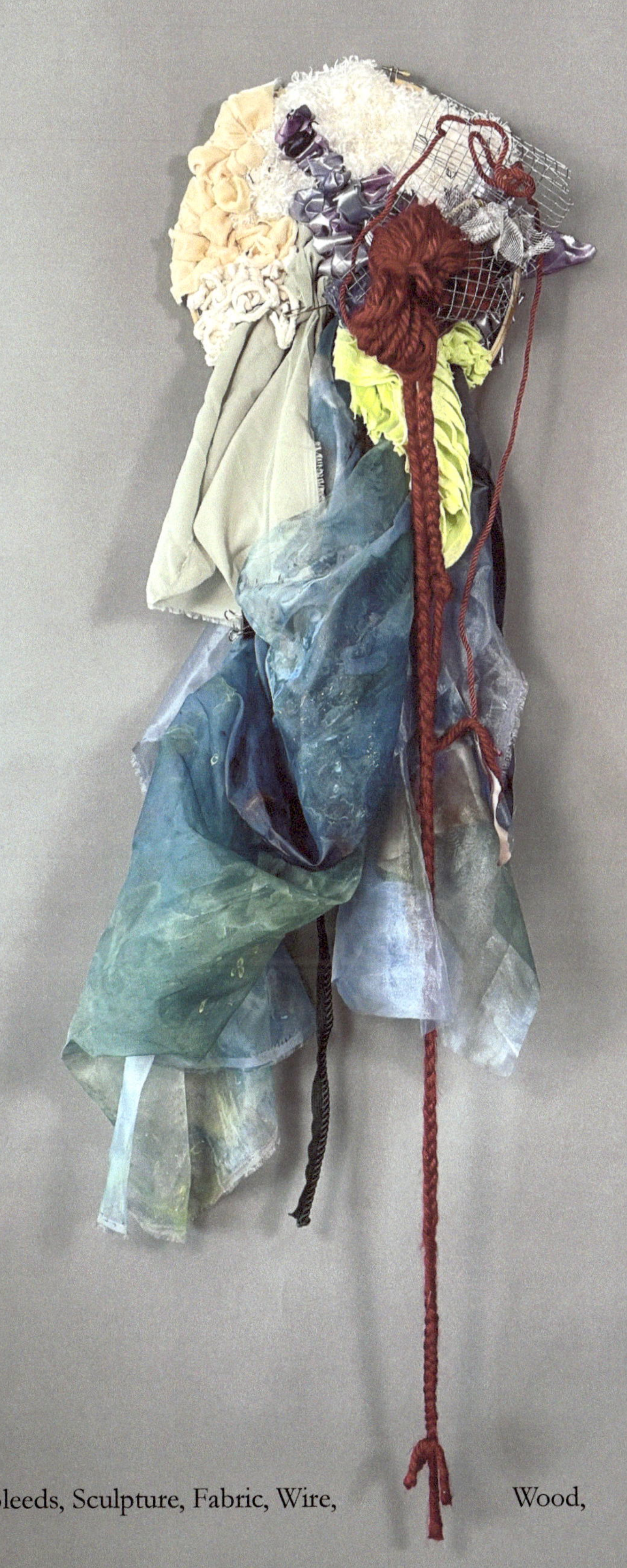

Mirzam Perez   It Bleeds, Sculpture, Fabric, Wire,   Wood,
66 x 24," 2023

Mourning Departure

Morning sky flings her gray veil lacy with fog across our land.
We huddle, frozen with grief, spreading ashes, wringing our hands.
Sun streaks whisper rise, spirit, rise as we stumble numb and blind.

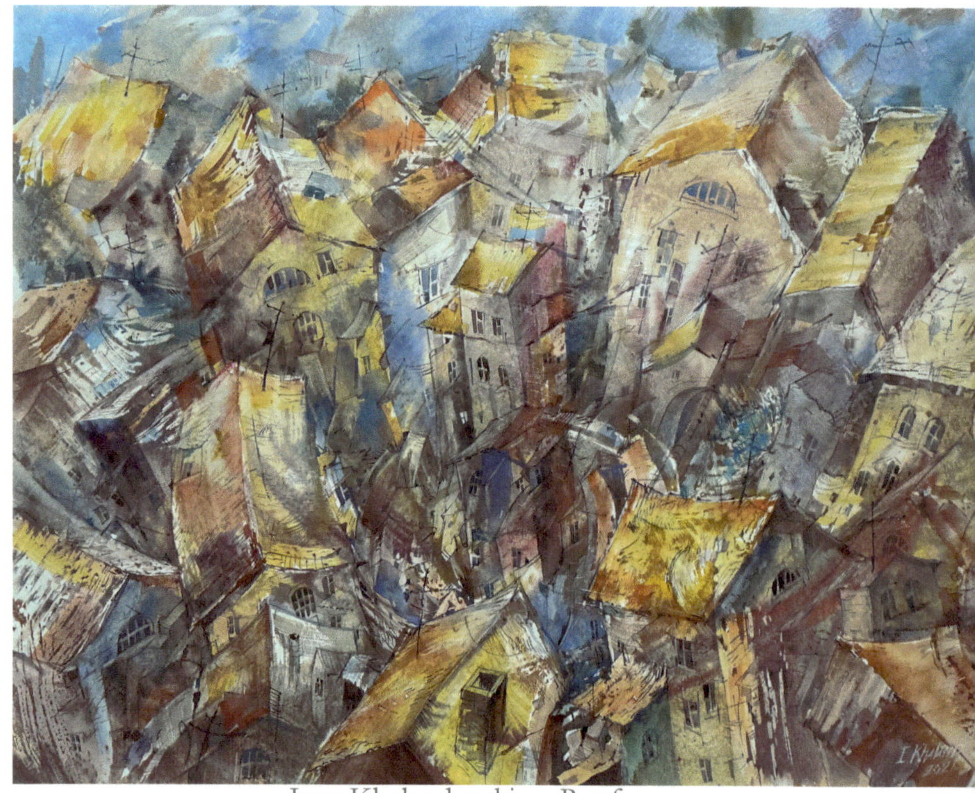

Igor Khalandovskiy   Roofs

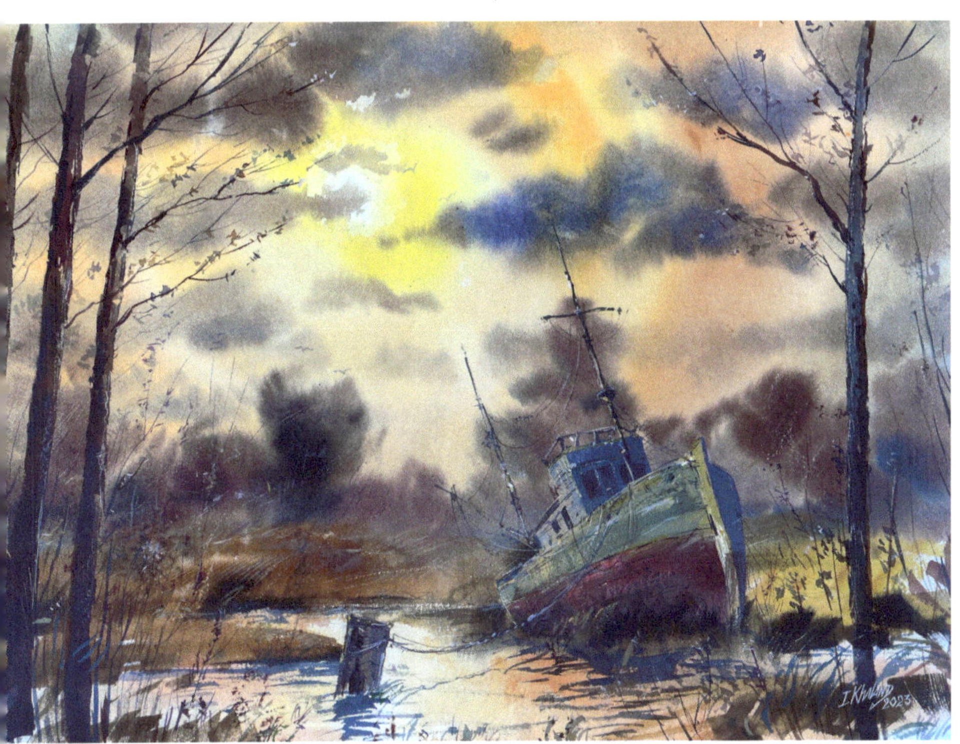

Igor Khalandovskiy   Wind Gust

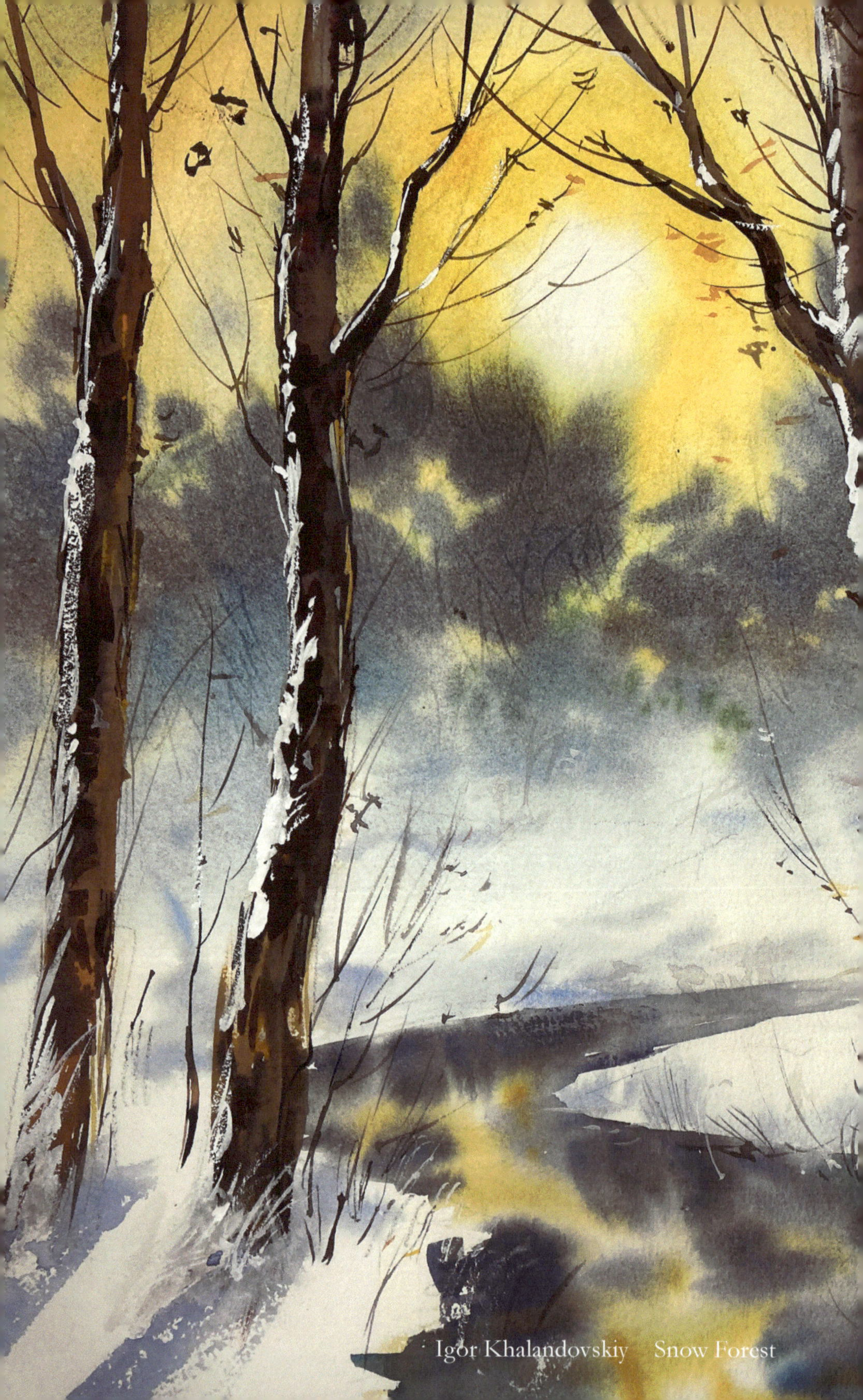

Igor Khalandovskiy   Snow Forest

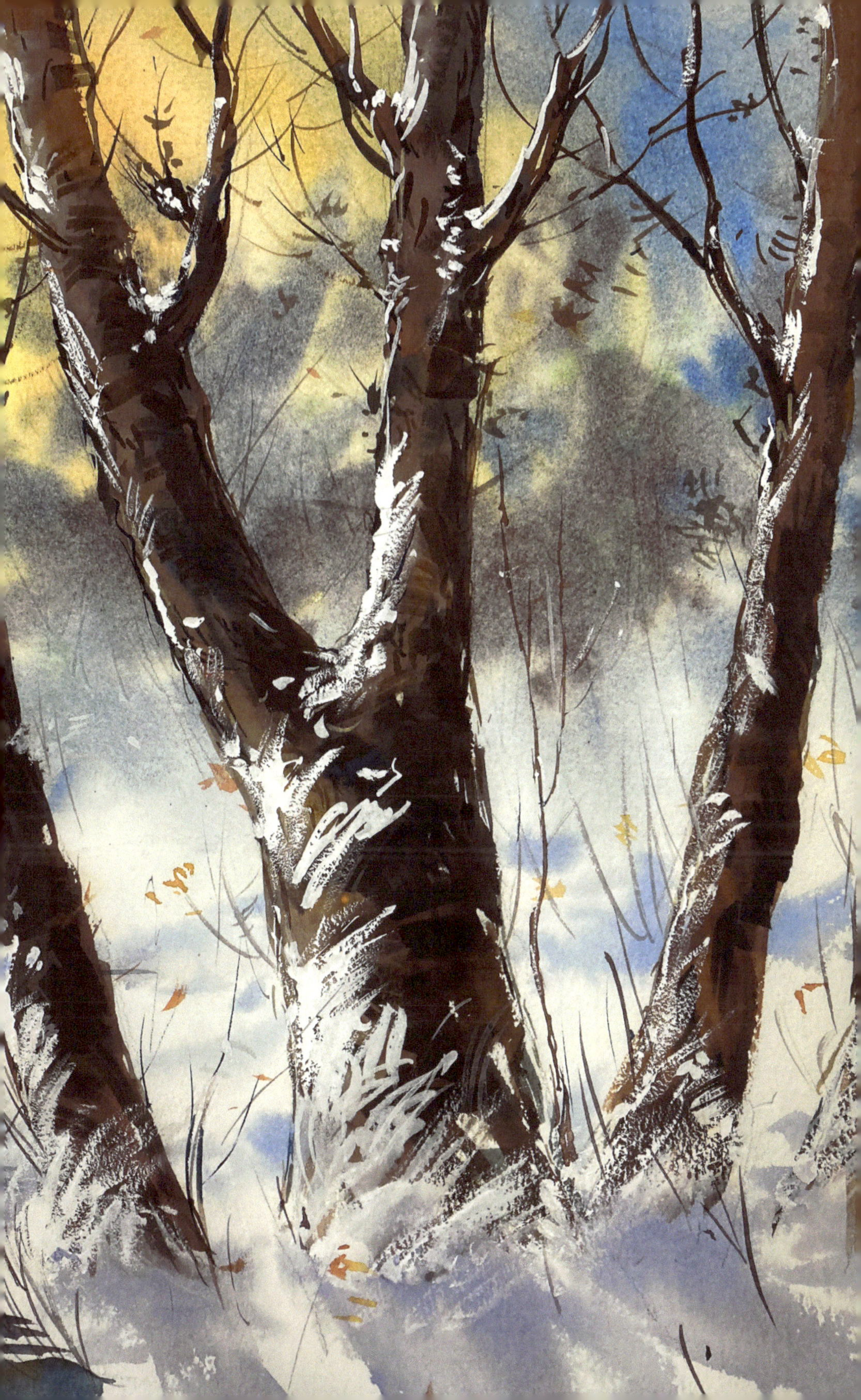

Previously Published Work

Julia Anna Morrison. "Moon Charger" originally appeared in *Counterclock Journal.*

Kelly Madigan. "Landscape Peopled with Figurines" was first published at *On the Seawall,* while "Heart of Wire and Wheels" first appeared in *The Midwest Quarterly,* vol. 4, Summer 2011 and "Regarding the Question of Ownership" in *On the Sealwall* (March/April 2024).

Marilyn Baszczynski. "pears" was first published online in *Halfway Down the Stairs* (March 2023).

ML Hopson. "A Black Child's Walk to See the Freedom Train" was first published in *The Pinder Poet: Cherishing This Heritage.*

Pat Underwood. "In Spite of Dying" and "Sockeye" were previously published in *The Briar Cliff Review* and *Gatherings.* "The Beach" was previously published in *Gatherings.*

Paul Brooke. The series of poems "The Ravine and the Organic Farm" was first published with *Writing the Land: Windblown I.*

Ray Young Bear. "The Firefly" was first published *The New Yorker.* "From the Insect World, a Fall 2019 Message" was first published in *The Washington Post.*

Tasha Jackson. "The Inferno Elegies" first appeared in the first issue of *Revolver Literary Magazine* (March 2023).

Vince Gotera. "How Clara Met Santiago on Good Friday: A Pantoum" appeared in *Crab Orchard Review,* 22.2 (Southern Illinois University), January 2018. "Encounter on Good Friday" was published in *Lupine Lunes: Horror Poems & Short Stories,* edited by Lester Smith, Popcorn Press, October 2016.

Acknowledgments

The Cities of the Plains anthology was a team effort and there are many people to thank:

Crey Abbas, Jayda Allen, Jake Frederick, Rebecca Gilseth, Elyas Jackson, Dom Judge, and Sammy Swacker from my Advanced Creative Writing class for proofing the whole anthology.

Leilani Buchi for her work on arranging the readings, food, and social media posts.

Jennie Knoebel for providing initial email contacts for poets and artists.

Pat Underwood for proofing the whole anthology.

Vince Gotera for the proofing suggestions.

Biographies

Akwi Nji has served as an arts ambassador in multiple roles including as an Iowa Arts Council board member and on the Brucemore board of trustees, producer of nearly 100 events in recent years, involving more than 300 writers and performers; and advisor of Arts Midwest initiatives. Her art serves as manifestations of her exploration of race, gender, Black history as American history, and a parallelism of current social issues with their historical and cultural counterparts, tensions between the 'outsider' and 'insider', and concepts of spiritual and geographic home. As a writer, voice artist, performer, and producer her collaborative partners include Emmy-award winning composers and nationally-renowned dancers and choreographers. She has been an Iowa Arts Council Fellow and, for her efforts in the business community, she was named one of Corridor Business Journal's Forty Under 40.

A'Ja Lyons is a writer, historian, teacher, and performer. She was born in the warm waters of Texas' Gulf Coast and naturalized in the Iowa cornfields. A'Ja's work utilizes environmental imagination to communicate historical, physical, and emotional context. She is the 2024 intern for Tulsa's Greenwood Rising museum in partnership with the National Humanities Center. A'Ja was a steward of Iowa State University English department's Everett Casey Nature Reserve from 2022-2023. She earned a Bachelor of Liberal Studies as well as a Master of Fine Arts in Creative Writing and Environment from Iowa State University. A'Ja is currently a first year PhD student at Oklahoma State University's Creative Writing program specializing in Creative Nonfiction. A'Ja can be found on Instagram @earthmamacentering calm and at ajalyons.com.

Alexandra Ackerman is a mixed media painter living in Iowa City, IA. Her artwork has been influenced by her years of experience working on farms and in gardens across the country. She is also inspired by folk art, patchwork quilts, abstract expressionism, and the midwest landscape. She earned her BFA at Massachusetts College of Art. She has participated in numerous solo and group shows nationally and her work can be found in many public and private collections. Recent exhibitions include the Iowa State Capitol, Memorial Union Gallery at ISU, and the Dubuque Museum of Art biennial.

Amenda Tate is an artist with a diverse background spanning metalsmithing, engineering, performance art, and visual art. She holds the distinction of being recognized as an Iowa Arts Council Fellow. Her creative practice is characterized by its interdisciplinary nature, rooted in engaging audiences through participation. Tate is particularly known for her innovative work that employs custom robotics to transform dance into captivating abstract paintings, alongside her ventures into digital interactive systems and filmmaking. Her art explores a range of themes, including authorship, gender, legacy, and the evolving role of technology in our sociocultural landscape. Tate's dedication to her craft has been celebrated with honors, including two Editor's Choice Awards at the New York International Maker Faire, as well as a special recognition award in the 2017 International RobotArt competition. Her commitment to pushing the boundaries of art has been further supported by grants, notably a project grant in 2020 and a 2021 Iowa Arts & Culture Resilience Grant, both awarded by the Iowa Arts Council in partnership with the National Endowment for the Arts.

Ange Altenhofen is an interactive sculptor and wearable art maker currently based in rural Iowa. Shortly after earning her MFA degree from the School of the Art Institute of Chicago, she was diagnosed with a degenerative eye condition that has deeply influenced and inspired her artmaking. Her work has been exhibited extensively both nationally and internationally; notable exhibitions in the U.S. include the MCA Chicago, the National Museum of Women in the Arts, and the Hyde Park Art Center which sponsored "Project Molehill," a hand-sewn climbing wall installed at the Cook County Administration Building in the Chicago Loop. She was also selected for the Artlink@Sotheby's International Young Art series which featured her interactive sculptures at Sotheby's Auction Houses. Since relocating to Iowa in 2015, she was named an Iowa Artist Fellow in 2019 and received a New York Foundation for the Arts Grant and a Rauschenberg Foundation Grant in 2021. Her newest interactive sculpture, "Grotto," is currently on display in the exhibition Transform Any Room at the Des Moines Art Center. The creation of "Grotto" was funded by a Project Grant from the National Endowment of the Arts and the Iowa Arts Council.

Anna Stoysich is a ceramic artist, illustrator, painter and teacher living in Malvern, Iowa. She graduated from the University of Nebraska-Lincoln with a BFA and an emphasis in ceramics. Anna has been awarded an artist in residence at the Archie Bray Foundation, apprenticed to ceramicist, Chris Gustin, in South Dartmouth, Massachussets, and exhibited internationally. Anna is an award winning artist; her most recent awards include second place in 3-dimensional art at Lawrence Art Festival and a merit award at Rockbrook Village Art Festival, Omaha, NE in 2023. Anna was awarded grants from the Iowa Arts Council in 2020 and 2021. Her recent exhibitions include the Nebraska Biennial at Gallery 1516, Omaha, NE, and 'Perspectives', a duo show with her husband Jorge Chavez Colorado at Moonrise Gallery, Elkhorn, Nebraska. Her outdoor public tile mural is scheduled for installation in June 2024 on the Southwest Iowa Nature Trail.

Barbara Edler, a lifelong Iowa native, currently resides in Keokuk, Iowa where she works part-time as the Keokuk Art Center's executive director. Prior to her current stint, she was a high school English and College Composition teacher for forty-two and a half years. Today, Barb loves spending time with her family and friends and writes poetry to heal herself.

Bob Lockhart is an Iowa-based artist originally from Mount Vernon, Ohio. He will be graduating from the University of Northern Iowa in the Spring of 2024 with his BFA in Printmaking as well as an Art History Minor. Bob has participated in a variety of exhibitions including the 2023 Juried Student Art Exhibition curated by Jason Sweet as well as consistently performing in the biannual performance art exhibition, Vertigo A Go-Go: A Night of Performance Art. Bob has also accumulated experience in public art fabrication through Public Art Incubator, directed by Dan Perry, working with artists such as SujinLim and Chris Wubbena.

Brittany Brooke Crow uses image-making to confront her fear of vulnerability while exploring intimacy, ways of seeing, and the expansive possibilities of creating photo-based art. Crow's self portraiture began as an exploration of the tangle of historical tropes, cultural expectations, and personal control that comes with representing the queer, female body. In 2020, Crow received an Iowa Arts Council Art Project Grant to support the creation of the photographic installation Exhibition(ist). One year later, Crow was named an Iowa Arts Council Artist Fellow. Crow pursues her arts practice out of Mainframe Studios in Des Moines.

Caleb Rainey is an author, performer, and producer. He hails from Columbia, Missouri, and holds a B.A. in English (Creative Writing) from the University of Iowa. His debut book, *Look, Black Boy*, became Amazon's #1 new release in African American poetry, and was awarded first prize in the North Street Book Prize. His second book, *Heart Notes*, was published in 2019 and featured on Iowa Public Radio. He released two spoken word albums, a studio version of *Look, Black Boy*, and a performance album titled, *Heart Notes Live!* He co-founded the literary magazine *Black Art; Real Stories*, was published in Iowa's Best Emerging Poets - 2019, the Little Village Magazine, and wrote a monthly column for The Real Mainstream. For three years in a row he was named Best Poet/Spoken Word Performer in Cedar Rapids & Iowa City.

Catherine Reinhart is an interdisciplinary artist based in Iowa. Reinhart creates fiber work and conducts social practice with abandoned textiles around themes of domestic labor, connection, and care. She received her BFA in Integrated Studio Arts in 2008 from Iowa State University. In 2012, she completed her MFA in Textiles from the University of Kansas. Her works have been exhibited locally, regionally, and nationally. She is the recipient of numerous local, state, and national grants. Reinhart was honored as a 2020 Iowa Artist Fellow, an Artist-in-Residence at Terrain Residency (2021), a recipient of the Alex Brown Foundation's Residency (2022), and an Artist-in-Residence at the West Cork Arts Center in Ireland (2023).

Charlie R. North grew up in a small town in Montana, where she realized her affinity for poetry. She has since planted roots in Iowa, where she and her husband raise their family. Charlie will obtain her Masters degree in English literature from Iowa State University in the next year. Her poem "Battered Secrets" was selected as a top finalist in Wingless Dreamer's anthology, *Calling the Beginning. Poet's Choice* and *Beyond Words Literary Magazine* have also published Charlie's work, and she won Lyrical Iowa's First Time Entrant Award in their 2022 print.

Cyril Mandelbaum is a mixed media artist who makes abstract and political art. She shares a studio space with Igor Khalandovskiy at Mainframe Studios. Mandelbaum works as a CPA and served on a number of boards, including the Des Moines Public Library.

Dawn Terpstra is a poet, writer and beekeeper living in rural Iowa. Her poetry appears in *Grist, 2River, Verse Daily, Pratik, Halfway Down the Stairs, Midwest Quarterly, Quartet, Ekphrastic Review,* and others. She is the author of a chapbook, *Songs from the Summer Kitchen* (2021). Her work has been nominated for a Pushcart Prize and Best of the Net. She is currently working on her MFA in creative writing at Rainer Writing Workshop, Pacific Lutheran University. She is the Poetry Editor for *River Heron Review.*

Elizabeth Rhoads Read received a degree in art and political science from Cornell College. She has spent years creating, exhibiting and teaching art. Her work has been exhibited in both the U.S. and abroad. Elizabeth's fiber sculptures can be found in private, public, and corporate collections. She is a founding member of the Cedar River Artisans and is currently on the Cedar Rapids Public Art Commission.

Ethan Edvenson is an emerging artist from Des Moines, Iowa who creates mixed media drawings. He conveys individualism, humor, truth, and eternity through gestural mark making, surreal imagery, and storytelling in his heavily layered pieces. Edvenson graduated from the University of Northern Iowa in

2020 with a BFA in studio art and a minor in Art History.

Geneva Toland is a writer, farmer, naturalist, and educator residing on Báxoje territory (Ames, Iowa). Her work has appeared or is forthcoming in the *Tiny Seed Literary Journal, Canary Literary Magazine, West Trade Review, HerStry,* and *Decapitate Magazine,* among others. She is currently a student in Iowa State University's MFA program in Creative Writing and the Environment and the co-managing editor of *Flyway.*

Igor Khalandovskiy was born in Ukraine in the city of Kharkiv. After graduating from high school, he entered the Kharkiv Art Academy, and spent seven years studying painting, drawing, graphic illustration and industrial design. Several of his art projects won awards for the best design at International Exhibitions. He graduated from Art University in 1991 with Master Degree in Fine Arts. For 27 years, Khalandovskiy has lived in the United States. Over the past fourteen years, he has been working as a teacher of the graphic art and design at Des Moines Area Community and Iowa State University.

Indigo Moore is a self-taught artist, currently located in Des Moines, Iowa. Their art is a representation of self, women empowerment, self-love, black beauty, and lived human experience. Indigo paints mainly with oils on canvas, incorporating acrylics and other mediums.

Ingrid Lilligren is a professor at Iowa State University, teaching all levels of ceramics. Recent exhibitions include The Des Moines Art Center; Whitechapel Gallery, London; Brunnier Art Museum at Iowa State University; Woodbury University, Los Angeles; and Museum of the Hand in Lausanne, Switzerland. Her art is held in public collections including Grinnell College, Iowa State University, the Sioux City Art Center, and private collections. Lilligren's art incorporates Braille to explore social, cultural, and political blindness.

Jan Friedman received her M.A. in Textile Design at the University of Iowa in 1980. She has conducted workshops in weaving, color, and dyeing throughout the country. Her tapestries and framed collage pieces have been featured in numerous invitational and juried exhibits and have been commissioned for corporate collections and private homes across the United States."

Jen Rouse currently directs the Center for Teaching and Learning at Cornell College. She holds an MFA from American University, an MA from Iowa State, and an MLIS from the University of Iowa. She has multiple chapbooks available through Headmistress Press, and her latest is forthcoming from Small Harbor.

Her work has appeared in *Poetry, The Inflectionist Review, Sweet Literary,* and else-where.

Joan Webster Vore grew up in Rockford, Illinois; lived in Hudson, Iowa for many years; and recently moved to and currently lives in Garden City, Idaho. She began her career as an undergraduate with a focus on drawing and painting, then explored and created a deep body of work as a fiber artist. Her work has continued to expand and mature as her interests led to large-scale environmental sculpture and installation artworks.

Jocelyn Châteauvert raised and educated in Iowa City, Iowa is a paper artist, who creates jewelry, lighting, sculpture, and installations from the paper she makes by hand. After earning an MFA from the University of Iowa, she taught electro-forming at Middlesex Polytechnic in London, and then established her career in San Francisco. She is recipient of a Smithsonian Artist Research Fellowship and the Craft Fellowship award from the South Carolina Arts Commission. Her work is in the collections of the Smithsonian American Art Museum, Museum of Fine Arts, Mint Museum, South Carolina State Museum and the Medical University of South Carolina.

Julia Anna Morrison has lived in Iowa City since earning her MFA in Poetry at the Iowa Writers' Workshop in 2013. Her first book of poems, *Long Exposure,* won the Moon City Poetry Prize and will be published this November through Moon City Press. Her poems and non-fiction have appeared in *Best American Poetry, The Adroit Journal,* and the *Iowa Review,* among many other journals. She teaches screenwriting at the University of Iowa and co-edits *Two Peach,* an online poetry magazine.

Kelly Madigan is a writer with roots in both Iowa and Nebraska, and an advo-cate for conservation in the Loess Hills. Her book *Getting Sober: A Practical Guide to Making It Through the First 30 Days,* published by McGraw-Hill, is an effort to quickly get tools into the hands of people struggling to get sober, and is based in part on her 30 years of work as a licensed drug and alcohol counselor. Kelly is also an award-winning poet and essayist, whose awards include a fellowship from the National Endowment for the Arts in creative writing, and the Distin-guished Artist Award in Literature from the Nebraska Arts Council. She teaches creative writing workshops with an environmental focus through Larksong Writ-ers Place. Her collection of poetry, *The Edge of Known Things,* was published by SFASU Press.

Kristin Roach completed her BFA at Northern Illinois University in painting with a minor in art history in 2008. Roach constructs her work using scientific data and cast-off/natural materials. Her site-specific installations use contemporary technologies to create an immersive environment of sculpture, light, and sound that explore themes of decay and restoration. Roach's art and zines are internationally exhibited and collected and her book, *Mend it Better*, has been published. She currently lives and works in Ames, Iowa.

Kyle McCord is author of seven books books including National Poetry Series Finalist, *Magpies in the Valley of Oleanders* (Trio House Press 2016), *X-Rays and Other Landscapes* (Trio House 2018), and *Reunion of the Good Weather Suicide Cult* (Atmosphere 2021). His work is featured or forthcoming in *AGNI, Blackbird, Boston Review, The Gettysburg Review, The Harvard Review, The Kenyon Review, Ploughshares, TriQuarterly* and elsewhere. McCord has received grants or awards from the Academy of American Poets, the Vermont Studio Center, and the Baltic Writing Residency. He has served as associate poetry editor of *The Nation* and currently serves as Executive Editor of Gold Wake Press and Acquisitions Director for Atmosphere Press.

Larassa Kabel was born in 1970 and received her BFA with honors in 1992 from Iowa State University with an emphasis in fibers. She currently lives in Des Moines, IA where she works as a full time artist and independent curator. She has received numerous grants and awards including an Iowa Arts Council Fellowship, and her work has been shown nationally and is in several corporate and private collections including the Des Moines Art Center, the White House and the World Food Prize.

Laura Travnicek is a painter living in Urbandale, IA. She received her BA in art education, with an emphasis in painting in 2007 from The University of Northern Iowa. After working as an art teacher in the public school system, Travnicek left her job to pursue an arts practice. Travnicek exhibits her work locally and nationally and has published work in the books, *Amazing Iowa Women and Amazing Iowa Athletes* by Katy Swalwell.

Louise Kames holds an MFA degree in drawing and printmaking from the University of Wisconsin-Madison, a MA degree in Art History from the University of Illinois, and a BA degree in studio art and art history from Clarke University in Dubuque. She is a professor of art at Clarke University where she Chairs the Arts + Media Department. Kames was a recipient of a 2022 Iowa Arts Council Fellowship.

Lydia Nong was raised in Iowa, where she also received her Bachelor of Fine

Arts from Iowa State University in the Spring of 2023. She is currently an artist in residence at Mainframe Studios in Des Moines, where she continues to pursue her passion. Lydia is a multidisciplinary artist who uses the human form to explore the strangeness of the human mind. Most often, she portrays dreams and visual metaphors of ineffable feelings.

Marilyn Baszczynski is a retired French teacher, originally from Ontario, Canada, who lives and writes in rural Iowa. She has two chapbooks: *Gyuri, A poem of wartime Hungary* (2015) and *daughter, while i'm still here* (forthcoming 2024); her poems appear in numerous journals and anthologies including *Abaton, Aurorean, Backchannels, Conestoga Zen Anthology, Gyroscope, Halfway Down the Stairs, Healing Muse, Last Stanza, Midwest Poetry, Scapegoat, Shot Glass Journal, Star82 Review, Slippery Elm,* and others. Marilyn is past-president of Iowa Poetry Association and is editor-in-chief of their annual anthology, *Lyrical Iowa,* since 2017.

Mario Duarte is an Iowa Writers' Workshop graduate. His poems and short stories have appeared in *Arkana, Bones, Ocotillo Review, Red Ogre Review,* and *Write Launch.* In 2024, his poetry collection, *To the Death of the Author,* and his short story collection *My Father Called Us Monkeys* will be released.

Mary Jones spent most of her life in Chicago, where she built her career as an artist, illustrator, and teacher. She has an MFA in Printmaking from Indiana University at Bloomington and a BFA in Art History from the University of Illinois Urbana-Champaign. She is included in the permanent collections of the Linda Lee Alter Collection of Women in the Arts at the Pennsylvania Academy of Fine Arts in Philadelphia and in the State Museum of Illinois. Jones has been an artist-in-residence at the Ragdale Foundation and at Anchor Graphics, Chicago. She was named an Iowa Arts Council Fellow in 2018 and a notable artist in New American Paintings, Midwest Edition #134. She currently lives and works in Indianola, Iowa.

Matthew Kluber holds a Bachelor of Fine Arts from the Rhode Island School of Design and a Master of Fine Arts degree from the University of Iowa. Kluber has exhibited paintings/projections, films, and drawings at galleries and museums including the following: the Museum of Contemporary Art Shanghai, China; FOCUS09/Art Basel, Switzerland; David Richard Gallery, New York; Art Basel/Miami; Haw Contemporary, Kansas City; the Orlando Museum of Art; Joseph Nease Gallery, Duluth; the Portland Museum of Art, Oregon; The Micro Museum, Brooklyn; the Austin Museum of Art, Texas; the Grand Rapids Art Museum, Michigan; the Des Moines Art Center; the Bemis Center for Contemporary Art, Omaha; and the Thoma Art Foundation, Chicago. He is a

Professor and Chair of the Art Department at Grinnell College.

Michaela Mullin is a Pushcart-nominated poet, arts writer, and editor living in Des Moines, IA. She earned her BA in English from Drake University, her MFA in Creative Writing from University of Nebraska, and her PhD in Philosophy, Art, and Critical Thought from the European Graduate School. She is a recipient of the Helen W. Kenefick Poetry Prize from the Academy of American Poets and the Thomas Dunn Scholarship in English. Her full-length poetry collection, *must,* was published in 2016. She was the Associate Editor at Nomadic Press, Oakland, CA, during its decade-long life, and she currently works at Moberg Gallery in Des Moines.

Mirzam Pérez is a Honduran-born, self-taught visual artist based in Grinnell, Iowa. She describes her art as a constant search for belonging and an active dialog with environmental issues, questions of identity, immigration concerns, and the unwavering human need of "fitting in." In her mixed media paintings, she uses bright fabrics as her working surface and contrasts solid-colored figures in the foreground with multicolored, translucent tints. Her textile sculptural forms combine her love of color and texture. She uses found fabric as well as fabric she has dyed herself to create pieces that focus on land, water and our stewardship of natural resources. Mirzam Pérez' art seeks come to educate, promote reflection, and ultimately, move us towards the protection of human health and natural resources. Her work emphasizes our interconnection, the layers of history and cultural practices that bind us, and that constantly remind us of the urgent need to conserve life and land in any region of the world.

ML Hopson, poet and spoken word performer living in Clive, IA, was a Court Appointed Special Advocate (CASA) for children for fifteen years and was Copy Editor for U. S. West. She is the author of two poetry books: *The Pinder Poet; Cherishing This Heritage* (Center Press Books 1997) and *Come Taste the Sugarcane – A View From the Staircase With Dialogue* (Palindrome Publishing of Iowa 2004). A civil rights activist born in Gowdy, MS, she is among the last generation of American Blacks to experience segregation in the South. Formerly broadcasting as the Pinder Poet at KUCB radio in Des Moines, her work appears in numerous anthologies and literary magazines, including *Will Work for Peace.* Hopson is a recipient of various poetry awards and served on the nominating committee for the Poet Laureate of Iowa in 2000 and 2009.

Molly Wood lives in Des Moines, Iowa. She graduated with her MA in Art History from Southern Methodist University in Dallas and has had solo exhibitions at The Dubuque Museum of Art and The Sioux City Art Center. She was one of five Iowa Arts Council Fellows in 2018. Her work can be found in the collections of the Sioux City Art Center, J.P. Morgan Chase, Bankers Trust, Farm Bureau and Principal Financial.

Nash Cox is a self-taught artist who works exclusively in watercolors to create highly detailed automotive paintings. Sourcing images from his own photographs, Nash's paintings present the viewer with the soul and history of each vehicle he paints. An internationally recognized artist, Nash's paintings can be found in private collections in the U.S., Puerto Rico, and Australia. A signature member of the Iowa Watercolor Society, Nash works from his studio and gallery located in Chariton, Iowa.

Pat Underwood of Colfax, Iowa is the author of three poetry books: *Gatherings* (Celestial Light Press 2007), *Portraits* (Finishing Line Press 2017), and *Where I Live* (Blue Light Press 2022). She is a contributor to *Voices on the Landscape; Contemporary Iowa Poets* (Loess Hills Books 1996), *Flyway, The North American Review,* and *The Briar Cliff Review,* among others. Underwood's poems received a 2001 Pushcart Prize Nomination, a 1996 Founder's Award, and a 2002 Founder's Award from the National Federation of State Poetry Societies.

Patricia Tiffany Morris is a writer, artist, illustrator, and creative, who owns her own Tiffany Ink Studio LLC. She designs fonts, alcohol ink paintings, and greeting cards and has numerous writing awards such as the National Federation of State Poetry Societies 2023 NFSPS Contest (3rd Prize).

Paul Brooke, Endowed Chair and Professor of Creative Writing at Grand View University, has published six books of poems (*The Skáld and the Drukkin Tröllaukin, Arm Wrestling at the Iowa State Fair, Sirens and Seriemas, Light and Matter, Meditations on Egrets,* and *Pantagruelain: Photographs and Poems of Torres del Paine*). His poems have been featured in *Scientific American, North American Review, The Antioch Review,* among others. Brooke has won many awards (like the Iowa Prize for Poetry and an Iowa Artist Fellowship) and has been selected for many residencies (like Gullkistan in Iceland). He is also a photographer specializing in nature and wildlife; that work has been featured in nine exhibits. His photography has been published in *Audubon* and *Wild Planet* magazines. In 2020, he coauthored *Jaguars of the Northern Pantanal: Panthera onca at the Meeting of the Waters,* a definitive work on jaguar behavior.

Rachel Morgan is the author of the chapbook, *Honey & Blood, Blood & Honey* and she is the co-editor of *Fire Under the Moon: An Anthology of Contemporary Slovene Poetry* (Black Dirt Press). Her work recently appears in the anthology *Fracture:*

Essays, Poems, and Stories on Fracking in America (Ice Cube Press, 2017) and in *Prairie Schooner, Salt Hill, Boulevard, Mid-American Review, Barrow Street,* and elsewhere. She was a finalist for the 2017 National Poetry Series, winner of the 2021 Fineline contest, and recipient of a fellowship at Vermont Studio Center. She is a graduate of the Iowa Writers' Workshop. Currently she teaches at the University of Northern Iowa and is the Poetry Editor for the *North American Review.*

Ray Young Bear first wrote poetry in Meskwaki and began to translate his work into English, publishing his first poem in 1968. His first audience that he considers while writing are his own tribal members. He always keeps his grandmother in mind while writing. He said, "My grandmother was always giving me advice on how I should watch what I say, because she would say that the single word itself is very, very powerful." He writes about the dislocation of contemporary Native Americans who are pulled by two different cultures. His novels, starting with *Black Eagle Child* (1992), describe his youth through the character of Edgar Bearchild. They combine first-person narrative, letters, religious imagery, and poetry. He often switches between English and the Meskwaki language to express himself more fully.

Seth Thill is a poet and librarian from Dubuque, Iowa. They are the Assistant Editor at the *North American Review,* and their work has been published in *Indiana Review, Plainsongs, Drunk Monkeys, West Trade Review,* and elsewhere. Their debut poetry chapbook, *Cover, Recover,* was published in 2022 with funding from the Hartman Reserve Visiting Artist Program.

Seso Marentes was raised on Des Moines' east side and attended Edmunds Academy. He began painting at an early age. He recalls drawing the character from the Lucky Charms cereal box when he was in second grade. His teacher then showed how people draw comic books, and he was fascinated with sketching cartoon-type characters. He graduated with a Bachelor's in Visual Arts from Grand View University. After that, he submitted work at the Des Moines Social Club and started a screen print design business. Today, he has a studio at Mainframe Studios and does a variety of paintings and "whatever art method speaks to him."

Shelly Reed Thieman writes to connect with the wounded. She is a messenger of imagery, a mistress of montage. Her work is heavily influenced by the discipline of haiku. Her poems have appeared in *Modern Haiku, Humana Obscura, december magazine, Conestoga Zen,* and many other journals. Forthcoming work will appear in *The Orchards Poetry Journal, Adanna Literary Journal, and Lyrical Iowa.* Thieman is a two-time Pushcart nominee.

Steve Rose has appeared in numerous publications, including *The Midwest Quarterly; So It Goes,* (a literary & arts journal in memory of Kurt Vonnegut); *The Journal of Medical Literature; Conestoga Zen, Dime Bag of Poetry;* and the *Nebraska Writers' Guild Anthology* (where his work has won awards numerous times). He has published two books of poetry: *Hard Papas in 2014* and *Nebraska and Other States in 2017.* Rose has served as a judge and reader for various poetry anthologies including *Lyrical Iowa* for almost two decades. He is a professor emeritus of Simpson College and a longtime resident of Indianola, Iowa.

Tasha Jackson is a genealogist from West Des Moines. One of her ancestors commanded the troops to fire the 'shot heard round the world' in the American Revolution, and her 9x great grandmother was convicted of witchcraft at Salem in 1692. She plays the guitar, and loves Doctor Who, learning new languages, the X-Men, going to concerts, writing, and reading (especially poetry from her two favorite guys named Charles: Baudelaire and Bukowski). Her poetry has also appeared in *Revolver Literary Magazine* and Simpson College's journal, *SEQUEL.*

Tibi Chelcea takes elements and processes of traditional art disciplines, such as printmaking and drawing, and combines them with parts and operations of digital technologies. His work demonstrates unexpected correlations between old and new technologies, and issues of consumption, serial design, automated vs labor-intensive processes, are brought to the fore. Exhibits have been shown throughout the United States (New York, Pennsylvania, Tennessee, Iowa, and other states) as well as Mexico, Egypt and Brazil. He has received a Pollock-Krasner Foundation grant and an Iowa Artist Fellowship. Born in Romania, he came to the United States to pursue a PhD in Computer Science. He has received several awards, fellowships, and patents in the field of electronic and digital design, which continues to be a major source of inspiration for his art.

Tom Riefe attended the Sam Fox School of Design and Visual Art, Washington University in St. Louis, and University of Northern Iowa in Cedar Falls. Since then, he has been in group exhibitions at the Kemper Art Museum in St. Louis and in outdoor shows in Knoxville, Tennessee; Hutchinson, Kansas; Mankato, Minnesota; and Cape Girardeau, Missouri. Riefe has public scultpures at Iowa State University and Minnesota State University.

Tracie Morris graduated with her MFA from Hunter College and her Ph.D. from New York University. She is the author of *Intermission* (1998), *Rhyme Scheme* (2012), and *handholding: 5 kinds* (2016). A consummate performer, her poetry was a mainstay at the Nuyorican Poets Cafe back in the early 1990s and she has presented in over 30 countries. Her work has earned her grants from the Asian

Cultural Council, Creative Capital, and the New York Foundation for the Arts. Currently, she is a Distinguished Visiting Professor at the University of Iowa.

Vi Khi Nao hails originally from Long Khánh, Vietnam. She graduated from Brown University with an MFA. There she won the John Hawkes Prize, the Feldman Prize, and the Kim Ann Arstark Memorial Award. Nao works across genres and disciplines, intertwining her art and writing together seamlessly. Her books include *The Old Philosopher* (Nightboats Books, 2016), *Fish in Exile* (Coffee House Press, 2016), *A Brief Alphabet of Torture* (FC2, 2017), *Umblical Hospital* (1913 Press, 2017), and *Sheep Machine* (Black Sun Lit, 2018).

Vince Gotera teaches at the University of Northern Iowa, where he was Editor of the *North American Review* (2000-2016). He is also former Editor of *Star*Line*, the print journal of the international Science Fiction and Fantasy Poetry Association (2017-2020). His poetry collections include *Dragonfly, Ghost Wars, Fighting Kite, The Coolest Month,* and the upcoming *Pacific Crossing.* Recent poems in *Dreams & Nightmares, The Ekphrastic Review, failed haiku, The MacGuffin, Philippines Graphic* (Philippines), *Rosebud, The Wild Word* (Germany), *Yellow Medicine Review,* and the anthologies *Multiverse* (UK), *Dear America,* and *Hay(na)ku 15.*

Yvette Sutton is a visual artist that lives in Des Moines, Iowa. Born in Akron, Ohio, she was there until high school when her family moved to Iowa. Her variety of works and different mediums gives each piece each own stage. She attended Grand View University to study Commercial/Graphic Arts. Even though she attended mainly for art she studied business as well. She eventually worked for Norwest Mortgage/Wells Fargo for 17 years.

Index